T0328947

Buried Together

Social Fictions Series

VOLUME 43

Buried Together

A Story of Quarantine and a Question of Conscience

By

R. P. Clair

BRILL

LEIDEN | BOSTON

All chapters in this book have undergone peer review.

Library of Congress Cataloging-in-Publication Data

Names: Clair, Robin Patric, author.
Title: Buried together : a story of quarantine and a question of conscience
  / by R. P. Clair.
Description: Leiden ; Boston : Brill, [2021] | Series: Social
  fictions series, 25428799 ; volume 43 | Includes bibliographical
  references.
Identifiers: LCCN 2021020322 (print) | LCCN 2021020323 (ebook) | ISBN
  9789004467415 (paperback) | ISBN 9789004467422 (hardback) | ISBN
  9789004467439 (ebook)
Subjects: LCSH: Beasley, Silas Mercer, 1834-1914--Fiction. | Conscientious
  objectors--Fiction. | Quarantine--Fiction. | CYAC: United
  States--History--1865-1898--Fiction. | LCGFT: Historical fiction. |
  Biographical fiction.
Classification: LCC PS3603.L3454 B87 2021 (print) | LCC PS3603.L3454
  (ebook) | DDC 813/.6--dc23
LC record available at https://lccn.loc.gov/2021020322
LC ebook record available at https://lccn.loc.gov/2021020323

ISSN 2542-8799
ISBN 978-90-04-46741-5 (paperback)
ISBN 978-90-04-46742-2 (hardback)
ISBN 978-90-04-46743-9 (e-book)

introduces the reader to a native prayer aimed at providing individual strength in troubled times. It's in the spirit of this prayer that Clair tells the story. That makes *Buried Together* a highly worthy read."
– Leonard Cox, Columbia University, Center for Oral History

"As a work of historical fiction and as a social justice novel, *Buried Together* offers truths and insights that have been left unrecorded in official documents. Through rigorous research and imaginative reconstruction, Clair marvelously weaves together her family's history with Cherokee history and culture, as well as American Civil War history. Her novel makes the past come alive on the page, and as I read, I felt as though I were present in the cabin with Silas Jr. and his family in 1865, dealing with one agony after another, held in the grip of riveting storytelling.

Intriguingly, the novel reveals how Cherokee removal, the Civil War, and outbreaks of measles, typhoid fever, and smallpox afflicted the Beasley family in the nineteenth century, and in so doing, the novel speaks to our present moment as well—a moment when we are facing a terrible pandemic, at a time when America is deeply divided and when cruel inequities abound. *Buried Together* is powerful storytelling, combining aspects of literature, history, ethnography, philosophy and ethics, public health, and social justice in a way that makes it a valuable text for classes in literature, history, Native studies, and American Studies."
– Nancy J. Peterson, Professor of English at Purdue University, author of *Against Amnesia: Contemporary Women Writers and the Crises of Historical Memory*

"Dr. Robin Clair's gripping, exquisite prose helps us feel as though we are alongside this family, in time, journeying into their lived experiences and like them, searching for connection inspired during moments of isolation. Clair's novel positions us all within the complex interconnectedness of religion, culture, social relations, economics, politics, and policies that has shaped our lived experiences over time... before, during, and after the Civil War era in the United States. Clair's historical novel brings to mind pressing social issues of the past that remain today, such as the forced migration of the silenced, the erased, in the United States and around the world. Clair invites us to consider epistemological, ontological, and existential questions all the while captivating our interest in what is unfolding on the written page. What does it mean to be a '*real* member of [a group]'? What does it mean to *be*? What does it mean to be *silenced* and how can that happen with or without our knowledge? Through Silas and his family, we are encouraged to interrogate power relations, the overt and the subtle, that permeate society and the so many ways they have done so throughout U.S. history. We cannot help but ask: Who gets to speak in the U.S., and for whom? How do policies and legislation make some people present in society and others absent? Through Silas, we question what it means to be free, and whether freedom is possible for everyone in a democracy.

Clair's message is of relevance to those who study and do peacebuilding for it speaks to the power of narrative and storytelling in peacebuilding scholarship and practice. The three main questions Clair addresses are central to peacebuilders: 'By what right do any of us take a human life? How has ethnic and racial divisiveness wrenched humanity apart? How do everyday actions promote policies of peace, or thwart them?' Through her account of Silas and others, Clair reminds us that we have much to do in the United States of America. That to heal *and to emerge as a more just society*, we must remember *and act*. For to do the work of peacebuilding, we must be at peace with ourselves, our choices, and our actions. Through Clair's account of Silas Beasley, Jr., the conscientious objector, she reminds us that everyday people *can and do choose* peace despite monumental political, economic, cultural, and social impediments to that choice. In this way, Clair's historical narrative is timeless."

– Stacey Connaughton, Ph.D., Director, The Purdue Policy Research Institute, Director, The Purdue Peace Project, Professor, Brian Lamb School of Communication, Purdue University, Associate Editor, *Journal of Communication,* and co-editor of *Transforming Conflict and Building Peace* (2020) and *Locally Lead Peace Building* (2019)

To the memory of my mother, Angela V. Belew Clair and to my ancestors who were the source of this narrative

To my family and relatives who I am sure will continue to debate the contested aspects of this story

To the memory of Esquire Dodd for his generosity and care of my ancestors

CONTENTS

Part 3: The Final Battle

ACKNOWLEDGMENTS

My mother, Angela Belew Clair, initiated my interest in the family ancestral narrative with her stories of Native Americans (Cherokee) on her mother's side and French pirates on her father's side (that's another story entirely, and one that she did not romanticize). When I was a young adult she passed along *The Silas Beasley Jr. Story*, a collection of Silas Jr.'s stories edited by a relative, Hattie Shackelford Sims (1978). My interest grew over time, but waxed and waned with a busy life. As the interest returned, my own children and husband endured my "preoccupation." I owe them a debt of gratitude, as I do for others who helped me along this journey.

When I joined Purdue University in 1991, teaching and researching mainly in organizational communication (e.g., investigating sexual harassment, work socialization) the ancestry research was a side project. During this early stage of the ancestral exploration, I met Selene Phillips (Ojibwa) who encouraged me to keep going, to dig deeper into the archival story, beyond what my family knew. Doing so meant traveling to the Qualla Boundary, NC, New Echota, GA, Cornwall, CT, and Austin, TX. Professor Catherine (Cat) Warren was kind enough to coordinate my trip to North Carolina, house me, drive me to the Qualla Boundary and even schedule a speaking engagement on my sexual harassment research at North Carolina State University in Raleigh. Her generosity was beyond words. I am ever grateful for her help. My husband and I traveled to New Echota; I am grateful to Tim for sharing this adventure with me. In addition, I traveled as far north as Cornwall, CT in order to gather facts, cultural-historical insights, and a sense of the environment where Kilakeena went to school, met Harriet Gold, and faced great prejudice. This trip was coordinated by my brother Bob Clair and his wife Kathy (and their young daughter Catherine came along for the trip). Thank you so much. I also traveled to the University of Texas at Austin, to conduct archival research at the Harry Ransom Library at the University of Texas at Austin. My son Cory and two of his friends joined me on this trip, in which I discovered that "Poor Sarah" was likely not written by Kilakeena or his benefactor; but, it did help me to learn more about both Kilakeena and his benefactor. This research trip was funded by the College of Liberal Arts, Purdue University. Closer to home, librarians at Purdue University assisted me with the genealogy, especially Larry Mykytiuk. Thank you. And it was there that I learned that Kilakeena's mother had the same last name as my third great grandmother, lived in the same general area, and during the same time.

I wish to provide a special acknowledgment to Hattie Shackelford Sims for her careful reconstruction of Silas Beasley Jr.'s memoirs. Silas Beasley's memoirs, which were first published in the *Lawrence Democrat* 1906-1908, were collected by Hattie Shackelford Sims who reconstructed what she could and added a family genealogy in 1978. I contacted the *Lawrence Democrat* and was informed that the originals no longer exist. Shackelford Sims' collection, titled *The Silas Mercer Beasley Jr. Story: A Brief Family History, 1725–1978*, however, is currently housed at the Lawrence County, TN Archives and is listed as available to on-site researchers. In the following novel where exact quotes or paraphrasing from Silas Beasley Jr.'s articles are referred to they are as cited in my personal copy of Shackelford Sims' collection and will simply be cited as Shackelford Sims, 1978.

My uncle's memoirs would still be tucked away in an archive if not for the Social Fictions editor, Patricia Leavy, who supported this project. I am grateful to the entire Brill team and especially Jolanda Karada.

My uncle's stories speak of his early childhood as an "Indian life;" he knew his Cherokee numbers, played with Cherokee friends, and never saw a White man until he was older. I contacted a Cherokee linguist, Marvin Summerfield to ask him questions. Marvin and I had long talks on the phone about indigenous language and my project, as well as some of the things he was working on. His main advice for me was to make the novel as realistic as possible. Keep researching. When I was nearly finished with the novel in June, 2020, I reached out to talk with Marvin and thank him in-person (at least over the phone in a socially distanced manner). That is when I became aware that Marvin had passed away during the Covid-19 pandemic, three months earlier on March 15, 2020. Marvin Summerfield was the founder and linguistics editor of the *Cherokee Observer*, a tribal newspaper. He was an activist for the Cherokee and his loss will be felt by many. Wado, Marvin.

Marvin was not the only person to help me who passed away during the writing of this novel. My cousin Jane Remke Jones told me many a family story and was the first to suggest to me that the family debated whether Sarah Reece (Reese), our shared relative, was of Cherokee or African-American and Welsh descent. Jane's many stories, told with a sweet Southern drawl, will stay with me for a long time to come. May she, and her husband Cal, rest in peace.

So many family members, including my brothers and sisters (Candy, Kate, Jo, Betsy, Bob, Jim and Drew and their respective life partners) have helped, encouraged, or corrected me along the way. In-laws have been especially encouraging of my writing career—thank you Hack family. Special thanks to my children and their life partners, Cory and Melissa, Calle, and Shea. Friends never gave up on me with regard to finishing this project one day—thank you Pam and Jim Finucane, Ralph and Ginny Webb and Stacey Connaughton. A special thanks to Leonard Cox who also read an earlier draft of the novel. And especially to my husband, who lives through these stories as they unfold, are worked through, edited, and finally put to bed, I say thank you. I love you.

ACADEMIC INTRODUCTION

Narrative Ethnicity refers to a person's ancestral story, the lived experiences and historical stories of ethnic identity. In other words, it is how the past and present position individuals and their families in contemporary culture. Such historical narratives are inevitably multiple, complex, and multi-layered by the many branches of a family tree. Ethnic and ancestral narratives are not only complex but might also be contested. As discourses they are malleable in some ways and set in stone in other ways; discourses can be embraced, embellished, challenged, debated, ignored, or in some cases, buried. My mother shared such a narrative with me when I was much younger. The story was researched by a relative, Hattie Shackelford Sims (1978), who wrote of Sarah Elizabeth Reese (Reece), our ancestor, my great, great, great, grandmother. Later, relatives discussed whether Sarah (Sallie) Reese was of partial Cherokee or African-American descent. There are valid arguments on both sides. Her father, it was suggested, was a Welshman from South Carolina named George Reese, who fought in the American Revolutionary War (Sims, 1978). But when seeking his pension later in life, I discovered, George Reese did not mention a daughter named Sarah Elizabeth among his children. He does however admit to being stationed in Cherokee Territory twice and taking two lengthy absences at that time from battle. Sarah's mother's name and heritage are conspicuously absent from all documents, suggesting an invisibility, an absent presence. And her suspected father does not claim the relationship. Here then, the branch of the family tree is broken; no one knows for certain Sarah Reese's ethnic identity. No one knows for certain her mother or her father's identity. My mother thought she was Cherokee; my cousin Jane thought she was African-American.

What I know reliably comes from my great-great-grand-uncle's published memoirs, which were transcribed by a relative. He was a conscientious objector during the Civil War and wrote about his 'Indian childhood.' I have added to this archival information with as much detail of the times and practices as I could. For the Cherokee history and culture, I have relied heavily on the work of James Mooney, an anthropologist who lived and worked among the Cherokee in the late 1800s along with other historical publications, carefully annotated. And for Silas' story I have relied on numerous Civil War documents, books, and articles.

Ironically, I revisited this family narrative during the pandemic of COVID-19. I say ironic because the main thrust of this novel is based on how my ancestors struggled through a previous pandemic—the pandemic of 1865-66; specifically, this is the story of their quarantine. I had made prior attempts at a novel and even published one article on the ancestral narrative earlier in my career (Clair, 1997). At one point, I came across a story, a conversion narrative, entitled *Religion Exemplified in the Life of 'Poor Sarah.'* I knew so little at that time about my own ancestor that I thought that 'Sarah' of *Poor Sarah* might be my great, great, great grandmother. The author of the story was in contention; some said it was Kilakeena (a.k.a. Elias Boudinot, a Cherokee who renamed himself in honor of his benefactor), others said it was written by the benefactor—Elias Boudinot, the philanthropist who paid for Kilakeena's education. As I dove into the research, I discovered that Kilakeena's mother was Susannah Reese, a Welsh and Cherokee woman, who was married to Oowatie (Bell, 1972), and I wondered if she could be related to Sarah Reese. Kilakeena was the famous, or infamous, Cherokee editor of the first bilingual newspaper in America, which used the Cherokee syllabary and English letters.

But what of *Poor Sarah,* her identity and the story's debated authorship, I was curious. Had Kilakeena written it? I wrote a grant proposal and received funding to explore archival data in search of setting the record straight. If Kilakeena had written the story, it would have been the first fiction authored and published by a Native American. If on the other hand, the benefactor had authored the story there might be interest in his work. Either man could have written the story, but I doubted that either one had, as it was written in first person in the voice of a woman and the editors acknowledged knowing the author who asked for anonymity and promised that it is a true story. I traveled to Austin, Texas and explored the Harry Ransom Center at the University of Texas at Austin. After conducting the preliminary research, I offered the mystery to my graduate student class, and Elizabeth Wilhoit discovered a third possible author. So, we traveled, in the form of a class field trip, to the Newberry Library in Chicago, to confirm our suspicions. Indeed, *'Poor Sarah'* was likely not written by either Kilakeena or Elias Boudinot. It was more likely written by a Connecticut woman, Phoebe Brown, who lived in the area where Kilakeena had attended missionary school. What may have created the confusion is that Kilakeena republished a translation of the story, using the Cherokee syllabary (Clair, Wilhoit, Green, Palmer, Russell, and Swope, 2016). And clearly, *'Poor Sarah'* of the story was no relation to Sarah Reese, my ancestor. In short, the research of my own ancestral narrative had nearly nothing to do with the conversion narrative, with the exception that it sent me on another quest to see if Sarah Reese was related to Susannah Reese, a Cherokee and Welsh woman, who was Kilakeena's mother.

As I mentioned above, it is ironic that I re-entered this narrative search at this time, that is to say, during the pandemic of 2019-20-21. The quiet of isolation, at least during the summer months, allowed me to reread the archival materials and to partially refocus the ancestral story to the time period of the previous pandemic that my ancestors experienced, including Sarah Reese and her twelve grown children. That pandemic took place in the aftermath of the Civil War, in which four of my distant uncles fought for the Union, two for the Confederacy, and one was a conscientious objector. To describe the pandemic of either era as providing quiet solitude is a misnomer of sorts. To speak of the quiet that allowed me to research and write, concomitantly speaks of my own professional privilege. As a professor at an elite university I had been given a chance to research in the summers. For many people the quarantine did not allow even a short period of reflection; instead, it meant suffering illness and death, working long hours as essential workers, or protesting racial injustice in the streets. It was anything but quiet. I was fortunate to have undisturbed time during the summer months of the pandemic to devote to the novel.

The solitude allowed me to make connections from the past to the present. By focusing on Sarah Reese and her children, and especially that of Silas Beasley, Jr., the conscientious objector, I was able to witness via diaries, memoirs, and other artifacts how Silas cared for the family during their quarantine. Small pox, typhoid fever, and measles devastated the country; thousands of soldiers and civilians of all races, recently freed slaves and Native Americans died from the diseases. Sarah Reese's family was no exemption. My ancestors' quarantine became my quarantine as I read and wrote, based on Silas Jr.'s memoirs, which, as I mentioned earlier, begin with his "Indian childhood" and continued into his life as a conscientious objector before, during, and after the Civil War.

I am not a historian, but I have done my best to convey the history through my uncle's eyes. His stories were published in the *Lawrence Democrat, 1908–1909,* a Tennessee newspaper and re-collected by Hattie Shackelford Sims (1978), a relative. Sarah Reese's story is based on my years of research and notations are provided throughout the novel. This novel may provide the resources for students of history to learn of the personal experiences of those who lived through the Cherokee Removal, the Civil War, and the pandemic that followed. I have framed this historical novel around Silas' vigil of his family (well documented in his memoirs), but as in most historical novels, and like authors of such novels, I have taken liberties to create the world that is left out of other accounts, to fill in the blanks. I have provided notations for those experiences that are grounded in fact. But I have also set the stage with the imagined idea that Sarah Reese took advantage of this quarantine time and situation to tell her son, Silas, Jr. about her life and the Cherokee Removal. Students of American History, American Studies, and Native American Studies should find this story of great interest.

Students of political science may find many of the stories quite interesting, as well. For example, the story of Charles Reece, a.k.a. 'The Whale,' who fought on the side of the Cherokee and traveled with Cherokee delegates, most notably with Kilakeena's uncle Ridge, to Washington D.C. to meet with Andrew Jackson, is fascinating. Political science students may find debating the outcome of that meeting and U. S. Supreme Court decisions concerning court cases that questioned treaties of special note. Further, they may discover insights regarding the arguments on secession or Silas' struggle to vote against secession as having parallels to voter suppression today. And students may find each of the brothers' decision, grounded in their individual views of politics and morality, to be telling of the divisiveness of the time.

Sociology students may consider the ways that different social circles responded to Kilakeena and his wife, Harriet Gold, fascinating. Some people embraced them as a charming couple and others held strong biases against interracial marriage. For example, in Cornwall, Connecticut, one woman encouraged them to marry while others created straw effigies of the couple that were dragged through the streets and set ablaze. Sarah Reese, my ancestor, was married at 15 years of age, which was customary for Cherokee girls, but in her case married to a White man twice her age, which was not the norm. This interracial marriage may be the explanation for why my kin lived among the Cherokee. The Cherokee appeared to be more accepting of interracial marriages. On the other hand, if Sarah was of African descent, then her marriage to a White man would have been illegal and thus it would have been of the utmost importance for them to stay away from White communities.

Anthropology students will find the two main stories (i.e., the Cherokee Removal and the pandemic following the Civil War) intriguing on several counts. I have relied heavily on the work of anthropologist, James Mooney to supply the legends, the medicines, and the practices of the Cherokee as they existed during the 1800s. This work is carefully listed in the endnotes of the novel. In addition, I traveled to New Echota and to the Qualla Boundary to gather information, hear stories, and talk with local Cherokee. I also interviewed Cherokee historian and linguist, Marvin Summerfield by phone, who advised me to write the story as realistically as possible. Before the covid-19 pandemic took hold, my previous travels also took me as far north as Cornwall, Connecticut where I met with the local archivist, saw the Gold family's house and the museum which stored a lock of Harriet Gold's hair. I held a piece of history in my hand.

Three fundamental theses drive this historical novel: By what right do any of us take a human life? How has ethnic and racial divisiveness wrenched humanity apart? How do everyday actions promote policies of peace, or thwart them? Silas Jr. chose to be a conscientious objector while four of his brothers chose to fight for the North, and two for the South, including the youngest. Their conversations are set forth as historical fiction allows. English literature majors might discuss and or critique the authenticity of such representations. Philosophy students might discuss the universality or relativity of morality, according to the times. Inserting additional plausible encounters for which Silas Jr. must reflect is meant to enhance the tension of the first thesis. Likewise, additional fictional characters, such as the "Unnamed Negro" and the "woman by his side," are crucial to contemporary literature that addresses moral and political questions. The novel can certainly be criticized for treating the freed slave and the woman by his side, as "essential accessories," a complaint that I raised with Lauren Hearit against Simone de Beauvoir's classic work—*Les Mandarins*, a novel about the working class in which no working class characters are developed (Clair & Hearit, 2017); but at the same time, I could not leave the character of the "Unnamed Negro" and his companion out of the novel as the Civil War rests on the fundamental principle that slavery is wrong. My justification is that the story of one man (Silas Jr.) and his family does not exist without the stories of *Others*. Further, these two characters remain unnamed for a reason, which the conclusion reveals. The Confederate characters are fictional as well. But since two of my uncles fought for the South and likely had Cherokee blood I have portrayed dialogue of the brothers from a Cherokee perspective. For balance, I have created both brave and cowardly Confederates. Bravery and cowardice is a theme well developed among the brothers' discussions of Silas' choice to be a conscientious objector.

Ethics, generally taught in philosophy classes, should take place in all courses, as our ethical decisions weigh on every aspect of our lives. We live them every day. Morality and the ethical choices that we make, and especially with regard to racial civility, should be the cornerstone of all humanities courses. Deciding whether to wage war, and on whose side one stands, if one chooses to fight at all, fills the pages of this novel. Today, students in every course may wish to discuss the *Black Lives Matter* movement. And it is crucial that we do so with an understanding of history and of contemporary conditions. As activist and scholar, Jolivette Anderson-Douoning (2020) offered, it is not only "that Black lives matter, but that Black life matters." How we nurture one another, how we give Black lives, and life, a chance to flourish with safety, with dignity, with equal access to liberty and happiness is paramount to classroom conversations, scholarly research, and community practices.

Peace Studies might use this book to place the current crisis in America in its historical place before addressing ways in which the country can be reunited. A living history of pain, over a century and half, does not heal without dedicated intervention.

Physical sciences should not be bifurcated from the humanities. The health disparities of the past can be linked to the present. Today's pandemic has demonstrated such health inequities across race and ethnicity, across gender and age, across occupations. As students of medicine and science explore the physical, they should keep in mind the socio-political. For example, how do politics and poverty influence pandemics and how do pandemics influence socio-economics?

This historical novel fits within the genre of social justice fiction. Grounded in facts of the past with relevance for today's world, it raises serious questions for students of sociology, medical anthropology, health communication, political science, history, diversity, philosophy, and ethics. I encourage students to explore the parallels across sub-disciplines and in particular explore how the humanities and social sciences can contribute to the current impetus to reimagine the world and move forward.

Sarah Elizabeth Reece, mother of Silas
Mercer, Jr. later part of 1800's.

Photo 1. Sarah Elizabeth Reese (Reece) (1809–1888). Original photo taken in the 1880s.
Photo source: Hattie Shackelford Sims (1978). The Silas Mercer Beasley Jr. Story: A Brief
Family History, 1725–1978 housed at Lawrence County, TN Archives available to on-site
researchers. I took the current photo of a copy given to me by my mother many years ago.

Martha Ann Beasley Plemons. Date-
bofore 1892.

Photo 2. Sarah Reese's daughter Martha who is described in the novel as looking the most
like Kilakeena. Photo source: Hattie Shackelford Sims (1978). The Silas Mercer Beasley
Jr. Story: A Brief Family History, 1725–1978 housed at Lawrence County, TN Archives
available to on-site researchers. I took the current photo of a copy given to me by my mother
many years ago.

Photo 3. Kilakeena (Buck) Elias Boudinot, son of Susannah Reese and Oowatie. Photo Courtesy Oklahoma Historical Society. Original glass-plate photograph of a painting of Kilakeena (Buck) Watie Boudinot is part of the Muriel Wright (Choctow) Collection. Permission to reprint granted by the Oklahoma Historical Society, July 2020.

Photo 4. Cover photo for The Silas Mercer Beasley Jr. Story: A Brief Family History, 1725–1978 (Shackelford Sims, 1978). I took the current photo of a copy given to me by my mother many years ago.

PART 1

THE WAR THAT FOLLOWS

CHAPTER 1

SISTER SUN AND BROTHER MOON

Recalling the Night of December 17, 1865

My mother always walked with a limp. As a boy, I never asked how her gait had become so labored. Perhaps, it seemed too brazen. Perhaps, I was more interested in the hidden talisman she wore, which on occasion—like when she hoed corn in the field or twisted hemp on her thigh while making rope, would slip from the confines of her calico blouse, where it had been tucked away. On those occasions, I would witness a sudden flash of black—a crow's feather, horse's hair? I couldn't be sure what swung free for a fleeting second before she would notice it, grasp it, and stuff it back down the front of her blouse. And then making some excuse, she would turn and limp away.

I admit I never thought to ask her about her limp, and I never dared to ask her about the talisman, until I was a grown man with my own family. It happened the night we sat together; awake in the dark, watching the others sleep. A cold night in 1865. The chill had come suddenly upon the mountains of Tennessee as it sometimes does. I kept vigil over the sick ones who moaned and stirred from time to time, listening to the wind match their whimpers. They lay on the cabin floor, on folded blankets, all except my father whom I had assisted earlier into the only bed. I kept guard that night, my rifle, readied, lay across my lap. Marauders and carpetbaggers, wretched veterans and impoverished, abandoned Negroes—ex-slaves who knew not where to go or how to feed themselves at the war's end—all wandered the area. As night grew deeper, I fought off an urge to lower my eyelids. It was then that I engaged my mother in conversation just as she raised herself up from the chair at the table to get a blanket. She took one beleaguered step.

"Is it getting worse? Your limp?"

"No better, no worse," she answered as she stepped carefully around the bundled bodies and returned to her chair with the blanket wrapped about her shoulders. The room became quiet again for a long time, until a moan from one of my sisters seeped into the silence. And then another painful groan followed from my elder brother. My mother began to hum a Christian hymn. She rarely sang the words, although she knew some of them. My mother had the sweetest and lightest voice for which I usually held great fondness, but that night I found the sound of her humming, in the dark, to be as thick as blood one moment and as thin as a ghost's wail, the next.

"Is it the ankle? Or the knee?" I interrupted her humming. She stopped, became silent, but eventually answered me.

"The ankle," she whispered, her voice faltering. Just then, one of the children whimpered and rolled over somewhat fitfully.

"How did you get hurt?" I asked. She breathed deeply but didn't answer me. "Does it give you grief all the time?" Tears welled up in my eyes. I'm sure she heard my voice crack ever so slightly. My tears had nothing to do with her ankle and she knew it. Part exhaustion and part fear. We had been traveling for weeks, over rough terrain, with little food. Refugees. While one war had ended, another, more covert one began. Several of my brothers had fought for the North. We couldn't stay in Georgia any longer. Threats against our lives had been made. I had to give up my home, again. I felt an immense sense of loss flood over me that mixed with anger and fear, exhaustion and hunger. I struggled to keep those emotions and sensations at a rifle's distance. I took a deep breath. She heard me.

"I'd never part with it," she remarked.

"The limp?"

"The limp, the pain. It reminds me of who I am. And," she paused, letting a sanguine silence fill the air, "that we move on." Leaning forward in the light of the coal oil lamp, and turning slightly toward me, she repeated the sentiment, "We do move on." My mother grew quiet again; she was not a woman of many words.

I watched her, my mother, Sarah Elizabeth Reese, 'Sallie' to my father, as she rocked back and forth ever so slightly. She stared into the darkness. Her black hair melted into the shadows, but the silver strands caught the light. As she rocked backward, away from the light, she looked her fifty-five years, but as she rocked forward into the eerie illuminations of the coal oil lamp she seemed much older. Her face, weathered with wrinkles, reminded me of ink lines on a parchment—a map with rivers and tributaries making their way across an ancient and rocky land. I wondered then what she had looked like as a girl and whether she had always walked with a limp.

"How old were you?" I asked.

"When?"

"When you hurt your ankle?"

"Oh, I don't know," she sighed. But she did know; I could tell. I endured the silence yet again. Everyone else slept.

"Tell me. Tell me about your limp."

"It's a long story," she countered. Her tone dismissed me gently, and seemed instead to be addressing someone else, someone far away or from her past, perhaps, as if she were speaking to the ghost winds, to the ancestors, instead of to me. She inhaled slowly rather than speak to me again, and then released a deep, low mourning note of a death song.

To this day, I remember that sigh. It crossed the chasms of space and time. It held a story that I wanted to know. The story of how she acquired a limp. Although in truth, I must admit that at the time, my main motivation was for her to distract me from other thoughts and to keep me awake, so that I could keep vigil over my sick family. But her story, her life, as I have mentioned, had piqued my curiosity as well.

"Tell me anyway," I prodded.

"It'll be morning soon; time to get some sleep." Raising herself up, she meant to leave me awake in the shrouded and shadowy confines of the cabin, but I caught her with the tone of my voice.

"Of course, you're right," I spoke as if defeated. "Sun'll be up soon," I agreed with her. "You're right," I surrendered again, but the tone I used reached out, imploring her, taking hold of her—a tacit plea. She heard my need and acquiesced by gently sinking back into her chair; I felt relief.

"Silas, I'm still cold," she told me with a shiver of her shoulders.

"I'll get you another blanket." I set the rifle aside, crossed the room, stepped around sleeping figures and eventually lifted another blanket from the stack in the corner of the cabin before making my way back through the bundled bodies. I covered her lap with the woolen blanket, one of many that the soldiers had given us several weeks ago as we left Georgia, and then I turned the knob, raising the flame on the coal oil lamp knowing it would only give the illusion of warmth. I sat back down. "I'll get firewood tomorrow," I promised.

"Will you tell me now?" I asked. She nodded, and then began her story.

"The Sun was a young woman who lived in the East. Her brother, the Moon lived in the West. The Sun-girl had a lover who would come to visit her every month. He came only in the darkness of the evening to court her. Always, he came at night; always, he left by morning. The Sun-girl had never seen his face because of the darkness. Sun-girl didn't know his name because he wouldn't tell her. Sun became curious and she developed a plan by which she would discover who her lover might be. The next time her lover arrived to court her, she slipped her hand into the ashes from the fire. Saying, *your face is cold; you must have suffered from the wind*; then, pretending to care for him, she rubbed her fingers about his face. Later, he went away again without telling her his name or showing his face." My mother's voice filled the dark and desolate cabin and I listened like a grateful child.

"The next night Moon climbed into the sky, but this time Moon's face was covered with ashen spots, and his Sister the Sun knew that it was her brother who had been visiting. Brother Moon was so ashamed to have his sister find out that he loved her that he kept as far away as possible. Brother Moon went to the farthest side of the sky from Sun. Ever since then, he tries to stay a long way behind Sun."[1]

At the end of this story my mother sat back as if she were done, as if she had answered my question. I let her rest for a time before asking, "What does this have to do with your limp?"

"The story is about love, deception, betrayal, and loss. So much loss. So is the story of my limp." Not only was my mother a woman of few words, those words were often cryptic.

"Who betrayed you?"

"My cousin betrayed me; he betrayed all of us when he ..."
Her words were cut short as she suddenly coughed uncontrollably and
shivered involuntarily; this time a hacking spell overcame her with
great force, wrenching her body forward and putting an end to our
conversation.

"Are you all right?" I leaned forward with concern. She didn't
answer. I feared that she was getting sick too, and that I would be alone
among the listless fever victims, who rarely had lucid moments. Maybe
she was already ill, maybe that's why her story sounded like nonsense
to me. My father had only spoken an occasional rational sentence since
he had taken ill, nearly a week ago. My wife clutched her bible and
prayed from time to time, but sometimes forgot the words or mixed
up the lines of the psalms when I know that she knows better. The
rest mostly mumbled or moaned. Perhaps, my mother was not rational
either—her story of Sun-girl and Moon seemed like fever-talk.

My mother stood up gripping the arms of the chair. I stood to
support her. She left her place at the oaken table and hobbled to a small
clearing in the grouping of bodies on the cabin floor. Walking behind
her, I took an extra blanket and laid it on the floor planks so that she
could curl into a spot not far from my father's bed. I had to straddle my
brother's sleeping form to do so.

"Don't walk over them, you can hurt their spirit," she instructed
and added, "go around." Without an argument from me, I followed her
instructions, stepping to the side of my brother's body and soul and
then supported her by her arm as she lay down. I covered her with the
blanket which I had previously wrapped around my own shoulders.
The air that fluttered as the blanket fell into place made her shiver
again, this time even more violently.

Now, alone, in the presence of my family—the sick and
sleeping—I felt abandoned in the darkness. I returned to my chair by
the table and thought of Brother Moon, alone now in the night sky—
sullen, brooding perhaps, as he journeyed across the evening's arch.
Yet, a thought came to me, *was it Sister Sun who betrayed Brother
Moon by exposing his true identity or Moon who betrayed Sister Sun
through his silent and deceptive pretense.* Either way, I felt a weight
of loneliness that Brother Moon must've experienced after Sister Sun

disappeared from view. The strong light was gone. The reflective remained, weak and lonely. My empathy for and fraternity with the lunar light—*Nunda*, however, was short lived as I began to wonder about my mother's final statement—*My cousin betrayed me; he betrayed all of us.*

Cousin? What cousin? How, when, under what circumstances had this cousin betrayed my mother? And I wondered what this had to do with her limp.

The unanswered questions became loose strands that fluttered like broken legs of a spider's web in a mild wind. My mind lost track of them, my eyelids dipped, I began to give way to exhaustion. I jerked myself forward; I could not take the chance of falling asleep. I felt a sense of betrayal at that moment, while sitting in the emptiness of night, everyone else lapsed into feverish dreams. I wanted someone to stay awake with me.

"What about the talisman? The one you wear around your neck?" I asked, attempting to stir my mother. No response came.

"What does it mean?" I pressed her for an answer.

"Malachi knows," she whispered and then I could hear her roll over.

Malachi, I thought. *Why should Malachi know? By what right, would my youngest brother have this knowledge, when I didn't,* I silently demanded. *I have always cared for my mother. Why would she share a secret with Malachi and not with me?*

"Why? Why did you tell Malachi?" I spurted aloud like a jealous child. And then I tried to steady my voice, but it was too late. I clenched my jaw. My mother didn't answer. I refused to ask again. I sat determined in the darkness to will an answer out of her. It never came. For long stretches that night, I sat feeling angry and resentful; it kept me awake. At the edges of those jealous thoughts, floated the enigma of my mother's life, about which I became even more intrigued, maybe obsessed. Her refusal to answer me and the mystery it left filled the emptiness of the bleak cabin, eating at me, occupying my mind; until, I heard stirring among the sleepers.

My sister Nan stood up, pulling her blanket about her shoulders and then dropping it to the floor. She seemed confused. I watched her for a moment by the dim light of the lamp and eventually realized what she needed. I went to her side, raised the blanket that she had dropped, and then took her by the arm to lead her toward the cabin door. I opened the door, letting the sharp, crisp air meet the musty odor of the cabin. Once outside, Nan stood with her feet a shoulder's width apart, pulled her calico skirt up about her hips and urinated like the Cherokee women of old.[2] I stared eastward; the sun was cresting behind a rolling Appalachian mountain. My breath appeared as white clouds in the chilly air; I blew on my fingers to keep them warm. My sister finished quickly. The stream was a pittance, leaving but a small puddle between her moccasin-covered feet. I realized then that I needed to find water for my ailing family. Nan turned and took my hand for assistance. Her hand felt clammy, covered in sweat. I searched her face for signs of hope, but her eyes were glazed and a red rash appeared on her neck. *She needs more than water*, I thought. *They all need more than water; they need a doctor and medicine.*

NOTES

[1] The story of Sun-girl and Brother Moon is adapted from James Mooney's *History, Myths, and Sacred Formulas of the Cherokee (1891–1900/1992)*. Mooney, an anthropologist, lived with the Cherokee, compiling extensive cultural information.

[2] Bernard Romans (1775) reported to European readers that Indian [Native American] women of the southern region stand to urinate while the men squat, "a savage man discharges his urine in a siting posture, and a savage woman standing. I need not tell you how opposite this is to our common practice" (p. 42). I would like to thank the curators at the Newberry Library in Chicago for allowing me to read the original works of Bernard Romans.

CHAPTER 2

REFUGEES AT THE MERCY OF MARAUDERS

The Morning of December 18, 1865

We had arrived at this cabin at dusk the night before and after getting everyone settled, it was too dark to forage the woods for berries or nuts; and of course, too late to hunt. I slept fitfully in the early evening and then stayed awake through the night. The Union captain who had been kind enough to send me to this place had warned of drifters of every kind and I took his caveat to task. But now it was growing light and I felt the need to rummage through the shelves in the small back room of the cabin, a kitchen pantry of sorts. I found no food, but I did find some utensils and an oaken bucket for hauling water. I gave thanks at that moment for the captain's and Mr. Dodd's kindness.

I look every bit the *Johnny Reb*; yet, I couldn't expect kindness from most Southerners. It never took them long to call me a half-breed after meeting my mother or one of my brothers or sisters. I, however, look like my father; I have the bluest of eyes and murky brown hair. I knew my best bet would be to tell a good and honest Union man of my troubles. So I sought the local commander of the Union forces and explained my situation.

"Sir," I introduced myself, "My name is Beasley, Silas Beasley, Jr."

"What can I do for you, Beasley?" the captain asked without looking up from his paperwork. He sat at a makeshift desk—a door set on a stack of bricks; the doorknob was still attached. An apple crate acted as a chair. Papers of varying sizes and shapes were strewn about in front of him, they could be vaguely defined as stacks, each secured from the wind by the weight of a rock.

"My family and I have been traveling for several weeks. First, from northern Georgia to Alabama and then from Decatur to Nashville, I've been gathering my brothers who have been released from their service in the Union army," I explained. He looked up briefly.

"And?"

"*Waay'll*, sir, my father has taken ill."

"And?"

"I couldn't let him sleep on the damp ground in the winter's cold. So I moved him and the rest of the family into an abandoned, freight car in Gallatin," I paused.

"And? On with it, Beasley."

"*Waay'll*, then the rest of the family took ill. Now, even my brothers, Union veterans," I added for sympathy "are sick. Not one of them is strong enough to move on. Not that we have a home to return to, sir. I'm asking if you might take pity on the seventeen of us," I pleaded, knowing if anyone would understand our situation, it would be a Union officer. He'd be able to imagine how unwelcome we'd be in the South after learning that several of my brothers had fought for the North. I didn't tell him about John and Malachi fighting for the Confederacy.

"How can I help?" he asked.

"Would you know of a cabin, one with a fireplace, that we might use?"

He pursed his lips and thought for a moment, leaning back slightly on his apple crate chair, half expecting it to have a back, he caught himself before speaking.

"I might," he considered. Then he slid one of the pieces of paper out from under its quartz anchor, signed it, and handed it to me.

"It's a pass so you can travel without being interrogated at every bend in the road," he explained. Then he sent me to find the man whom he knew to have an old cabin in the area. "If Esquire Dodd will let you use the cabin, I'll have my men help you move," he offered. I nodded and tipped my worn hat at his generosity. "Watch out for marauders," he called after me, adding, "Confederates are on their way home, too, son."

I traveled the good part of the day down a wide, dirt road—an old cattle drive path—to reach Esquire Dodd's estate. Along the way, I passed one mutilated man after another. Trying not to let my gaze linger on their absent body parts—a leg, an arm, a hand, an eye—I focused my gaze straight ahead until I reached Mr. Dodd's home. Fact is, though, most of them looked so dazed they wouldn't have noticed if I had gawked.

Mr. Dodd's estate stretched out in rolling hills before me, which I tried to imagine in the height of spring. The present, dormant state of the apple orchard and pear trees had a haunting, knotty look. The patchy snow interlaced with mud and yellowed grass would be rich in green splendor come April and May. For now, the woods seemed a drab brown not even encrusted in winter's gleam. I turned the reins of my horse down the entry path, a drive which appeared to be more than a country-mile long.

I knocked on Mr. Dodd's door and waited. I surveyed the front porch, which stretched the span of the entire house. The surrounding area remained quiet, somber under the winter stillness, a snow drift lay on its northern side. No birds chirped, but turkey vultures flew overhead, circling. This would be a livelier scene come summer, I imagined, I pictured lemonade being sipped or watermelon in mouths of children. Seed spitting from the front porch steps. My daydreams disappeared as I heard the squeak of the front door. I turned.

"Sir," I said, removing my hat, "My name is Beasley, Silas Beasley, Jr." I extended my hand. Mr. Dodd was an elderly fellow. Lean. He stood not much taller than me. With wisps of white hair and reddish skin, I guessed him to be near or past my own father's age— seventy. "The captain sent me, sir."

"Captain Worthington?"

"Yes, sir."

"In that case, it's nice to make your acquaintance, Mister Silas Beasley," he extended his hand to meet mine and then allowed me to proceed with my request. When I finished my story, Esquire Dodd tapped his lips with a crooked and quivering finger, and letting a good part of his hand come to rest under his chin, he offered, "It's not much, but I have an old cabin, up yonder." Coming out onto the front porch and moving along, holding the railing and taking slow steps, he eventually pointed, with a shaky finger, to the distant cabin. I nodded.

"Thank you, sir." I put on my worn hat.

"The river is north, behind the cabin, best to take the old deer path down past the evergreen and the pink and grey boulder. You'll see it."

"Yes, sir," I acknowledged adding a nod.

So it came to be that the captain's friend, a generous man and Union sympathizer, offered without hesitation this cabin in the woods, an old tenement house, dirty from neglect, but holding possibilities for warmth and shelter. The captain allowed me the use of an extra wagon; we had one, but that wasn't large enough to hold my entire family and only my mother and I were capable of walking, and she of course, was limping. A soldier helped me to ease my family members, one after the other out of the boxcar in Gallatin, into the wagons for the bumpy ride to Mr. Dodd's cabin, at which time, everyone but my mother and me were sick with some complaint or other. And now, even my mother seems to be shivering with chills from a fever as she lay blanketed on the floor. After I had taken Nan to relieve herself, I scanned the dismal scene before making my way to the kitchen pantry of the cabin.

I gathered the haversack that I found hanging on a hook and slung it over my shoulder. I took the bucket by its rope and then went to the other room. I slung my rifle, a Springfield musket, over my shoulder. It was the only shooting weapon we had as my brothers' Enfields were confiscated by the army upon their release from duty. William, although an officer, was also relieved of his rifle, and he had no side arms. Each brother had a knife, as did I. Mine still sheathed at my side. Oh, and blankets, the army gave us plenty of blankets, but I was the only one with a rifle.

After gathering these supplies, I quietly left my brothers and sisters, mother and father, wife and children in the cabin, letting them sleep their sickness away and I followed the directions given to me by the elderly gentleman, Esquire Dodd, to find the river behind the cabin. The woods were thick with thin saplings that begged to be covered in dogwood, redbud or laurel leaves. The ground, upon which I planted one hand-sewn boot after another, lay bare except for dried leaves blowing across it. Though still chilly, a winter thaw had melted earlier snows down to patches with thicker drifts in more shadowed areas. The only bit of color came as I passed the pink and blue-grey rock, feldspar, that Mister Dodd had spoken of earlier. The river should be clear of ice, I figured. Then, having reached my destination. I kept my eyes open for drifters.

I heard the river before I saw it, more than a trickle but hardly a rushing sound. I quickened my pace along the deer path, my moccasin-boots colliding against pebbles that slid downward toward the embankment. And just as the stream came into view, I slowed my step and took caution, as I heard something. The rustle of a bush? I listened. Just the water rushing downstream, I assured myself, and then almost immediately, questioned that conclusion. Each step forward came with a hint of my hesitation. I heard another sound. Was it the wind? An animal? I continued, taking more cautious steps, moving from one brush-covered area to another, while scanning from over my right shoulder to over my left. That's when I spied them, hiding in the greenery of a grove of hemlock trees on the other side of the river. I thought I had heard something, and indeed I had!

Two Negroes cowered in the dried thicket by the river's edge. Had they heard my steps, I wondered. Poor wretches, I thought, how they shivered.

Clad more thinly than myself, their bodies tightened against the bite of winter's chill. The man, covered in one cotton shirt over another and trousers, faded union-blue, lacking the stripe and baggy in size but thin in material that were equally wanting, made his way to the riverbank. His boots had seen better days, I noticed, but at least his feet weren't bare. His eyes seemed alert for trouble, which made his expression cautious, ready. His features, distinctly African, without a hint of Caucasian influence, were strong. He reminded me of the only Negro man whom I had ever spoken with in my lifetime—Nate Butler. I wasn't sure at that moment whether it was his facial features or his broad shoulders that reminded me of Nate. In any case, it made me feel kindly toward him.

Behind him, a woman crouched against the cold. Her clothing, more stylish than his, still offered little protection against the elements. Her peach-colored, calico dress covered her legs, which were drawn up tightly toward her. Her arms, covered by a loose knit navy shawl, were wrapped around her legs. Her feet were covered in slippers, not meant for such harsh conditions. Perched snugly about her head, tied in a knot at the nape of her neck, was a kerchief. She didn't have the same chiseled features as the man. Instead, her face was rounder, more child-like. Her eyes, like a doe, were deep brown and filled with fear.

I imagined that she could have been like Nate's woman, Elizabet, a house slave, back before the war.

I recalled Nate Butler's first words to me—*I'm no man's slave.* And he wasn't a slave. His grandmother had bought his freedom from Master Butler. In my ignorance I had thought all Negroes were slaves. I was astonished to learn that Nate was a working man, much like me. But then there were a lot of things that I learned after leaving the mountains of North Carolina, where we lived prior to moving to Georgia. Oh, and as for Nate, he admitted to never having known a brown-haired, blue-eyed Indian, which gave us both a good laugh.

At any rate, they seemed harmless enough, these two Negroes. "I won't hurt you," I called to them. They didn't answer. I took slow steps as they could be armed, although I knew that wasn't likely.

I spoke more softly as I moved toward the water's edge. I kept my eye on them as I lowered my weapon and the bucket, as well as my canteen.

"I've just come for water for my family," I reassured them, squatting by the river's ice-cold stream and letting the bucket plunge downward. I noticed that they each kept looking around and then again at me. I reclaimed the bucket, now filled to the brim with water. I filled my canteen, as well.

"My family's sick an' I haven't got much, but you're welcome to some parched corn and coffee," I told them. I looked behind me in a pointing way and added, "We're staying in a cabin up yonder." The woman looked up the hill, and then at her companion with concern; his eyes followed her gaze. This now raised my curiosity in a way that makes a man's palms tingle and his eyes dart from here to there. Suspicious and concerned, I scooped up my rifle first and then the bucket and canteen, and hastened back up the hill.

As the land began to level and I could see the cabin come into view, I made out two figures, white men, dressed in gray, entering the cabin door. I dropped the bucket; swung my canteen off in order to get at my rifle; and, ran to the cabin faster than a cougar in pursuit. My legs burned and my breath came in hot rushes, while my head exploded like gunpowder with worry for my wife and children as I rushed uphill. I bolted through the doorway.

There a man stood holding my sister Nan, her arms mostly dangling weakly at her sides.

"No!" she cried in protest and made a valiant but nearly vain-filled attempt to fight him off; she managed to claw his face. In anger, he ripped the front of her dress open and laid bare her undergarment, inspecting her with a hungry look and mocking laugh. My entrance stopped his laughter.

The other man was bent over, reaching for my wife, Julia, who tried to squirm away. He had his hands on her as I raised my rifle; it was loaded. I cocked the hammer. The man holding Nan dropped my sister to the floor and turned to face me full front. He had a jagged scar on his fleshy cheek, just under his right eye. And now he had fresh scratches to compliment the scar, thanks to Nan. Reaching up slowly and demonstrating that his hands were empty, he then proceeded to use each of his hands simultaneously to slide his greasy hair behind each ear. "No harm done," he determined.

The second man began to back away. He was wider in girth, darker complexioned, but roughly the same height as the first man, and both were at least a hand's length taller than me.

I moved a step into the cabin. We eyed each other. The second man had a Whitworth rifle over his shoulder. Just one rifle between the two of them, I noted. I took one step into the cabin, toward my right. They stepped to the other side. We circled, step by step, until I let them reach the egress. We faced each other.

"Now, get out!" I commanded. Still, they stood obdurately in front of the open doorway. One of them glanced at my wife again. Their audacity inflamed me. My brother William was trying to raise himself up but he was overcome by a weakness that made him fall against the wall.

"Get out!" I repeated, but neither one of them moved. The second man looked at my children on the floor.

"They're either barefoot or wearing moccasins.[1] I don't know fo' sure what they are, but it don't matter much. But that one's got Union written all over him," the second man taunted, pointing to William.

"We just want some food," the other said to me. I knew better.

By this time, I figured I'd given them enough warning. Wishing for the first time in my life that I held a Henry Repeater within my hands, and standing there, staring at them as if I did, I leveled my rifle in defiance and took aim.[2]

"By God, I swear one of you is about to die," I announced.

"Now, now, we're leavin'. No reason to get your feathers ruffled," the one with the scar on his cheek blurted. I think they saw the fire of hell in my eyes and this time they backed away, out the door.

"We can see you ain't got no food or nothin' else that we want," the same man protested.

"You just let us go now and we'll be on our way," the second veteran proposed. Their voices were too calm for my liking. My eyes were squeezed so narrow and my trigger finger so ready that they must've figured that if they didn't talk calm, I would shoot one dead and beat the other to death with my rifle. And that was close to the truth, except for the promise that I had made. They had entered my home, abused my sister, and touched my wife. My teeth were clenched so tight they felt like steel, two barrels soldered with anger. They could see it.

Those two Rebs walked into the clearing in front of the cabin, still making meek excuses. I followed without a word. I didn't have to talk; my rifle, still pointed at them, spoke volumes. In short order, they mounted the one horse they had and rode off down the trail.

I watched until they were out of sight. After my heart stopped racing and my anger subsided, I realized that these were not the kind of men who would walk away easily. Not to mention in detail, but there was plenty in this cabin that they wanted.

NOTES

[1] Silas' memoir tells that "each member of the family had one pair of moccasins a year" Shackelford Sims (1978, p. 1). Based on Silas Beasley's memoirs which were first published in the *Lawrence Democrat* 1906–1908, Shackelford Sims reconstructed what she could find and added a family genealogy. Shackelford Sims' collection is currently housed at Lawrence County, TN Archives available to on-site researchers. My mother gave me her family copy many years ago.

[2] With respect to Civil War era weapons, the Springfield musket was the most commonly used and was used by both Northern and Southern soldiers. It took approximately 20 seconds to reload. The Enfields were also musket-loaders and were fairly accurate. Both the Springfields and the Enfields used minié balls. The Whitworth, a muzzle-loading weapon, was used primarily by Confederate soldiers. It had long range accuracy, but required special ammunition—hexagonal bullets. The Henry Repeater rifle, which was invented before the war but not issued to Union soldiers until 1863, could fire at least four times as fast as the musket-loader rifles.

A SICKNESS TAKES HOLD

Afternoon of December 18, 1865

"If I'd had my rifle, I would've ..." my brother William began weak of wind but strong with determination.

"It's all right," I assured him.

"No! It's not all right," he declared. He banged his head backward against the wall in frustration, adding, "If I were stronger, if I had a rifle ..."

"Just rest," I told him, knowing what he was going to say—*I would've killed those bastards.* I didn't want to have this argument with William again, at least not now. I could see the sickness in his glazed eyes. I was grateful that he had made an attempt to get up while those no-good Rebels were here. He even leaned forward as if he were reaching for something, a rifle, perhaps. Good, let those scoundrels wonder if we have a few rifles beneath some of these blankets.

"There are minié balls in my bag, if you need ammunition, and dry powder," William said, before slumping down into his blanket. I moved toward William's haversack, but stopped in mid-step. My son, William's namesake, Willie stood up and came toward me.

"Papa," he said as sweet as any child, "I'm scared."

I lightly tussled his hair and ran my hand along his cheek. His skin was hot to the touch.

"Papa," he complained, "I'm thirsty, too."

"I know," I told him, remembering that I had dropped the bucket and let my canteen slip from my shoulder so I could get my rifle ready. I smoothed my son's hair, where I had given it a rumple.

"When do you think they'll come back?" I put the question to William.

"Probably not till nightfall or dusk. Yeah, dusk so they can see just enough for whatever they plan."

"S'pect I could go for water now, since it'll be a while before they come back," I thought aloud. My brother nodded. But as I took a step toward the door, Willie threw his arms around my legs. I set my rifle aside for the moment and scooped up my son. Carrying him, I went to the chair by the table. Of course, everyone was awake now. Each one looked in need of reassurance that everything would be all right, but I couldn't give it to them. I said nothing; I just rocked Willie back and forth as I took in the scene before me.

My father looked the weakest. He was the first to take ill, or at least, the first to mention his symptoms. He quivered with chills, complained of aches, and had been unusually irritable. Once I realized he was sick, I sought a place of cover in which to sleep. He'd suffered too many nights of open winter air. The abandoned boxcar in Gallatin hadn't been much, but it had provided shelter from the wind. The next morning more of my kin complained of ailments. Most of them shivered from both the cold and their fever's chills. I needed to find a place where I could build a fire for them and put them to rest on a dry floor. This cabin, with its fireplace would prove to be better than that boxcar, I was sure. My mother, whom I thought was well, began to shiver last night. Today, she moaned from time to time, but didn't speak. William seemed to be the strongest of my brothers and even he had trouble raising himself up to protect our sister and my wife. My brothers Reuben, Joseph, John, and Thomas had slept through the night and barely more than opened their eyes with surprise when those marauders entered the cabin. Four of my younger sisters, Martha, Mary, Elizabeth and Lydia, drew strength from each other as they huddled in fear from those wretched intruders. Nan had been sleeping next to my wife Julia and our three children. I realized as I looked around the cabin that whatever ailed my father, seemed to have taken hold of each and every one.

"Papa, everything'll be all right," my boy told me. I pursed my lips and fought back tears. He had said what I should have. He swiped his long, blonde bangs out of his eyes and leaned his head against my chest.

"You need a haircut, boy," I lightly teased. Leaning forward, I breathed in the smell of his hair.

"Yes, sir," he answered me. I kissed him atop of his towhead and sat with him for a spell. After a time, my four-year-old son fell asleep in my arms and then I put him back on the floor. My daughters, Sara and Nannie curled around their brother. Just babes, I thought, Sara only two and half years old and Nannie barely a year.

"Are you all right?" I asked my wife who lay next to the children.

"Yes," she whispered gripping her Bible to her breast.

"And you?" I asked Nan. Nan nodded, holding her calico blouse together. I expected nothing less from my sister, Nan, and my wife, Julia.

I stood again, but this time without making a move in any direction. Like an old man who's lost his thought and his way, I stood immobile, staring into space. I guess I just didn't know where to go or what to do.

"Have you slept yet?" my brother William asked me.

"No."

"Silas," he lectured me, "You need to get ready." I looked at him. He could barely raise himself up on his elbow before, and now he managed, and only with intense difficulty, to get himself into a sitting position. Leaning against the wall, he motioned weakly for me to join him.

I sat next to him as he gave me instructions. Even his voice came with strained effort.

"You need to cut holes in the chinking between the logs. Make 'em big enough to see through, big enough to put your rifle through. Do it on all four walls, four directions."

"There are seven directions," my mother interjected from her place on the floor. We ignored her.

"See what else you might have in the way of lanterns in that kitchen," and as an afterthought, he added, "and utensils. Bring me utensils."

I followed my brother's instructions carving chink from between the logs. It wasn't as hard as I expected. The daub was old and the surrounding wood splintered away at my hunting knife with ease.

"Not too big," William warned. When I was done, I collected some of the utensils from the kitchen—two copper spoons, two forks, a handful of gourds wooden spoons, and a tin cup. "They'll have to do," William judged.

"There's a fire poker," my sister Nan added. I nodded. I helped my brother with the copper spoons, lashing pairs together with thin rawhide cord, and then I returned to the kitchen in search of other metal pieces. We had to make it appear that my brothers had roused themselves for the occasion and were keeping vigilant post at their keyholes. It had to appear that we had more than one rifle and more than one healthy man. I stuffed cloth around the edges of the tied spoons and shoved them through two of the holes.

My musket stood readied by the fireplace as I made my rounds, checking on each of my brothers and sisters. I couldn't count on a single one of them to help me; they were too debilitated with fever. And I was suffering from hunger and exhaustion. So I sat in the chair by the table for a moment of rest. But an anxious feeling moved through me that started in my toes and kept my knee bouncing with a twitch. My old musket loader was good for getting deer, but against two soldiers, mean ones, at that; well, I just didn't know. Time passed more slowly than I believed it could and now I was beginning to wonder if I shouldn't have gone for water and searched for berries. But I was just trying to think of what else I could do to protect my family. Someone coughed.

"Shh," my brother John warned us.

"I heard something, too," my brother Joseph whispered. I hadn't heard anything but the cough. Everyone lay quite still, except me. I stood slowly and silently and moved toward my musket. As I picked it up, I heard a sound on the front porch. Making my way to the door, I determined to take the offense. I flung the door open and pointed my rifle.

"No, sir! No, sir! Don't shoot," the Negro said holding up his hands. "We just refilled your bucket for ya, sir." There at his feet sat the oaken bucket that I had abandoned in my earlier rush to the cabin. He'd even returned my canteen. He looked to his left. From around the corner of the cabin came his woman. Shivering. It took me a minute to gather my senses, for relief to replace anxiety. At last, I spoke to them.

"Thank you," I told them and after a moment's hesitation I offered them food. "Corn, I've extra parched corn. It's not good for making meal, but it's somethin' and we have extra blankets," I told him, adding, "Wait here."

Too stingy to give him my only haversack to carry it in, I bundled the parched corn and coffee beans in a towel that I found in the kitchen and tied it with twine. I returned to the open doorway with two blankets, Union blankets, and the wrapped package of corn and coffee.

"Thank ya, sir," he said turning away. "Sir," he turned back again, "They's a bit more than a furlong away. An' they settled in. Just over that ridge," he shared with pointing finger. "I been keepin' an eye on them. They got a campfire goin'," he told me. His woman moved closer to him, reaching for a blanket. They started to leave, when the man turned around once more, "I know you didn't intend it, sir, but you give me, us, a chance to get free of them. But I can see ya'll in worse shape than us," he determined, looking around the cabin. "An' if you want me to stay and help ya, I will, sir," he offered.

I couldn't speak. An odd mix of reactions ran through my brain, one that I was proud of and the others not so, but even that got muddled. On the less noble side, I was embarrassed to have a Negro judge me and my family as worse off than he and his. *Worse off than Negroes*—that didn't seem right, an insult I thought that made me shake my head. Yet, at the same time, his generosity touched me so and to give it to me, of all people, made me feel small. It was my brothers, Reuben, William, Thomas and Joseph who deserved his kindness, not me. I never raised my rifle against a Confederate soldier before that day. On the more noble turn, staying to help us would probably only bring our illness upon them, whatever it was, and I didn't want to make anyone else suffer as we were suffering. Besides, how was he goin' to help; he didn't even have a rifle. In truth, I think, as I look back on it, that my noble consideration—being concerned about their health, was probably an afterthought and it was my pride that got the best of me—being compared in the worst way to Negroes just made me feel ashamed.

I nodded my gratitude, but told him we'd be fine.

23

"You go now. Go quick," I told him. He nodded and took to the woods, his woman at his side.

I carried my canteen and the bucket of water into the cabin and set my rifle against the wall. I found a ladle in the kitchen and started passing out sips of water to my family. One by one, they settled down again and fell back to sleep. I went about my business, preparing the cabin for an assault of some kind.

"Silas," my brother William spoke softly, but sternly. He paused until I looked straight at him. "Silas, you might have to kill a man."

CHAPTER 4

REMEMBERING THE DIFFERENT DIRECTIONS OF 1861

Late Afternoon of December 18, 1865

I didn't answer my brother. Instead, I took my thoughts outside with me, but I never let the cabin out of my sight as I gathered wood for a fire. I dug through underbrush to find the driest limbs for tinder and held them in a bundle under my arm. During this task, William's words echoed in my mind, *Silas, you might have to kill a man.*

That statement took my mind back in time to the last day all of my brothers and I had been together. April 30, 1861. That was the day that we learned that Fort Sumter had been attacked. Reuben, my eldest brother, had brought word to us after he placed his wife and children in the care of his father-in-law, in South Carolina. Reuben arrived at our log-hewn house several miles north of New Echota, Georgia, the capital of the Cherokee Nation, to tell us of the matter.

"Lincoln sent word to the Governor of South Carolina that he intended to bring relief to Fort Sumter," Reuben informed us.

"What kind of a relief?" my father had asked him.

"Food and provisions, not ammunition."[1]

"I knew this was coming," my youngest brother Malachi interjected.

"You know everything," Thomas retorted. Thomas and Malachi were the youngest of my six brothers, 21 and 19, respectively. Thomas would be leaving home at the end of that summer according to family tradition and Malachi would farm for my father for two more years before receiving his horse and rifle and the profits from his plot. That's what a man did in those days—farm for his father 'til he turned 21 and then go in search of a wife. Often times returning to live with them, extending the family.

I had left home in the early months of 1858. Although there's a whole story in between, I returned in the fall of 1859 with my wife, Julia, expecting Willie. By April 30, 1861, when my brothers and I debated the possibilities for war and the politics behind it, Julia was plump with expectation of our second born; that's to say, Nannie was on the way. When Willie was on the way we proudly told the family that if the baby was a boy we'd name him William John Reuben Beasley after my eldest brothers. And our second child honored my sister, Nan, in name. Shortly after that announcement the conversation had turned to one of politics, in which, my younger brothers, Thomas and Malachi continued to argue.

"Hush up, you two," my father ordered. "Tell me, then what happened at Fort Sumter?"

"There's not much to tell. They've all been afraid that Lincoln was goin' too far with his demands."

"What do you think?" my father asked Reuben.

"I think it was time for the showdown."

"Me, too," added William, "The South is being just plain greedy with demands on the west."

"What's he talkin' about? The west?" Malachi asked.

"I thought you knew everything," Thomas quipped.

"Everybody's pushing west. There's a lot of land to be had. And gold," my father explained. My mother glanced up at him. She'd been twining rope on her thigh. She curled the hickory strands around her hand and lifted her work. She raised herself up and left the room, limping. After she had departed, my father continued the conversation.

"See, son," my father began, looking at Malachi. "I think they all want a piece of those western lands. The Northerners and the Southerners. Gold lust drives them. But the North also wants land, to open it to homesteaders, individual families. An' the South, well you got them rich plantation owners who want to go sweep up huge pieces of territory and then use their Negroes to work the land. The Northerners don't want that to happen. Anyway, when Lincoln ran for President, he did so, on a slavery restriction platform. Meaning nobody could own slaves in the western territories and everybody would have an equal chance."

"Except the slaves," William countered.

"What do you mean?" Joseph questioned.

"I mean, the Negroes'll still be slaves in the South."

"William, you an abolitionist?" Thomas asked.

"I don't think any man should be put to slavin'. It ain't right."

"I agree," announced Reuben. "Everybody knows that Lincoln's goin' to free the slaves the first chance he gets. He don't think it's right either."

"To be quite honest, I don't see how a man could see it any other way," John added.

"*Waay'll*, I 'spect, plantation owners see it a might differently," my father added. "Probably, when the cotton tax was levied on 'em years ago they thought the North was being greedy. I imagine that still smarts for them." Was my father defending South Carolinian elite or maybe he was just explaining. "That's a man's livelihood in the South. An' the North just kept pelting away until the Southerners thought they'd lose their slaves, their cotton, and their rights to land west of the Mississippi. And in the South. But by and large, I think it boils down to a combination of fear and greed. Greed makes men see differently and when they're afraid of losin' what they got, they near get crazy," my father surmised. "I know firsthand. So does your mother," he told us. He stood up then and left the conversation saying, "*Waay'll* boys, I leave it to you to figure out."

I heard him say, "Well, boys," in his usual long drawl, like a meandering honeysuckle vine, the word *Well* dragged and trailed into *Waayy'll*. It always meant one of two things either he had pondered something long and hard or he was about to give some issue great say. This time though he wanted us to ponder it. *Waay'll*, I thought, *what will each of us decide*? I realized then that I had taken up this linguistic signature, like father, like son. The room was quiet as we took up his advice. Why I focused on the way he said *waay'll* at that moment is beyond me, especially when there were more serious matters at hand. Each of my brothers seemed to contemplate the matter. But I had another thought, I was sure that he'd gone to check on my mother. He was good that way. Caring for her.

I never knew the whole story of what happened to my mother's family, but I had an inkling. And sure as betting on a winning horse after the race, it had something to do with greed, gold, land and the Cherokee. More importantly, I knew the issue brought tears to her eyes so that she would have to swallow hard to keep them back. So I never asked for the details. Nor had I asked her how she'd come to acquire her limp, although I had an idea that it all went together somehow.

"It's important to remember who they're taking that land away from," Malachi exhorted, after a time. "Haven't the Cherokee been through enough? And now they want Oklahoma, too."

"True enough, but it's important to focus on the future, as well," William added.

"What do you mean exactly?" Malachi asked.

"I mean there's goin' to be a war, Malachi. One big, bloody war."

"Are you goin' to war?" Malachi asked.

"I am," William told him.

"We plan to join the Union Army," Reuben added. Malachi looked to William.

"It's true, Malachi. I'm not rich and I don't own slaves. I don't think slavery is right. Lincoln's boys, they'll make things square."

"So first you'll kill Southerners and then you kill Indians?" Malachi quipped with more than a dab of sarcasm in his voice.

"That's crazy talk."

"William, think about it. Whoever goes West, whether it's the North or South, they'll go against the Indians."

"I can't help that. But the South is wrong, Malachi," William's words lunged at my youngest brother. "They argue on the pretense of States' Rights. It's not States' Rights they're protecting; it's slavery they're protecting and it's not even most of the South. I heard from several South Carolinians that they never wanted to secede. It was the Governor and the plantation owners who wanted to secede. They'll make all kinds of fuss about States' Rights and the freedom of Southerners. They are politicians and plantation owners. They'll blow their horns until they have every man fightin' for the South. Those who won't, will be shamed by the label of traitor. Lincoln says, it's time to be bold. Our minds are enslaved to the idea that slavery is necessary, and acceptable. We need to free ourselves from bondage in order to free the world. He said, "It is not 'can *any* of us *imagine* better?' but, 'can we *all* do better?' The dogmas of the quiet past, are inadequate to the stormy present. The occasion is piled high with difficulty, and we must rise—with the occasion. As our case is new, so we must think anew, and act anew. We must disenthrall ourselves, and then we shall save our country."[2] William's ire was up, he quoted Lincoln and argued until Thomas directed a question to my youngest brother.

"What about you, Malachi?"

"I'll do whatever the Cherokee decide to do. If they go with the Confederates, so will I."

"I side with the Union," Joseph announced without being asked.

"What about you, John?" Thomas called for an answer.

"I was born in Cherokee Territory, in North Carolina. My neighbors and friends were Cherokee," he spoke as if beginning an important stump speech, but he truncated it, adding only, "I'll join my younger brother and stand with the Cherokee." When John finished, Malachi gave him a quick wink and confirming nod. Then it was my turn.

"Well?" William asked of me. I had assumed he pictured me, my blonde hair, blue eyes, and whitest of skin, a ridiculous figure among the Cherokee. I didn't look much like my brothers. I didn't answer right off. Julia, who had been sitting quietly by the fireplace, looked in my direction.

"Silas?" Malachi impatiently asked. I glanced at Julia, her fullness, a baby on the way, before I spoke.

"I'll not kill any man," I declared at last. Two of my brothers jerked back, eyes wide. A silence followed that set my brothers' brains to thinking; then just as quick, a skirmish of conversation followed.

"Have you no convictions, man?" William asserted.

"How can you make such a proclamation?" Thomas contested.

"Are you saying you won't go to war?" Joseph queried.

"Where's your gumption?" John challenged me.

"Whoa, whoa," I stopped them all as I started to explain. "I've given my word to someone," I told my brothers without saying to whom.

"I swore that I'd never be judge, jury and executioner; that I'd never take another man's life in war or loss of property," I testified.

Although I didn't detail my explanation, I remembered the exchange with Julia, keeping it to myself. I'd been farming a large tract of land for her father so that we could be married. I'd cleared it, planted, and weeded that plot under the hot South Carolina sun only to come out one morning near harvest to find over a quarter of my crop stolen away. I snatched up my rifle with my calloused hands, stalked those culprits through the field and into the woods, to no avail. I lost their scent at the river. But something told me they'd come back and so I stayed up all night, sitting, waiting with my rifle across my knees and hatred in my heart. In the morning, Julia found me, still awake, still seething. *Melons*, she had chastised me with a clucking tongue. *To think that you sat out on my father's porch all night in hopes of killing the men who stole your melons. It is killing you have on your mind, isn't it?* I had nodded to her without a word. *Shame on you, Silas Beasley, Jr.! The Lord would have you recognize those men's needs, not their crime. And to think, you would shoot them dead!"* Of course, I didn't tell my brothers how she had scolded me. I had thought judiciously about the matter and in the end I decided she was right, it took days of reflection, and much walking, but no one needed to know how I came by my decision or that she helped me write that promise in the front of our Bible—to kill only in direct defense of myself or my family and only then if there was no other way.

"Silas," my brother William had said to me, "You're a coward! Plain and simple!" I could hear the oxygen being sucked out of the room. A collective gasp filled the air. Aghast, everyone looked to see my reaction, including Julia.

For me, the room went lightning white. My breath came quick and sharp like a knife had pierced my chest. *A coward!?* They were all staring at me with intense expectation and a hot anticipation for what would happen next. *A coward? A coward! How dare he call me a coward?!* I seized solid with every muscle in my body clenching tight. Anger seared through me and radiated out of my steely glare. I wanted to lunge forward. I should've seized William by the throat and choked the insult into oblivion; instead, I sat with fire raging through my veins and a war whoop building in my throat. I should've lunged forward. Thomas and John would've held me back. They would've stopped me before I wrung William's scrawny neck. I should've grabbed him; I almost did. What stopped me, even now I wonder. My oath to Julia or my love for my brother.

"He's not a coward," Malachi had jumped to my defense. I was grateful it was Malachi and not Julia defending me. Sometimes, women don't understand the ways of men. No one moved as William and I continued to glare at one another.

"None of my brothers are cowards," Malachi countered. "I'll best the man who says they are!" Then he rolled up his sleeves and looked at the lot of us, when no one spoke again, Malachi continued, "All right then, we leave tonight. Each of us. All seven of us. Reuben, William, Joseph, and Thomas to the North. John and I to seek the Cherokee decision. And Silas to the caves, where he can live close by here, hunt during the day and farm and help care for the women and children. He'll take care of the family but join no army and still prove that he's not a coward; he's our brother. He will protect the family. Now, I say, we pack our things and leave tonight."

As astounding as it might seem, Malachi's words became law. The youngest of us had spoken and we listened. We left that night, in different directions.

NOTES

[1] Lincoln was elected in November 1860. South Carolina seceded as a result of the election. Seven states formed the Confederacy by spring of 1861. The South claimed all military holdings as their own. Lincoln refused to turn any forts over to the Southern forces. Instead, he attempted to supply Fort Sumter with provisions. The confederacy attacked Fort Sumter on April 12, 1861 (American Battlefield Trust, 2021).

[2] This quote is from Lincoln's (December 1, 1862) annual address to Congress, concluding remarks. So William could not have actually quoted these words in 1861.

CHAPTER 5

BRAVE WOMEN

The Night of December 18, 1865

I returned to the cabin with an armload of firewood and the recollection of that momentous night still swirling in my brain. Nearly four years ago we had gone our separate ways. Now, under the most wretched of conditions, we were together again, all but Malachi. I kicked the snow from my boots against the side of the porch, one light tap each, so as not to awaken the sleepers inside the cabin. Then I shifted the dried branches to my left arm and opened the cabin door, letting in light and cold simultaneously. After shutting the door, I tiptoed past the bundled bodies to the hearth.

Cracking branches and wedging dried leaves between the spaces of the grating, I built a base for a fire. Using my father's tinderbox, I struck a spark, blew light breaths onto the brush and placed twigs and leaves under the angled space created by the branch that leaned against the log. The grating was small and the fire would need refueling often, I thought. For now, I was satisfied with it. Sparks jumped up the daub-lined flue and flames gave the cabin a warm glow.

I ladled another drink of water to my patients, starting with my children just because they were closest to where I had left the bucket.

"Willie," I lifted his head, "Here, son, have some water." He obeyed without a word.

"More," I coaxed, but he turned his head and groaned. The girls were more difficult to handle. Awkwardly, I scooped up Sarah, the baby, into one arm and tried to put the ladle to her lips but she wouldn't drink. I ended up spilling it on her; she cried. I set both the baby and the ladle down, wet my fingers in the bucket and placed them in her mouth. She sucked for a moment, but not with any enthusiasm. I then took Nannie, our two-year-old daughter, from Julia's protection.

Nannie arched her back and cried aloud, fighting me as I tried to spoon the liquid into her mouth. The adults were more pliant, of course.

Each was parched and feeling poorly. I gave Julia a sip of water; and then, she fell back into an uncomfortable sleep. My sister Nan was next. She too slid backward after taking a mere sip of water as though it had taken the strength and determination of a besieged army to do so. Her torn dress flapped open and I couldn't help but to see that a rash was spreading across her upper chest and lower neck, likely it covered her stomach. I could see that same rash on my children's bellies. I covered my sister with a blanket, which seemed to make her more uncomfortable, itchy. She scratched at herself and threw the cover off and then pulled it back with a shiver. Pausing a moment, I looked past Nan to Julia lying next to her, their heads nearly touching. Nan's black hair fell in an interlacing fashion about Julia's auburn tresses. Such an unlikely pair to have become friends, I thought. After all, Nan derived her name and temperament from her namesake the great woman warrior, *Nannye-hi*.[1] And Julia, … my thought was interrupted.

"Silas," a whisper came from the corner.

"What Lydia?" I answered.

"I don't feel good."

"I know. What can I do for you?"

"I don't know."

"Do you want some water?" I asked, standing up.

"No."

"Some food?" I walked closer to her and watched as she sat up.

"Sit by me?" she requested. I made room between my sisters Lydia and Martha, wriggling my way in and waking Martha in the process.

"Tell me a story." Lydia reached for my hand as I settled in.

"I'm not good at stories, Lydia." Lydia was the youngest of my sisters, barely thirteen-years-old. I stroked her smooth, dark hair,

"Why don't you try to get some rest," I added.

"I can't," she said weakly.

"Maybe Nan will tell us a story," Martha suggested, trying to be helpful in her own meek way. Martha is the most beautiful of my sisters with her doe-like eyes that seem eternally moist like morning dew. Her lips are just plump enough to remind one of a baby rose bud and they curl into a smile like a ribbon fluttering on a breeze. Martha's wide eyes and gentle lips grant her an innocence and youthful look that is immediately balanced by the maturity of highly-sculpted cheekbones. She hides too often behind her sleek, raven-colored hair, making herself tinier and tinier and more difficult for others to see. People have remarked about the fact that she looks like my mother's cousin, *Kilakeena*.[2]

"Nan," I asked. "What do you think? Are you well enough to tell a story?"

"Tell one about *Nannye-hi*," Lydia interjected.

"Will you, Nan?" Elizabeth pleaded, raising herself up on one elbow.

"Will I what?"

"Will you tell us the story of *Nannye-hi*, the beautiful warrior woman?" Lydia asked.

"She was beautiful and strong. Wasn't she?" Mary entered the conversation.

Elizabeth added, "And a Chieftain's daughter."

"Yes, yes. She was all of those things—tall and beautiful and brave. She married the handsome and courageous *Kingfisher*. By the time she was my age, seventeen, she had borne him two children and made diplomatic ventures in his name. Once when they had traveled to the southern borders of our territory, they came under attack," Nan seemed to take strength from her story. She sat up. "Can I have more water, Silas?"

I took the bucket and ladle to her. She sipped several times from the ladle before continuing the story. I returned to my place by Lydia.

"During this fierce battle, *Nannye-hi*[3] took cover behind a fallen log near her husband's side. She reloaded his rifle for him and chewed on bullets so that these enemies would surely die from their jagged wounds. The air grew thick with smoke. The sound of the rifles blasting met the cries of warriors dying. Suddenly, *Nannye-hi* felt a spray of something warm and wet across her face. Within a breath, a cold shadow crossed over her. *Kingfisher*'s strong body crashed to the ground beside *Nannye-hi*.

"The young woman threw herself over her husband's body. Warriors yelled to one another, *Kingfisher has fallen! Kingfisher has fallen!* A fear spread among the warriors. Retreat seemed inevitable. Yet, *Nannye-hi* would not have it. She raised herself up from *Kingfisher's* body. She let out a war whoop that called the warriors to arms. She took up *Kingfisher's* rifle and fired at the Muskogee warriors. One by one, the brave young *Tsaragi* men, who had been ready to retreat, turned and faced their enemy, again. So it was, under the leadership of *Nannye-hi*, the Cherokee won the battle. And *Nannye-hi* became a Beloved War Woman of the Nation." My sisters all fell silent until my brother Joseph raised their ire.

"I've heard that *Nannye-hi* was a traitor," he asserted.

"No!" Lydia contested.

"She wasn't a traitor," Nan agreed with Lydia. "You don't know the whole story."

"Oh, and just what is the whole story?" Joseph coaxed.

"It was after *Kingfisher's* death. Our warriors planned an attack against a white settlement where *Nannye-hi* had met a man, a white man, with whom she'd fallen in love. When she heard about the attack, she warned the white settlers, but she also knew that our warriors planned to take the lives of all the whites on that night—women and children not just the men. *We are not murderers of the innocent*, she declared."

"Tell us more," Elizabeth pleaded, leaning forward toward my sister Nan. Nan inhaled, gathering her strength.

"A long time ago," Nan began, "the Birdtown village had been viciously attacked by whites who set fires to houses, trampled the harvest, and shot their rifles at fleeing Cherokee. When the air cleared of smoke and the people returned to their homes, they discovered two Cherokee bodies, an elderly man and his granddaughter. The bodies lie together; shot and trampled. Their families cried. The people of the village demanded revenge in order to restore balance to the world. *Two white people must be killed*, they determined. So the men of the village mounted their ponies and rode to the nearest white settlement where they kidnapped a white woman and a teenage boy.

"The woman and the boy were brought back to the village so that the people of Birdtown could witness their execution. Cherokee warriors tied each captive to a stake, surrounded their feet with kindling and prepared to set them ablaze, when *Nanny-hi* came out of her abode. She strode before the captives, measuring them with her eye. The men stood by with torches ready. *Nannye-hi* raised her hand and commanded, *Let the woman go.*

"Only the Beloved Women have the right to make life and death decisions," my sister reminded us. "So the men untied the woman and delivered her to *Nannye-hi.*

"*Nannye-hi* then signaled her approval and the warriors set kindling under the boy's feet afire. They burned him alive."

"That's awful," my wife Julia cringed. Nan ignored Julia's comment.

"The woman became *Nannye-hi*'s instructor in all things good that she could teach her from the white people's ways, including dairying, spinning, weaving, and bee-keeping. And *Nannye-hi*, in turn, taught the other women of Birdtown. Harmony and balance were restored," Nan finished.

"Good story, Nan. *Wado*," Lydia thanked her, weakly adding, "Silas, I still don't feel good."

"I don't want the children to hear such stories," Julia snapped, while trying to cover Willie's ears and acting as if she hadn't heard of such atrocities. Julia continued, "Silas, tell them, these are heathen stories." She prompted me.

"Oh, and white people aren't heathens?" Nan asked sarcastically.

"What do you mean?" Julia sounded offended.

"What about the story that you told us?"

"Which one?"

"The one about the Machabees, where the King ordered an Israelite boy to eat pork thus forsaking the Laws of his God and when the boy refused the Syrian King ordered frying pans and cauldrons to be heated and then he had the boy's tongue cut out. And when he still refused, the soldiers tore off the skin from his face, and chopped off his hands and feet, and at last threw him into the red, hot frying pan."[4]

"Yes, but those were the pagans who did that to the Hebrews," Julia explained.

"So, these Pagans taught the Hebrews and the Hebrews taught the Christians?"[5] At this comment, Julia sounded stunned.

"What do you mean?" she claimed indignantly.

"I mean the Spaniards were far more vicious than any Indians," Nan exclaimed.

"No, that's not true. Silas, tell her," she called on me again. Nan persisted.

"Your hero, Columbia,"

"You mean Columbus," Julia corrected.

"Yes, Christopher Columbus. He and his men were monsters, murderers,[6] and rapists.[7] Weren't they Silas?" Now my sister Nan invoked my support; I didn't answer her, either.

"Julia, Andrew Jackson sent his men into the field after the Battle of Horseshoe Bend, to take a nose count, literally cutting off the noses of the dead and dying—men, women, and children. Then soldiers cut up the bodies, making hats out of women's wombs after tossing babies aside, making horse's reins out of men's hides," Nan continued. "Is this Christianity?"

"Hush, now." My mother sought quiet, but Nan continued. "They sliced 'em up the back side as if they were skinning a rabbit, and one boy, who was shot but not yet dead, was set afire by the soldiers. As this boy tried to crawl away, the soldiers caught his flaming body grease and poured it on their potatoes."[8]

"Lies," Julia exclaimed. "Silas, tell her," Julia commanded as she reached up from her blanketed bed.

"Silas!" Julia invoked me yet again with what must've been all her strength.

I didn't answer her. I didn't answer either one of them.

"Hush now, all of you," my mother repeated more firmly. "Get some sleep." And with that each settled down, but not without a few murmurs and disgruntled pleas.

NOTES

1. *Nannye-hi* means One-Who-Wanders-With-The-Spirits-in a good way (Gridley, 1974).
2. To compare photocopies of Kilakeena and Martha see the preface of this novel.
3. For stories of Kingfisher and Nannye-hi (a.k.a. Nancy Ward) see Gridley (1974, pp. 39–46). In addition, Mooney's, *Historical Sketch of the Cherokee* (1975 published separately and with additional and preface materials; also the Kingfisher story is available in Mooney (1891, 1900/1992)), which was reprinted from his extensive reports housed by the Bureau

of American Ethnology in the 1800s and includes a biographical sketch of Nancy Ward. In addition, note that a previous reference places the Wolf Clan to the north. It is believed that the Wolf Clan encampments encircled the Nation (interview with Marvin Summerfield, 1997, Cherokee linguist and activist). Furthermore, the reader may find it interesting to know that stories of women warriors are not uncommon among the Cherokee. Mooney (1891, 1900/1992) reports other stories of women warriors in his collection (e.g., see the story of *Cuhtahlatah*—Wild Hemp and others, pp. 394–395).

4   Mooney (1891, 1900/1992).

5   Friar Bartolome de Las Casas, who wrote the *History of the Indies* in 1552, reported the following: [The Spaniards] "made bets as to who would slit a man in two, or cut off his head at one blow; or they opened up his bowels. They tore the babies from their mother's breast by their feet, and dashed their heads against the rocks...They spitted the bodies of other babes ... on their swords, ... [They hanged Indians] by thirteens, in honor and reverence for our Redeemer and the twelve Apostles... All this did my own eyes witness" (Las Casas, as cited in Josephy Jr., 1994, p. 114).

6   Columbus and his men attacked a group of peaceful Indians cutting off one man's head and taking the other men and women as slaves. Columbus gave one of the women away as a gift to a friend. Columbus's friend then raped the woman. The following is his account of what happened: "I took a most beautiful Carab woman, whom the lord Admiral [Columbus] made a gift to me; and having her in my berth, with her being nude ... the desire to enjoy myself with her came over me; and wishing to put my desire to work, she resisting, she scratched me with her fingernails to such a degree that I would not have wished then that I had begun; but with that seen ... I grabbed a leather strap and gave her a good chastisement of lashes, so that she hurled such unheard of shouts that you could not believe. Finally, we reached an agreement in such a manner that I can tell you that in fact she seemed to have been taught in the school of whores (see Josephy, Jr., 1994, p. 123).

7   Spaniards became known as The-Ones-Who-Chase-Women-and-Make-Them Cry. The native people had no word for rape in the 15th century (Josephy Jr., 1994).

8   For a detailed description of the carnage in battles prior to and following the Battle of Horseshoe Bend see Thurman Wilkins (1986). The reports are based on eye-witness accounts.

CHAPTER 6

MEETING JULIA'S CONVICTIONS

December 18, 1865

I don't know why I didn't answer Julia. It certainly wasn't the first time that she had beseeched me on behalf of Christianity—*Silas, tell her*. Nor was this the first time I had ignored her requests. At times, she became quite petulant with me.

At any rate, I left Lydia's side and returned to my place at the table. I couldn't explain to myself why I wouldn't answer Julia or why I was annoyed that Nan had now added to this strategy, I paused to think—*this tactic, this maneuver, this way to manipulate me to support each, to take sides, doesn't sit well with me.*

What kept me from saying, *That's right, Julia.* A part of me, felt that I should. She is my wife, after all. And I had become a Christian. But by saying yes to Julia, was I necessarily saying that Nan was wrong? After all, Nan wasn't wrong. Besides, if I agreed with Julia, I would have to endure Nan's silent censoring of me; but, if I supported Nan then Julia's wrath would have been a maddening series of reprisals, from vigilant Bible quotes to fervent interrogations about my faith.

I recalled when Julia and I met—in the fall of 1858 at a Sunday Meeting. It didn't take me long at all to decide that Julia's church was for me. It'd been my father's religious home at one time, as well, and he had mentioned it to me on occasion. But what most confirmed me to that Church might well be credited to Julia.

I'd seen some of the countryside and even made my way into Charleston not long after my twenty-first birthday. I left that town somewhat disappointed by the women I had met or had simply seen. Many of them floated down the sunny streets, covered by parasols, and humming like birds. They seemed flimsy somehow, like down feathers or dandelion wisps. Plus, they could judge a man worthy in a single glance and dismiss him just as quickly. Julia was different.

Julia had a solid stature. She had a beautiful face with a broad forehead and a sweeping smile. Wide eyes set against dark auburn hair that she pulled loosely up in a bun atop her head. Her dresses were modest and swished about her full hips, while the debutantes of Charleston wore crepe dresses that buoyed from hoops in wild circles around their ballet feet. Not Julia. Her clothing was usually dark in color, subdued, and her shoes were sensible, as some folks like to say. There wasn't anything tiny or dainty about Julia accept maybe that lace collar that she'd add for accent to her button-up dress. Julia had a waist bigger than mine and arms strong enough to milk cows, bale hay, churn butter, and hoe all day. Her bosom was ample, maternal, you might say, before she ever had a baby. She could mother a small town if need be and she certainly took to mothering me, teaching me religion and etiquette.

I became her project within a few days of meeting her. She asked me at the first Sunday meeting what skills I might bring to a family and I answered the way I thought my father would've liked a gentleman to answer:

"Miss, my father told me never to brag that I could bring down a quail with ease if it took me more than a sheet full of lead to do so. But, ma'am, I believe I can honestly say that I *can* bring down a quail in a single shot if that's what you're hankerin' for dinner." To my surprise and pleasure, the lady did laugh.

"So you're a hunter," she had queried lightly.

"Yes, Miss, I am."

"What else do you hunt besides quail?"

"When I was fourteen an Indian friend of ours gave us a dog for hunting raccoon. Ole Tige we called him and I would have to say that Ole Tige is probably the better hunter of the two us. For he never once barked up a tree where we didn't find a raccoon sleeping. So I have had many a raccoon meal. But if I were to brag for just a moment, I would have to say that deer and wild turkey are the tastiest meals I've brought home to my family." She let me finish my bragging although it became evident that she became most curious when I mentioned our Indian friends.

"Real Indians?"

"Yes, Miss. Is there another kind?" This again, although I didn't intend it to, made her laugh.

"You grew up with Indians?"

"Yes, Miss."

"Can you read? Do you know your Bible?

"No Miss, not much."

"Oh my!"

That was the sweetest and most heartfelt, *oh my*, I ever did hear. After that I became Julia's project. She had her father give me a job on their farm and she gave me a few reading lessons and a lot of religion lessons, daily. Julia herself read the Bible at breakfast, lunch and dinner. At first it seemed to me that she practically ate Bible verses. As the months passed, I learned not only to eat Bible verses along with her, but to relish them. I did tell Julia that hunting and preaching were similar in many ways and that I thought a man might spread the word of the Lord to others, like myself, if he made it clear through these comparisons. For example, I told her, that:

"A rifle, a preacher, and a teacher are much alike."

"In what way?" she asked me.

"Well, Miss, I own a splendid fashion old flint lock double-trigger rifle. Now when I go hunting I clean out my gun, well-pick the flint to insure as far as possible success. That is the first step any hunter must take—make sure the rifle is clean, inside. That's how a rifle, a preacher, and a teacher are alike, for if any one of them is dirty or crooked inside, they are not trustworthy."[1] This parable pleased her and she smiled and asked for more. I obliged, of course.

After months of Christian education under the guidance of my then hoped for wife-to-be, I had taken to further developing my analogies into parable-like stories in such a way as they nearly became full-fledged sermons for the Appalachian hunter-preacher. For example, I eventually told Julia the following:

"Time is a gift from the Creator that can be experienced down to its tiniest component. And if we're patient enough to detail our experiences we can see just how each experience relates us back to the Creator. You take hunting, for example, I remember a time that we had run out of meat. So I planned a hunt. I planned it in my mind in silence and in good faith before I even cleaned my rifle or took my first steps toward the forest. After entering the forest, I went from place to place that I knew would be good feeding grounds for deer at certain times of the day, but I spotted nothing. Sunset found me a mile from home, hungry, tired and much discouraged. However, as I turned my course for home, I resolved to keep up my courage as long as the fading twilight would permit me to see how to shoot. I could think of only three spots where it was likely that a deer might be feeding at that time of evening. So I went on my way. I had approached the last one, although it was quite dark in the valley, the western slopes that I had reached were not so dark and I discovered about sixty yards away something that resembled a deer.

"It was so still that I knew that if it was a deer it would likely spring away the next second. Time was precious. I strained my eyes to their full strength. I decided it to be a deer; my gun was still on my shoulder. I dropped it on my arm, set the triggers, pulled back the hammer, raised the gun to my shoulder, charged myself with good aim, placed my index finger of my right hand an eighth of an inch in front of the trigger with order to wait for further orders. I directed my aim very carefully at the command of my brain when the aim was found correct the order to hold until the finger is instructed and moves up to the trigger. All this had taken about five seconds, from the time that I had decided as to game. The finger being instructed to move the trigger in a reasonable length of time to press until the trigger was released and started on its journey of a half inch to the dog of the lock, the dog being loosed from the hold of the tumbler; the hammer with flint in teeth immediately started on a trip to about an inch and a half to the steel; the flint and steel must now take time to create a spark of fire, before anything else is done, then the entire muscle and structure was commanded to hold steady until the ball could be discharged. If the effort to create fire had been a failure, then the result would've been like that of a preacher, trying to preach without the fire of the Holy Ghost in his heart.

"But at the first stroke of the flint a spark was struck which started on its way to the pan that held the priming powder, at a distance of an inch. As soon as it reached the powder, it began to kindle a fire, as soon as the powder in the pan was all burned the fire passed through the touch hole into the charge which was placed behind the ball waiting its turn to act. As soon as the fire broke out in the gun a rush sped the maddened ball through the only outlet on a straightforward path regardless of what might be hurt or in its way. Although the rush of the ball was so rapid, I was compelled to hold still until each inch of the whole length of the gun barrel were passed through an inch at a time. As soon as the missile was free from the gun I was powerless to do more, but to hope that no intervening obstacles would turn it from its path. I do believe a preacher must know his flock in the same way that a good hunter knows his rifle. And I do believe that the preacher must sit back powerless after giving the people the Word of God.

"In this particular case, the bullet made its way straight through the intervening sixty yards and at a speed faster than it would take sound to travel the same distance. As soon as I heard the deer fall I said in my heart, *It is finished; it is mine.* I had toiled all day with only faith, hope and courage, as my incentives. I was now ready to go home with the reward of my labors. On my way to the game, I examined the ground over which my messenger, that is the bullet, had passed, and found many intervening obstacles, which might have turned its course, such as I couldn't see in the dim twilight of the moment in which my victory was won.

"The lesson I learned from this is the great importance of faith, hope, courage, endurance, patience, and trust. I trusted myself and my gun because I had tried both. Yet I, gun, and powder were all powerless without fire. A preacher, man or woman, well charged with the Holy Ghost, having the fire of Christian love burning upon the main altar of the heart can kindle a flame of Divine Love in the hearts of others by simply presenting the fervent truth of the gospel in its simplicity."[2]

Julia sat before me that day, listening with full rapture as could be seen in her still posture, poised on the edge of the seat with her wide-open eyes. I waited for her assessment.

"As sure as there is a heaven above, Silas, you were meant to be a preacher," Julia had complimented me and there is nothing finer than to have a woman praise your strengths, unless maybe it's to have her overlook your weaknesses.

45

"Oh, and always reload your weapon right away. You never know what the Lord will bring your way," I added. She laughed again in a most delightful way.

I had met the expectations of a husband-to-be and then on the day I told Julia, *You are the reason the sun shines*—the Good Lord delivered my wife to me. I must admit to a twinge of guilt and a stain being placed on my soul when I used that phrase, *You are the reason the sun shines,* as I had stolen another man's poetry, a man who'd I'd met along the way.

Nevertheless, not long after that she accepted my proposal and the suggestion to come and live with my family. We planned to return to the mountains, farm, hunt, and preach for the rest of our happy lives. We didn't have much time for happily ever after, what with the war years creeping up on us.

So I wondered, as I remembered my conversion and my proposal, and that I had stolen another man's poetry, pretending that it was mine, was I only pretending to be a preacher. *Silas, tell them,* I heard her words echo in my mind.

Of course, I didn't want to offend Nan either. But I knew my silent response went beyond politeness. They were so filled with their convictions that they simply overwhelmed me. I loved them both; I didn't mean to deny either one. They seemed ablaze with their beliefs. I, on the other hand, found neither side really fulfilled me.

I sighed and shifted in my seat. As I looked over this dreadful scene, bundled bodies clustered in this wretched cabin, Julia sleeping on the floor with our children in the folds of her blanket, I thought, *I should've answered her.* But then I looked at my sister Nan's black hair, dusty with dirt and falling over her torn blouse, and wondered how I could possibly deny her. *They're so different,* I thought *and yet so very much alike.*

Silas, tell them—the words haunted me. Who am I to tell anyone, anything? I stared into the fire. But I suppose they each have the right to seek my loyalty; after all, each had stood up for me. But does loyalty demand that I choose between them—Christian or Cherokee? Julia is my wife and Nan is my sister. Why does Nan have to fight so? Many Cherokee have become Christians. I shook my head, stood up and stretched my legs. I looked at Julia.

Silas, tell her, the words echoed in my head, as did my silence that followed. I looked at each of them, sleeping on the floor. My silence was inexcusable, considering what they had each done for me. But how was I to choose between them?

NOTES

[1] This piece of wisdom and the following story/parable comes directly from the pages of the S.M. Beasley story as provided by Shackelford Sims (1978).

[2] Some minor adjustments have been made to grammar, spelling, and wording.

CHAPTER 7

A RIFLE, A LOCKET, AND COMBS

December 18, 1865

In my pretense to be a preacher I had promised Julia a certain kind of life. As I sat in this cabin surveying the scene, I realized that I had in some ways cheated her. But at the time, I hadn't meant to misdirect her. Truly I felt the Holy Spirit in me when I was with her and meant in every way for us to farm and hunt and preach until our dying days, but the civil unrest between the States most certainly took that away.

During the war years, I mostly hid from both the Union and the Confederate armies, each of whom wished to conscript me and any other poor fella they could get their hands on. So I hid by day and went to see my family by night. At least it was hide and seek until Julia took my combs to an officer in the Union army and showed him, as she put it, their abundant qualities to save a soldier's sanity, worth a prayer and whatever's in your pocketbook. I had spent so many long and solitary hours in the caves that I'd taken to whittling. I whittled combs of great beauty, but those weren't the ones that both the Northern and later the Southern armies exchanged for my freedom from their pursuit. No, it was the fine-toothed combs that they wanted. I whittled the teeth of the wooden combs so fiercely close together that these combs could pull the lice from a man's hair and not leave a single egg behind. For that, a stable supply of combs, the Union officer promised Julia that he would leave me to my work.

Nan, however, was the one who braved the battleground and made her way into the mountains to find me when I hadn't come to them at our pre-specified day and time. She had saved my life in a different way from Julia.

My family would call me with a secret code that they'd beat out on a hollowed log that would echo through the mountains. I'd know from the beat whether the soldiers were near or far. They'd sent me

49

several messages that the regiments had moved out of the area, but I hadn't heard because I was ill. Days passed and still I hadn't sneaked into my family's house to bring them fresh deer meat and visit my kin. The soldiers eventually moved back into the area and Nan, with cannons blasting around her, made her way into the mountains to find me.

As I have mentioned, I had taken ill. Too sick to even answer the drum beats, I'd laid on the cave floor waiting to die. Nan found me. She guided me out of the cave, placed my hands on the horn of the saddle, and half hoisted and partly pushed me atop my horse. I slumped in the saddle.

"My rifle," I managed to say.

"I have father's rifle; we'll be fine," she told me. Nevertheless, she returned to the cave to hide mine deeper inside. She then came back to me, mounted my father's horse, and took mine by the reins. My head spun and my eyelids felt like rocks. I burned with fever and felt half crazy. I entrusted myself to my sister, allowing my horse to plod along. We curled down and around the mountainside so hidden under lush autumn foliage that we hardly knew night from day. Yet, nearing sunset we found ourselves, lowering our heads under the lacey branches of the hemlock trees that grew near home. She had been glancing back at me on a regular basis but now her worry eased. And just then, when we expected it least, we heard the gruff voice which startled us.

"That's far enough," the voice commanded. By now my fever was so extreme that I hoped and thought I might be hallucinating. But Nan turned around first and as I saw the look on her face I realized that this was no dream.

I looked up to see a man adorned in a patchwork coat of square pockets, all black on black, over a black and white checkered shirt that was partially covered by a black and gray striped vest. His hat another shade of dark; his boots faded black leather, his gloves the same monochromatic theme; and yet, he seemed so colorful to me. Must have been the patterns. He sat without speaking again for some time, aiming his rifle at us, stroking his beard, which was thick enough to match any fur I'd ever tanned, which made me think he might be the Bear-man that the Cherokee speak of around midnight campfires. Even his head was covered in a mass of curly black hair that bulged from underneath his hat. His black eyes were as beady as an opossum's eyes. He licked his teeth, which is when his black ensemble was interrupted by one sight—red blood trickling over his yellowed teeth, not an oddity for these impoverished times, I supposed, but his bleeding gums seemed like an infinite fountain.He circled around in front of us. I tried to steady myself in my seat, but the more I tried the more unbalanced I became. Wooziness was coming over me. The woods were beginning to spin. His words were not quite clear.

"I'm not a greedy man, but I am a practical one." Then looking directly at my sister he added, "The Union army pays me well for bringing in deserters like him."

"He's not a deserter; he's my brother."

"That don't matter to me." He eyed me and I could barely lift my head.

"How do you plan to buy your way past me?" he asked of my sister. She didn't respond.

"The way I see it, you got three things here that interest me, besides this here deserter. That rifle," he nodded toward my father's gun, which sat sheathed in a holster and strapped to the side of my father's horse, which Nan rode. "Your horse, …" and here he rode up alongside of Nan and used his rifle, the tip of the barrel, to knock her blanket free. It fell from around her shoulders and onto the rump of the horse. She sat very still. I tried to upright myself, but my head was pounding and I couldn't see.

"How old are ya?" he asked gruffly, his breath on her face.

"Almost fifteen."

"That's almost old enough for me."

"Leave her be," I managed to say. He laughed.

"Like I said, I'm not a greedy man; at times, I can be downright generous. Give me the rifle and I'll let you be." Nan hesitated. He glared at her. I wanted to say, *Give him the rifle*, but I'm not sure if the words came out of my mouth. Nan reached to the side and slid the rifle from its leather sheath. She handed it over.

"And promise you'll come see me when you do turn fifteen," he contorted with laughter, his bloodied teeth dancing behind pale lips. But when she didn't answer him, he grabbed the rifle from her hands, set it across his thighs, and quickly grabbed her by the chin. He forced a kiss on her mouth and then refused to release her jaw.

"Promise," he demanded squeezing her face tight. "Promise!"

"I promise," she lied defiantly. He laughed a mighty laugh that rolled throughout the holler, turned the reins of his horse, and rode away.

I didn't have to be able to see Nan's face to know that there were tears in her eyes, anger in her heart, and embarrassment in her soul.

By the time we made it home, I could stay in the saddle no longer. I let myself fall from my horse. Nan went to get help. My father arrived to assist me into the house.

"Where's my rifle?" he questioned Nan as he noticed the empty sheath. He was wrapping my arm around his shoulder and half dragging me into the house.

"Lost," she said.

"Lost where?" he scolded.

"I accidentally dropped it over a ravine."

"I knew I shouldn't have entrusted my only rifle to a girl. Now what are we going to do?" He was angry.

Although I could barely think, I silently vowed to myself, at that moment, that one day I would buy a rifle for Nan to give to my father.

Days later, while I was still weak with a fever, a Confederate officer and his men arrived at the house. My sisters had already taken the pains to construct a hiding place for me under the floorboards of the living room. At the sound of the Confederates' horses' hooves, I climbed into this unholy grave for the living and Julia and Nan covered it with a rug and the dining table. I heard the door barge open.

"What do we have here?" A brusque voice called out. Silence followed. From my hiding place, I waited with tense anticipation for someone to speak. I heard something hit the floor and the shuffling of quick steps. One of my children had dropped something, I thought; I braced myself.

"Where are the men?" the voice came again. And then I could hear his slow footsteps making their way around the cabin, I envisioned him intimidating the women and children, each in turn. "Answer me, woman," he shouted.

"You, child, where are the men hiding?" He must have knelt in front of my son's face as I heard a sliding motion as he stood back up. I held my breath. *Please, Willie, don't speak.*

"You, old woman, tell me, where are your sons?"

"They've followed the seventh direction," my mother asserted.

"Don't talk crazy, old woman. Just tell me where they are."

"I've told you. Now leave my home, and my homeland." I heard a shuffling of feet.

"You, old man, where are your sons, sir?"

"Off to war," my father answered.

"This isn't over," the deep voice railed.

"Here, take this," I heard Julia say and in time I also heard the front door closing. Julia gave the officer some food and a bag filled with combs for his men; and then, she followed him out onto the front porch where she presumed she was out of earshot, but my unholy grave left me in the crawlspace and within easy hearing of their conversation.

"It's not enough." I heard him say.

A moment later, I heard her say, "Take this. It's solid gold." The only piece of solid gold jewelry that Julia owned was a locket that she wore around her neck, given to her by her mother and father. It then contained a lock of Willie's hair.

"I'll take that horse, too. And I want a steady supply of these lice combs. If your husband agrees to deliver the combs, then I'll stop hunting him." Somehow the Confederate officer had heard about my combs. While I still lay in the dark underground hole, I swore that someday I would replace the gold locket that Julia had given away on my behalf.

The officer and his soldiers left without looking any more deeply into the matter of my whereabouts. Thus, the Confederate army stopped trying to conscript me and I subsequently made combs for both the North and the South.

Although certainly not amusing at the time, I smiled now at the thought of it. For in the days and weeks that followed I set up a comb factory of sorts in the mountains of North Carolina that helped to protect me and to support my family, throughout the rest of the war. Julia delivered these items to both the Northern and the Southern forces, without prejudice.

My smile faded, now, as I looked across the room at my wife and sister curled uncomfortably on the floor of this God-forsaken cabin. I owed each of them more than a rifle or a locket. I owed them my life.

I set my musket aside and went to my wife and sister's side. Glancing down on Julia and Nan, I meant to find a way to comfort them. I pulled the blanket about their shoulders.

"More water?" I offered to Nan and then Julia, but neither one responded. Each pale and pock marked, too weak to take a sip of water. I shook my head. I took in the image of Julia's auburn hair interlaced with Nan's black strands. As I knelt on one knee, I smoothed a lock of hair away from Julia's face; she suddenly flinched with fear.

"No," she cried out; her arm flew up as if to protect herself. She started to squirm away, just as she had when that Rebel soldier had taken her by the arms.

"Julia, it's me, Silas," I spoke softly, taking her wrists in my hands and lowering them to her sides.

Never before had my wife cringed at my touch. Never! Anger rose up inside of me that curled my fingers into a fist. "I swear before God, I'll kill those men, if they come back." With this promise made, I started to stand up.

With a weak whisper, but a strong grip at my pant leg, Julia addressed me, "Silas, please don't. You promised. Remember what the Good Book says, 'Revenge is mine, sayeth the Lord!'[1] Promise me you won't kill those men." I didn't answer.

"Their blood will be on my hands," she pleaded. Still, I didn't answer her.

"Please."

I swallowed hard and then assured her, "It'll be all right." I stroked her hair; and then lowering myself, I lay by her side, my hand draped over her waist. My children nestled next to her. I was drifting off to sleep when, in the darkness, I heard my sister Nan say, "Revenge is the only reason to kill."[2]

NOTES

[1] *Deuteronomy* 32:34–36 also see *Hebrews* 10:30–31 Bible.

[2] The Cherokee, of the time, believed that revenge was one way to restore balance and harmony after someone had been murdered. Only one revenge murder was allowed. The avenger could take the life of the murderer or anyone one of his family members and then the matter must end. The only other recourse for a murderer and his family was for the murderer to seek refuge in the peace city. Upon reaching the peace city the murderer and his or her family members could be spared.

CHAPTER 8

MY FATHER SITS SENTRY

December 19, 1865

"Silas." I heard my father's voice; I wavered between wake and sleep. I wondered how long he'd been calling me as I forced my eyelids open. I rose onto one knee, and then stood; I left Julia's side and took the water to him.

"Are any of your brothers well enough to help you?"

"No, sir."

"Has Malachi returned yet?"

"No, sir."

"He'll come," my father promised.

"Yes, sir," I said, ladling water for him, but I knew that there was no way for Malachi to know where we'd gone. In a moment of desperation, I'd moved the family quickly and without informing anyone. I wasn't sure if Malachi would ever find us with him being west of the Mississippi with the Western Band of Cherokee, unlike John who'd enlisted with Thomas' Eastern Band of Cherokee.[1] "But Arkansas is pretty far away," I added.

"No, he'll come," my father asserted with sureness.

"Silas, the pine tree holds the strongest medicine," my mother inserted. I'd give her water in a moment, I thought.

"Silas," my father continued, "You need to get more water and firewood."

"*Tsiskwa'gwa*," my mother moaned. Again in a tortured voice, she repeated the word, "*Tsiskwa'gwa!*" I looked to my father again.

"What's she talking about?"

"*Tsiskwa'gwa* was a woman from the Bird Clan. She taught your mother all about healing medicines," my father informed me and then took a shallow breath that wheezed like the whistle of the wind through a crack in the wall as he exhaled. He held his chest as he did so.

"Give me the rifle, son" he told me. "You go get more water and wood."

"Are you sure you're strong enough?" I hesitated, not sure whether to give him the rifle. My father, seventy years old and sick with a miserable fever and wracking cough, would barely be able to balance the rifle on his knee, if he could sit up.

"Don't make me tell you twice, son."

I gave him the rifle.

Standing outside, I realized that my hesitation was more than uncertainty about my father's ability to handle the rifle. A branch snapped; I turned and reached for my gun, but my hand came up light. Being without a weapon, especially in the stark brightness of the day, nagged at me with each step. The wintry landscape reinforced these feelings in me as the sun shone brightly exposing naked trees, a vulnerable landscape. Their crisp shadows crossed the thin layer of snow that covered the ground. Markings which were as vivid as fresh ink on a sheet of white stationery, reminding me of when Julia begins to write a letter home to her parents or documents a date in our Bible. In order for me not to pen my presence onto that wintry scenery, I would have to be as a deer. Camouflaged. Invisible. This is achieved by becoming a log, a tree, a stump, a bush or forest animal. In spirit. I could be like the *Ani Kawi*, the *Deer People*—the deer, just by thinking it so.

I scanned the woods both close and far. This time, I found nothing of concern. Each of my steps crunched less underfoot as I became more like the deer. I found a recently fallen branch, a pignut hickory, with many dead twigs still attached. I dragged it back to the cabin. It would dry quickly and burn slowly, but it might pop and spark more than other woods. I used my foot to crack it into smaller pieces before bringing them inside the cabin.

The open door sent a rush of cold through the cabin. Mice scattered across the floor; one sped over William's shoulder. My father shuddered. We were the only two to see the rodents. Mostly hidden under blankets, the rest of the sick curled tightly against the frigid gust of wind; others didn't even flinch. My father looked up at me as I stepped around figures and walked across the room. He didn't speak, but gripped the rifle tighter. After stoking the flame, I took the bucket and my canteen and left again.

I thought about what roots might be hidden under this thin layer of snow that I could boil for them, but I couldn't think of what might cure them. Maybe it didn't matter. Not a single one of them seemed able to eat much and barely took water.

The ice dappled-snow sparkled in front of me as I made my way to the riverbank. I filled the bucket. My fingers felt the sting of the icy water and winter breeze against my metal canteen as I refilled it, as well. As it met that familiar weight, fullness, I capped it and slung its strap over my shoulder and across my chest. Then I reached for the bucket. Water sloshed as I carried it by its short hemp handle. The fibers of the rope were fraying and threatened to turn to slender icicles in my hand. I headed back to the cabin. Off to my left as I neared the cabin, I saw a pile of brush with dried leaves trapped inside—excellent fire starter, I thought.

I reached the porch without losing too much of the liquid, set the oaken bucket down on the front stoop of the cabin, and returned to the pile of brush and leaves. This would come in handy should the fire die out at any time. I started to scrape the leaves and sweep them into a pile with my hands when I stopped, thinking of a better idea.

I returned to the porch and threw the door open, witnessing much the same scene as before; the winter's wind coursed through the cabin with an invisible force that made mice scurry and human figures roll over. Lydia groaned. I caught the door and shut it, but didn't latch it. I took an army blanket from the stack and reopened the door, more carefully this time, just enough to slip out, not letting the wind rush in, and closed it tight. Taking the blanket to the pile of brush, I spread it on the ground and filled it with leaves and sticks and such and then folded the corners of the blanket toward the center and brought it to the porch. I left the bundle outside by the door.

From the porch I scanned the surrounding area. A thin trail of smoke could be seen in the distance. Could belong to those scoundrels, I thought.

I gathered the bucket by the rope, opened the door, and entered the cabin. I stepped around figures and set the pail of water by the fire, long enough to search the kitchen for a kettle. An iron stand with a welded hook waited by the fireplace; it begged for a pot to be hung, for stew to simmer or water to boil. A low shelf in a dark corner of the kitchen looked like it might have pots or pans of varying sizes on it. Crouching down I peered in the dim light to see and then I pulled out the stack of pans, using both hands. Instantly, a half-dozen or so mice came screeching out, racing in every direction. Dropping the stack of pans, I sprung backward falling on my ass. Quickly shifting away from the mice, I sent the pans scraping along the floor. I regained my footing, grabbed a frying pan and smashed away at the vermin missing every single one.

"What in blazes?" my father yelled out to me.

"Mama, Papa," my son Willie called. My daughters began to cry. Every sleeper was shaken awake by the commotion. My mother made it to her knees and then her feet as I reentered the main room of the cabin. I went to her first, placed my hands on her shoulders and lowered her to the floor.

"Silas, find the longleaf pine trees. Strip the needles and sprinkle them around the cabin, inside and out. The mice don't like the smell of mint. These trees are the next best thing to mint plants."

"Alright, I'll go in a bit."

"You're a good, son."

"Now, go back to sleep," I encouraged. Then I went to Willie and took him in my arms. I took him to the chair. My wife set the girls at ease by stroking their hair and making shushing sounds, low and gentle. Slowly, silence, if not serenity, eased back into the surroundings, until we heard only the wind whistling through the cracks in the cabin door and the holes in the chinking.

Willie slept in my arms for a good hour before I put him back on the floor. My towhead boy nuzzled down next to his mother. I glanced around at each of them, my kin. No one seemed to need to go outside to urinate, but then few had asked for water since the earlier hours of the day at which time I had helped each of my brothers to go outside and had given water to each of my sisters—Martha, Mary, Elizabeth and Lydia and later to Nan.

Four of them huddled in the corner of the cabin, moaning low groans from time to time. Only Martha's face showed. The others covered their heads under blankets—blue blankets, gray blankets, Indian blankets. I stood and watched over them for a bit. Martha without a doubt had the sweetest features of all my sisters and like I said, I had heard on more than one occasion that she resembled my mother's cousin, *Kilakeena*. I now wondered if this was the same cousin who betrayed my mother.

My mother was too sick for me to ask, but my father had somehow rallied and remained alert through most of the day. Holding onto my rifle, leaning against the rough log hewn wall, from his seated position, he mostly watched as I went about my duties. I gathered the longleaf pine needles and brought them back to the cabin. I sprinkled them inside and out. As the day wore on, my father drifted in and out of slumber without changing his position. When late afternoon was upon us, I gently took the rifle from his loose grip. It startled him.

"Silas?"

"Yes."

"Is it late?"

"It's time for me to keep watch," I reported. A winter's moon had risen before the sun had set. If those bastards were going to do anything, I felt now was the time. Yesterday had come and gone without further incident, but I didn't trust those malevolent, ill-disposed, evil vermin. I sat in the chair across from the cabin door. My mind drifted, but my eyes did not. Those two Rebs reminded me of two cowardly and lazy connivers I had dealt with during the war years. Two fellers had come across me in their own search for a cave to wait out the winter months without being conscripted. Neither one had much conviction of any kind, not for the South, not for the North, certainly not for religious ideas. No one would ever confuse them for conscientious objectors. As far as I could tell, their only conviction was to stay away from work; they were a lazy pair. Their appearance and behavior betrayed them for what they were, laggards. They'd taken advantage of my work ethic while they stayed with me in that cave, eating the fish that I caught and cooked, borrowing my canteen and supplies, drinking my coffee, and eating the meat that I hunted, carried, and prepared. I thought of them as highwaymen who had moved in with me. Probably my biggest mistake was letting them know I'd sworn not to kill, for it gave them license to steal, or so they thought. I only got rid them by refusing to fish and hunt. Eventually, they got so hungry they moved on, but not without attempting to persuade me.

"Silas," one of them cajoled, while rubbing his scraggly growth of beard as he sat leaning against the cave wall, my cave wall. "You haven't been out to fish in days. Aren't you gettin' hungry?"

"No," is all I said.

"Silas, what about those berries you found last week, couldn't you gather a few of those when you go for your usual walk?"

"No," I repeated.

"Silas," the other laggard joined in the conversation. "I'll go huntin' with you. You get your rifle and minié balls and we'll go up the other side of the mountain and find us some deer."

"No." I sat silently, recalling the last game that he hadn't helped to shoot; it was a deer. Nor had he helped carry it back, skin it, gut it, clean it, or cook it, but somehow he managed to eat it just fine.

"Silas," the second one coaxed, "we should build a fire. Someone let the last one burn out." *Someone, hmpph.* I didn't move.

"Silas, my clothes are startin' to collect fleas and my hair is gettin' lice. C'mon, be a good feller and keep the fire alive. The smoke of a fire'll keep the li'l varmints away," he had said, scratching himself the whole while from the top of his head to the crotch in his worn out trousers. He had cooties, I concluded.

"No," I announced, thinking they were the only two vermin that I wanting to be rid of.

It went on similarly for four or five days, until they'd run out of dry jerky and parched corn and realized they were not going to bait me into doing all the work for their lazy hides. After they moved on, I went cage-fishing, using walnuts for bait and brought back a good half dozen trout which I sizzled over an open flame. I do remember being as hungry then as I am now. It would've been less torment on my own stomach if I'd been able to point my rifle at them and then send them on their way. My only regret as to how I sent those two laggards on their way is that while I was outlasting them, my family was waiting for me to arrive with meat, fish, or other fresh food. My family was going hungry at the same time.

Now, I looked at Willie, asleep on the floor, his chest rising and falling with each breath. Laboriously. As the fire sparked and my family slept I became drowsy. I know my head bobbed once or twice as the time wore on me. I may have even fallen asleep.

"Silas," my father woke me.

"Silas, keep an eye out, son." I jerked awake, blinking between sleep and wide-eyes that feigned alertness. I wiped the sleep from my eyes, stretched my legs, poked the fire, and then returned the poker to the hole in the chink of the west wall. On a whim, I pulled the poker out again. I peeked out; the sun dripped a blood red color behind the rolling Appalachian Mountains. The woods were still. Winter still. I stuffed the hole again with the poker, my artificial rifle. This ploy would only work if and when the sunlight catches the metal in a certain way, thus confusing a man into thinking that the gleam, seen from a distance, is a rifle. If a man got close enough that the poker was in his ken, he'd figure out the deception. It certainly wouldn't work after dark. My sister Martha moaned and turned under her blanket. My wife mumbled something incoherent. My son stirred briefly.

I sat back down and sought conversation to keep stimulated.

"Did you know Mama's cousin, *Kilakeena*?" I asked my father, the only lucid member of my family at this point.

"Did I know *Kilakeena*? I sat at the front of a cave with a rifle across my knees, protecting my family, much like you're doing now, because of *Kilakeena*. Did I know *Kilakeena*? Yes, son. Everyone knew of *Kilakeena*, all too well."

NOTE

[1] The Cherokee Nation attempted to remain neutral but eventually joined the Confederate forces. Also, the Cherokee were not of one mind and some splintered off, joined Union forces, and formed traditionalist parties ("John Ross," 2021). For a general overview of Thomas' Legion comprised of Highlanders and Cherokee see Thomas' Legion (2020).

KILAKEENA

The Night of December 19, 1865

"Kilakeena, he was your mother's favorite cousin."[1] My father's voice wavered, but not his words. He was one of those people whose age is demonstrated in visual, as well as, aural tensions. His lean muscles were covered in loose skin; his bright blue eyes suffered from clouded vision; his slim, but friendly smile was framed by a sallow complexion; and now his strong words were betrayed by a weak, cracking voice. This struggle between what was and what will be leaned toward a destiny of decline. Both age and this illness were taking a toll. His breathing worried me. Though I thought he might be too weak, he took up the story after taking a bit of a breather, literally, short, wheezy inhalations followed by slow, wheezy exhalations.

"I remember when I first saw Kilakeena, what he looked like—hair the color of midnight and soft as dawn, eyes deeper and more mesmerizing than a doe. He had high cheekbones and a straight nose. His lips curled sweetly like ribbons on a Cherokee hunting shirt. And his build was willowy, yet strong. There was always a crowd around him. Young men or young women, adults or children, it didn't matter who, everyone was drawn to Kilakeena. He was seventeen years old when I met him and your mother was just twelve years old." My father leaned back, lowered his eye-lids, and continued the story as if he could see into the past.

"Two-Turtles introduced me to them, to his family, as well."

"Who is Two-Turtles?"

"Two-Turtles was your mother's adopted uncle," my father explained, opening his eyes. "His father, dead, and his mother and sister carried away by the Muskogee when he was young. He always wore two turtle shells strapped to his thighs. The shells were filled with potions that a shaman had given him to help him find his mother and sister. Two-Turtles and I became traveling companions who always returned to New Echota for the Cherokee festivals. I can still see your mother at the festivals—The Ripe Green Corn Festival; oh, how she danced," he reminisced, closing his eyes again. "Her favorite was the pheasant dance, a rejoicing dance."[2] My father paused, presumably, he envisioned my mother dancing as a young girl.

"Did she have a limp then?" I asked. He opened his eyes again.

"Oh, no, her limp was the result of an accident that happened much later. One could probably blame Kilakeena for that, too. But anyway, as I was saying, when she finally turned fifteen, I married her, your mother. I was thirty years old."[3] He paused his story and then breathed as deeply as he could, as if taking in all the years that had passed. The air rattled through his lungs and came back with a rough cough. "Forty years gone by now." His words floated afar; his voice waned. He drifted into a sudden sleep, until he jerked alert and continued abruptly.

"But Kilakeena, you wanted to know about Kilakeena, didn't you? *Waay'll*, I should tell you the story about Ridge and Charles Reese for you to understand," he drawled. I really didn't want to hear old war stories about Ridge and Reese. I was more curious about Kilakeena, but I let my father talk on.

"When Ridge and Reece returned from fighting at the Battle of Horseshoe Bend, where they had teamed with Andrew Jackson and his men to defeat the Muskogee, they found the women and children hiding in the caves. Their homes and crops destroyed by yet another battalion belonging to Andrew Jackson. So Ridge and Reese left the smoldering fires of their homeland, rode their ponies to Washington and demanded to see General Andrew Jackson. Without flinching, Ridge stood eye to eye with the General while Reese translated his demands.

"*I gathered five hundred volunteers to fight with you, Andrew Jackson. Did I make a mistake? In our absence your soldiers frightened our people, destroyed our homes and burned our crops. Is this how the Americans repay loyalty?* Ridge told his friend Charles Reese, The Whale[4] to translate and demand to know.

"*No, of course not,* Andrew Jackson apologized. *These young men will be punished for their deeds. Let me give you a gift to set the matter right. Return tomorrow and I will make amends.*

"The next day Andrew Jackson presented Reece with a silver rifle; and then, he handed Ridge a uniform with epaulets and gold buttons, making Ridge a Major in the U.S. army.[5] Ridge donned the uniform; he wore it on his pony as he rode out of the capitol. And he wore it into New Echota when he returned home. Major Ridge became one of the most important men in the Cherokee Nation from that day forward. However, his fame would turn to infamy as the years passed, as it also would be for his son Scaleeloskee and his nephew Kilakeena." With the word Kilakeena I perked up and paid better attention, but it didn't matter as the story was interrupted again.

My father coughed, not a single, short cough, but rather, he had a ragged, lengthy coughing spell. At the end of it, he cleared his throat and struggled to speak, "I think Ridge knew that the white man was the most two-faced being to ever walk the face of the earth," my father coughed again. "It pains me sometimes to say that I'm a white man, as hypocritical as all the rest."

"Don't say such a thing," I comforted him.

"I'm not the man you think I am," he whispered.

"Of course you are," I told him. He sighed. I needed to distract him, I thought.

"Tell me more," I coaxed, referring to the story, but only silence followed. I tried again, "What happened to Kilakeena?" A pause filled the air before my father spoke again.

"Ah, Kilakeena's parents sent him to a local mission school to learn English and those missionaries sent him to Cornwall, Connecticut to study at a school for Indian boys.[6]

"Kilakeena's skills in oratory and rhetoric flourished. He became adroit at math and science to the point that he calculated a lunar eclipse, which had his schoolmaster in such a state of excitement that he sent Kilakeena's calculations to a Professor at Yale to see if the boy was right.[7] The missionaries figured that they had themselves the best example of how Indians could be civilized and therefore saved. They began to show off Kilakeena like a prized possession, a newly discovered jewel from an exotic land. Nearly everybody on the eastern seaboard wanted to see Kilakeena, a 'real Indian' boy. His beauty was unparalleled, long streaming black hair and perfect features. Every time Kilakeena spoke in public, people would pass the hat and fill it with coins. Eventually, he changed his name to honor his benefactor, Elias Boudinot. And his public appearances raised so much money that the missionaries set out to find more Indians like Kilakeena. They looked for the brightest and most beautiful from tribes as far away as Hawaii.[8]

"Waay'll, when Ridge heard about this, he wasn't about to be left out. Ridge was brother to Oowatie, Kilakeena's father. *Scaleeloskee*, he said to his son, *it's time for you to study the White man's ways like your cousin Kilakeena.* The missionaries were thrilled to have the son of Ridge among them. They'd heard about Major Ridge, who had connections to General Andrew Jackson.

"There were just two problems that the missionaries hadn't counted on," my father kept me waiting, running a finger over his cracked lips and swallowing with difficulty.

I got up from the ladder-back chair, set the rifle down and brought the bucket to his side. I ladled out a drink for him. As I handed it to him, I noticed that the marks on my father's skin were not the same as the ones on Nan's skin. The sores looked different in shape and color. More like the marks on Julia's skin. I scooped more water and handed him the dipper, again. He took it tentatively. His hand shook and water bounced within the cup of the ladle all the way to his dried lips.

"Are you hungry?" I asked him. He shook his head and took another sip of the clear, cold liquid. When he was done, I returned the ladle and fetched myself some parched corn and jerky. I retrieved the poker from the wall, peered out and saw nothing but darkness. After adding logs, I stoked the fire and decided to save the coal oil lamp for another time. As weak as my father remained, he continued to tell me the story of Kilakeena Elias Boudinot, my mother's cousin.

"They hadn't figured on how harsh the climate would be for boys who'd lived their lives in warm environs. First, the Hawaiian boy took sick and died, then Scaleeloskee, Kilakeena's cousin, became ill.

Ridge's son was a frail boy from birth and as a teenager he had a slender frame, underdeveloped muscles. Ridge was beside himself, when he heard that his son was dying. He traveled day and night to reach the boy. As fate would have it, the family caring for Scaleeloskee had a daughter, with hair as red as Julia's hair." We both looked in Julia's direction. She opened her eyes at the mention of her name and then her eyelids fluttered. My father lowered his voice to a strong whisper.

"Scaleeloskee fell in love with the girl, his health improved and he asked her parents if he might marry her. This was the second thing the missionaries hadn't reckoned on. The parents were put off that an Indian would want to marry a white girl. At the thought of it, the girl's parents sent her away. In the meantime, Scaleeloskee's illness returned. Fearing what would happen if Ridge's son died while in their care, the parents allowed their daughter to return and agreed that the couple could marry on the condition that Scaleeloskee would not need the use of crutches for his weakened condition. They never expected him to heal fully.

"When Ridge arrived to find all that had taken place he threw his broad shoulders back and paced with long strides within the narrow parlor of the Northrup's house.

"*My son will be Chief one day*, he declared. *How dare you question his right to marry your daughter or belittle him for his ailment?*[9] He took his son home, vowing to never let him return to the missionaries again." My father took a shallow breath and lowered himself onto the palette. I let him rest for a bit before I asked for more of the story.

"And what became of Kilakeena?" My father didn't answer. I looked at him in the dancing shadows of the firelight. His eyes were closed; he had fallen asleep. Again, I found myself sitting sentry in quarantined solitude.

NOTES

[1]   There is no proof that Sarah Reese (Reece) was Kilakeena's cousin, much less a favorite cousin. However, Kilakeena was the son of Oowatie and Susannah Reese (Reece) and he would have been about 5 years older than Sarah Reese, Silas' mother.

[2]   See Mooney (1891, 1900/1992) for a description of the Pheasant Dance.

3   Marriage laws at the time suggested that White men and women married at the age of 21; indentured servants could not marry until their debts had been paid; slaves were not allowed to marry by law, nor were interracial marriages allowed between Blacks and Whites (see Wood, n.d.); whereas, "The usual age of a Cherokee girl was 15" (see *Cherokee and Sioux Courtship*, 2020). Sarah Reese was 15 when she married Silas Sr. He was 30 years old. Julia was 23 years old when she married Silas Jr. and left to join his family.

4   Charles Reese was called 'The Whale.' My educated guess is that he came by this name because some Cherokee were called by where they came from or how they came—as in I came by way of the Ridge might be known as 'Ridge' according to Klausner (1993). Charles Reese's (Reece) family came from Wales. The converted spelling and interpretation from Wales to Whale was likely a simple misnomer. The Reese family had multiple full-blood Cherokee members, one half-blood Cherokee, and 10 Quadroons according to the census of 1835.

5   Also of note, The Cherokee chiefs called for neutrality in the American/Creek War due to the fact that the Cherokee had sided with the British during the Revolutionary War. Now that the Americans were in power, Ridge asked if he could volunteer to serve with the Americans in the Creek War, thinking it politically astute. The Whale joined him in this endeavor. And at least one scholar has suggested that The Whale was not Charles Reese but a third man, who fought with them, an additional warrior who was hurt in the battle (see Wilkins, 1986).

6   Elias Boudinot LL.D. a lawyer and president of the New Jersey Bible Society sponsored Kilakeena Elias Boudinot's education. In short, Kilakeena took his benefactor's name for his English/American name. The most notable and debatable story surrounding the two is that each has been credited with writing the novella entitled, *Poor Sarah: Or, Religion Exemplified in the Life and Death of an Indian Woman*. After extensive research ranging from interviews with Cherokee linguist, Marvin Summerfield (personal communication, 1997) to uncovering archival originals of other work by Elias Boudinot LL.D. at the Harry Ransom Humanities Research Center at the University of Texas at Austin and reading the English translation of the Cherokee version, it is my humble opinion that neither Kilakeena Elias Boudinot nor Elias Boudinot LL.D. wrote the story. I believe instead what happened is that an anonymous woman wrote the story, and Kilakeena came across the story while he was in Connecticut attending the missionary school. He likely translated it into Cherokee. Some individuals thought the Cherokee version (1833) was the original, thus crediting Kilakeena with the original story, however, an original English version was submitted to the *Religious Intelligencer* (Vol. IV, No. 31), New Haven, CT and published on January 1, 1820. The narrator of the story is depicted as a woman living in Tolland, CT. The publishers assure their readers that they know the author and that the story is true. In later years, my graduate students undertook the task of searching out the author for a class assignment and Elizabeth Wilhoit was the first of us to suggest she had found the author—Phoebe Brown (see Clair, Wilhoit, Green, Palmer, Russell, & Swope, 2015). Early funding for this research came from the College of Liberal Arts at Purdue University.

7   Kilakeena's lunar calculations were correct (see Wilkins, 1986).

8   See a *History of Cornwall,* a pamphlet supplied by the Cornwall Historical Society during my travels. The same information can be found under the title "An experiment in Evangelization: Cornwall's Foreign Mission School (n.a. November 10, 2020).

9   Even the famed Sequoyah suffered from hip displacement, a common ailment among the Cherokee (see Klaussner, 1993).

CHAPTER 10

BLAZES

The Night of December 19, 1865

I slept on and off, figuring that if those two Rebs had planned a malicious attack, then they would have done so by now. Although I didn't want to play into their hands if they had schemed something for the morning; so, I slept lightly with my head on the table and rifle across my lap. Sometime during the night, I heard a thud.

I jerked awake, looked around. In my daze, I decided that I must have been dreaming. I laid my head back down on the table. Within a moment I heard a second thud above me. I tossed my blanket back and grabbed my rifle. I hastily made my way to the cabin door, stepping on someone in the process; whoever it was let out a light cry.

I unlatched the door and flung it open, yelling, "Who's there?"

I heard footsteps fast and loud and then I made out two figures darting toward the woods, heading away from the cabin. I fired a shot into the air. The blast echoed in the night. Then I reloaded in the dark, something I could do blind folded if the need arose, and now was one of those times. I knew my rifle inside and out, every inch of her.

My horse circled in front of the wagon and back again. Whinnying, uncomfortably and snorting, too. I had tied her reins securely to the wagon wheel and looped it across the opposite wheel from underneath the carriage of the wagon. That had worked to confound those Rebels had they tried to untie her. That must've been what they were up to, but between the Rebel bastards and my gun shot blast, my horse refused to settle down.

"There, there." I pulled down on the reins and tried to calm her.

"They're gone now. Settle down." I stroked her mane, but she reared up again. Something wasn't right by her. Her agitation increased. She jerked away from me and continued to circle on her tight rein. I let her be.

I went back and stood at the open archway, holding my ground, peering into the woods. My father called out.

"Silas, are they gone?"

"Went eastbound through the woods," I told him.

"Go back to sleep," I added without taking my eyes off the woods.

"Silas, son, quick!" my father yelled.

"What?" I didn't want to look away in case those bastards were circling back on us, but my father didn't answer. I turned. He had lost his voice and was pointing up. I looked up. Smoke was coming down through the thin ceiling between the log beams.

Smoke billowed through the rafters spacing. I dropped my rifle and ran to the front yard, just beyond the wagon, past my horse to see how bad the fire might be. "Oh, sweet Jesus!"

I ran to the porch, took a running leap onto the railing and hauled my body upward, swinging onto the roof. I flung my shirt off and tried to beat the flames into submission. They shot up too quickly. I made my way to the edge of the roof, slid myself part way down, hanging by my hands and then jumped down. I leapt over the porch stairs, grabbed the blanket that I had used earlier to gather kindling. I shook the blanket as fast as I could and flung it up around the porch banister. Then I jumped again and swung myself hard to reach the roof, but I knocked the blanket down in the process.

"Damnation!" I yelled.

"Silas," my mother called out. She was now on the porch, trying to throw the woolen blanket up to me, but it fluttered down. She wasn't strong enough to hurl it to the roof. I started to come down.

"No! Wait," she yelled. She folded the blanket over and over again until it became a small bundle, then she tossed it upward once more; it reached me. I disappeared from her view as I ran to the flames. I beat them back as best I could. As one area of flames settled down, others flared up. I looked around. The flames made a semi-circle on the roof. The center for some reason was fine. I didn't have time to investigate. I had to stand on the edge of the roof in order to smother the flames, moving in a circular direction.

Balancing on my tip toes at one point, I teetered on the edge, but pulled forward, just in time. I went back at the fire with all my strength, forcing the blanket down. I was on all fours, slapping at it. I stood again, stomped on the woolen blanket, eventually suffocating the fire on the northeast side. Then I moved to the southeastern section of roof that had a blaze. I moved in close to cover the flame, just then it burst upward. I felt the heat in my face; the flames roasting my skin. Sparks jumped dangerously close to my eyes. The smoke filled my lungs.

I threw the blanket down again. It was scorched. The malodorous smell of burnt moss that filled spaces between the beams twisted with the fibers of the woolen blanket, giving off a fetid smell with traces of kerosene that filled the air. I threw myself on top of the last spot and rolled. My back and chest burning in the process; I leapt to my feet and jumped back. The flames disappeared; the fire merely smoldered. Wisps of smoke drifted through the air.

As it cleared, I saw why the center of the roof had staved off the flame. A clean white patch of snow sat on the middle region of the roof. I went to the center of the snow-capped cabin; my blackened foot print marred its pristine surface. Gathering handfuls of snow, I then scattered it where the fire still smoldered. Then I packed snow around the scorched edges to assure that the flame wouldn't rekindle itself.

At last, I breathed deeply, the air had cleared for the most part and while I could still smell the burnt wood and the blanket, no more smoke came into my lungs. I squatted on the rooftop, resting for a moment and assessing the damage. We'd be all right, I thought. I wanted to lay in the snow and sleep right there on the roof. And then I felt my chest, my back, and realized why sleeping in the snow seemed so comforting.

I made my way back to the front of the cabin and lowered myself over the side to within about five feet, scraping my arms in the process. "Bastards!" I scoffed as I dropped to the ground.

While I had been struggling with the flames my mother had carried Willie to safety. Julia had my girls in her arms. And Lydia, Martha and Mary were on the porch. The others hadn't made it out. None of my brothers were strong enough to walk. My father never left his cot.

I took Willie from my mother's arms.

"Can I play on the roof, too?" Willie asked me. I couldn't help but to smile.

"Maybe when you're well," I told him

"And swing from the porch?" he wanted to know. I smiled again.

"Yes, and swing from the porch," I promised.

"Have you ever seen a monkey, Papa? A real monkey?"

"No, I haven't, son"

"They live in the jungles of Tennessee," he told me as a matter of indubitable fact.

"Is that so?" I said playfully to him as if he had taught me something new. Both Julia and I smiled at that and she found the strength to touch Willie's warm cheek. Willie laid his head on my chest. It pained my burned skin, but I'd bear it for the love of my son.

"Do you think they're satisfied now?" Julia asked. I didn't answer her right away. And then I remembered how Willie had comforted me earlier.

"It'll be all right," I reassured her. I took them back inside. They were weak and dazed. I laid them each back down. I drank heartily from my canteen, and then I served water from the bucket for each of them in turn before I returned to my seat and placed my rifle over my knees. Pleased with the fact that I had put out the fire, I hardly noticed the pain. I had taken care of my family, saved the cabin and scared those rascals away. Perhaps, they would know that they couldn't get the better of me. A man doesn't have to go to war to prove his courage or his worth. After all, I'd run them off twice now.

Quiet returned. Most of my brothers and sisters went back to sleep. My back burned and I wanted to pour water on it, but we didn't have enough. After a while, I quietly made my way to the door, stepped outside and rubbed my chest with snow. Placing pieces of packed ice on my shoulders, I stood letting it melt down my back. Afterwards, I walked the perimeter of the cabin, making sure those ex-confederates were nowhere to be found. I brought a sack of clothing in with me from the wagon to find a clean shirt. Done dressing, I returned to my seat again and let the darkness surround me. I sat for a good long time in the silence before anyone's words ushered forth.

"Silas?" my brother William spoke.

"So did you shoot to kill or did you just shoot over their heads?"

CHAPTER 11

I AM FREE

Night to Early Morning of December 19, 1865

I never answered my brother William. He already knew the answer. No, I didn't shoot to kill; yes, I shot over their heads. His words had dripped with disgust. I could almost read his mind, *they'll be back. They'll be back. Why didn't you shoot the bastards? You coward!* Not even a thought in his head that I had saved the cabin and scared them off. *What good does it do to scare them off,* he'd have argued, *just to have them come back again.* I gripped my rifle tighter.

I didn't speak again until I was sure that my brother had fallen asleep. I could easily have gone a lifetime without ever speaking to him or anyone else again if it hadn't been for my father.

"Silas?" I didn't answer.

"Silas?"

"I'm here," I reassured him after a moment.

"Don't forget the fire," he reminded me. I looked up at the ceiling.

"The fire's almost out," he pointed toward the fireplace. I raised myself up and put more branches on the fire, feeling glad that it hadn't gone out entirely, since I'd tossed the kindling aside in the yard as I had gathered up the blanket to put out the roof-fire. The thought of it all made me tired. Nevertheless, I retrieved the poker from the wall to give the dying embers a turn. The metal poker in my hand prodded another thought, the thought of William's hair-brained scheme, a lot of good that poker in the wall had done us. I didn't return it to its ill-gotten place after stoking the fire; instead, I took a rag from the kitchen and stuffed the hole. As I poked it in, I realized that I wasn't sure whom I was angrier at of the three: William or those two fool Confederates. So I shook my head and tried to focus on my father.

"Are you cold?" I asked him.

"No, not much." I brought another blanket to him, just the same, and put it over his frail form.

"I was telling you a story before, wasn't I?" I felt immeasurable gratitude toward my father at that moment, for I knew that I would have to stay awake, watching for those Confederate arsonists and I preferred to have a story instead of William's insult weighing on my mind.

"Yes, but if you want to rest, it'll keep." I was hoping that he would rather tell me the story of Kilakeena.

"You need to know the whole story," he asserted as if the story of Kilakeena really was relevant to me and yet at the same time, at some point in my life he'd kept something from me. But before I could ponder it further, he began.

"*Waay'll*," he started off slow, saying the word 'well' as if it were a swollen honeydew melon begging to be sliced open on a humid summer day.

"Kilakeena fell in love with a white girl, too. Harriet Gold. Pretty girl, I heard, though I never actually met her."

"Were they married?" I asked hoping to enjoy vicariously, that is, a sweet moment, but a part of me was still also wondering why he felt I deserve to know the *whole story*.

"*Waay'll*, yes, but first Scaleeloskee and his wife were married. Then Kilakeena got sick from the cold of Connecticut himself and had to take leave. He wrote to Harriet and their correspondence eventually led him back to Cornwall. However, a problem existed. The townspeople were angry that an Indian, meaning Scaleeloskee, had married one of their white girls. So they swore that if Kilakeena tried to return to get Harriet, they'd kill him. They were so angry that they made straw effigies of Kilakeena, Harriet and the woman, who had introduced the pair, Mrs. Northrup. They dragged those straw effigies through the village to the town green where they set them afire.[1]

The word, afire, alone was enough to make me picture the flames that had blazed from the roof, only moments earlier. The skin on my chest and my back still felt the sting.

"So, Kilakeena had to make his way back to Cornwall with some ingenuity. He took sap from a pine tree and smeared it on his face, mostly around his chin, and then he covered the area with deer hair, making a beard. After putting his hair up under an old hat, he pulled the hat down to cover his eyes, and then he took up a cane and hobbled down the main street of Cornwall."

"So he donned a disguise before going to get Harriet. Did it work?"

"Yes, indeed-y; it did."

"He was clever," I concluded.

"Oh, he was clever and even comical, at times. One time he was traveling south trying to catch up with his cousin, Scaleeloskee who was headed to Charleston. Kilakeena found a short cut, beat him there, bought a parasol and sat himself down on the beach. There he stayed, under that pink parasol, waiting for Scaleeloskee to arrive.[2] Just as pretty as you please, saying *Sir, whatever has taken you so long? An Indian could turn red under such a scorching sun if left too long.*" I smiled at the image of Kilakeena, an Indian, a *real Indian,* as my wife Julia might say, with a pink parasol, twirling it as he waited for his cousin, Scaleeloskee. I must admit I was beginning to wonder how such an amiable fellow could have betrayed my mother and brought my father to the brink of a cave with a rifle on his knees or what any of this had to do with me; however, I didn't ask that question. Instead, I queried about their journeys, "Did they travel to the coast a lot? Kilakeena and Scaleeloskee?"

"*Waay'll,* I don't know about those two, Scaleeloskee and his wife, but Kilakeena and Harriet did a lot in the beginning. From Boston to Charleston, they were quite the couple. He gave speeches, you see, to raise money to buy a printing press. He had this idea that he could publish a bilingual newspaper—Cherokee and English, wanted to call it the *Cherokee Phoenix.* He figured he could send the newspaper north to liberals and philanthropists to raise money for the Cherokee to build schools. And Sequoyah's syllabary meant most Cherokee could read.[3] But that's when it all started to go sour, if you ask me."

"When Sequoyah invented the syllabary?"

"No. When Kilakeena turned evangelical and started talking about religion and civilization."

"How so?"

"Kilakeena cut his hair and dressed like a white man. He told the Cherokee to take up Christianity if they wanted to be saved. People were threatened by it all, if not offended."

"Who was offended?"

"Your mother, for one. She believed the more Kilakeena tried to *save* the Cherokee by turning them into white people, the more the *Cherokee* disappeared."

"Hmmm."

"Then Andrew Jackson became President and the Cherokee thought he was their friend. I don't know what they were thinkin'. Cause he wasn't anybody's friend; he was a politician; the worst a white man can be." My father continued talking, but I cocked an ear as I thought I heard something outside; my father talked but I only heard part of it. "European immigrants … So Jackson figured he'd start giving them land, … he was going to have to take it away from somebody and that somebody was the Cherokee … Indian … Act …"

"Did you hear that?" I broke in on his story. He was saying something about Jackson declaring an Indian Removal Act, when I hushed him. We both listened. We could see through the aging slats that daylight was making its mark. I thought I heard a rustling. I brought the rifle to my side.

Stepping gingerly toward the west wall, I pulled the plug from the wall and checked in that direction. I saw nothing. I did the same at each portal. Finally, I opened the door with caution. A squirrel jumped past me so fast that I lurched backward with a start. I had to laugh at myself.

"Just a squirrel," I told my father in a loud whisper as I closed the door.

"Silas," he called to me. He wiped sweat from his forehead. "I'm feelin' parched, son. I'd take another dipper of water." I filled the dipper half-way and placed it into his trembling hand. In the shafts of daylight that came through the worn chinking of the cabin walls, I could see that his skin was as pale as a white winter's moon. He swallowed hard and grimaced.

"Son, promise me somethin'," his voice waned for a moment. I took the dipper from his hand and then faced him straight on.

"You have a voice that could send my soul to heaven when the time comes. Will you sing for me, Silas? I like the song that Julia sings, '*I am free. Washed in the Blood of the Lamb*'."[4]

"You'll get stronger," I reassured, but his voice verged on the ebb of decline.

"Promise me that you'll sing. Sing me to heaven," he whispered weakly and added, "Promise."

"I promise."

He closed his eyes; his mouth opened slightly.

"Papa?" I begged.

"Papa?"

NOTES

[1] See Wilkins (1986) for the story of Harriet and Kilakeena.

[2] Wilkins (1986).

[3] Being able to read English or Cherokee was noted on the census of 1835. For example, Charles Reese's family is listed as having 11 Cherokee, 1 half-breed, 10 quadroons (quarter Cherokee in this case); 6 read English, 8 read Cherokee; 8 females, 5 of whom were spinners and 3 of whom were weavers.

[4] This specific song is listed as Silas Beasley Sr.'s last request in the *S.M. Beasley Jr. Story* as collected by Shackelford Sims (1978).

CHAPTER 12

A PROMISE TO KEEP

December 20, 1865

I stepped outside, after having repeatedly tried to raise my father. Each attempt had been in vain. All the while I knew that he was gone. Dead. I had tried to give him water, begged him to open his eyes. "Papa, please don't leave me yet," I had pleaded. Nothing worked. No one heard my pleas, but me. Everyone else slept. And I wished and prayed that he were only sleeping, but I knew that he would never wake. Outside, the sunlight felt harsh against my face. I sat down on the porch step, wondering what to do next, feeling the emptiness swell inside of me. My guts twisted. I wanted him back. I wrapped my arms around my stomach and rocked back and forth, until the thought returned to me that my father requested a song at his funeral. He asked me to sing him to heaven. I needed to bury my father—an insurmountable task, I thought, under the circumstances.

Insurmountable or not, the task had to be done. I stirred with renewed purpose, scanned the area while circling the perimeter of the cabin, checking in every direction for those Rebs. I saw no campfire in the distance and decided that those two Confederates had probably moved on; so, it should be safe for me to leave my family and seek Esquire Dodd once more to ask a favor of him. I unhitched my horse and made a steady ride to the Dodd estate.

"Mister Dodd," I began after arriving. He must've heard my horse for he met me on the porch as I climbed the steps of his veranda.

"Beasley. How fares your family?"

"My father has passed," I said biting back my lip.

"I'm so sorry," he sympathized, his white eyebrows arched with surprise and then drew in tight with concern. "What can I do to help?"

"Sir," I hesitated. "It's the measles that killed my father, I think. But the rest, for the most part, have small pox, if I'm not mistaken." Lowering my eyes, I informed him of this apologetically.

"It can't be helped, but anything I can do for you without endangering myself, I will do."[1] His generosity brought tears to my eyes; for a moment, I couldn't speak. He then asked, "What do you need?"

"I haven't a shovel," I admitted my need, looking away.

"Oh my," Mister Dodd sighed and nodded thoughtfully before speaking again. "It wouldn't be right to just hand a man a shovel on such an occasion. Bring the body in your buckboard this afternoon to the place over that ridge," he pointed, "and around the bend. That's where the family cemetery is located. I'll have everything ready."

"I don't mean to put my troubles on you any further, Mister Dodd, but …"

"What is it, Silas?"

"Sir, do you know a doctor who might look in on us?"

"I'll take care of it." With the matter concluded he turned toward the door.

"Sir," I stopped him. "I'll a find a way to …"

"Not now, Beasley. Go take care of your family."

I rode back slowly, listening to my horse's hoofs clunk against the hard-packed dirt road. I bounced with the wagon's rhythm, without awareness. My mind meandered with the winding road. My body went numb. I could hear the wind whip through the trees, but it seemed to exist in another world, one apart from me.

Back at the cabin, I went through my usual chores—gathering firewood, stoking the flame, bringing water, ladling it out, taking each of those who needed to an outside bush, before I sat down beside my mother.

"Mama." I hadn't called her that in many years. "Mama, Daddy's dead."

"Hush now, Silas," my mother whispered. She tried to reach my lips with her finger, but her arm was weak. I touched her hand. It was warm. Then I touched her cheek; it burned.

"Do you understand, Mama?" She didn't answer.

"William?" I tried to wake my older brother, but it couldn't be done. Not a single one was strong enough to come with me to bury my father. I stood there looking over the scene with arms dangling at my sides, wondering where I would gather the strength. I felt tears edging up in my eyes; one plopped down my cheek. I sniffled the rest back inside of me.

I drew in a deep breath that gathered the air around me, stale and sickly as it might be, I pretended it renewed me. Then looking toward my father, the corpse, I took a second, very deep breath.

I lifted the Bible from Julia's side and set it on the table. I stepped gingerly around my mother, still as superstitious as any nonbeliever,[2] reached my father, wrapped him in a blanket and awkwardly carried him over my shoulder to the buckboard. There was nothing graceful about it. I went back for the Bible.

I arrived at the Dodd family cemetery by afternoon. I looked about and discovered a freshly dug grave near the north end of the ridge. I steered the horse over rough pasture to the site. There I found a shovel leaning against a mound of dirt, which was piled next to the burial pit. The final resting place was lined with a blanket. A second blanket lay folded like a pillow next to the grave.

I banged my father's body against the buckboard in my awkward attempt to unload him, and then while leaning him against the side of the buckboard, I spoke senselessly, "Sorry," apologizing as if he could hear me. Hooking my arms under his armpits, I half dragged him, half carried him, nearly dropping him on my way to the hallowed pit. I sat on the edge of the grave with my father's body across my lap, cradled in my arms. I can't say how much time passed before I laid his body at the edge of the grave. I didn't have the heart to roll it into the eternal resting spot. I knew the sound—the thud of his body against the hard dirt floor, would break my heart. So I left him at the edge for a moment. Eventually, I made the leap into the grave. I gathered him up in my arms and lowered him gently before lifting myself back out. I stepped on him in the process; I didn't mean for that to happen. Standing above him, I draped a second blanket over him; it fluttered into place. And then I began to shovel dirt.

Work is many things, I thought later, one of which is release. I shoveled dirt back into that hole and over my father's body until I could shovel no more. Maybe I shoveled more than I had to shovel. I shoveled till my arms ached. Then I put the tool in the buckboard and took the Bible from the seat. I meant to read a short passage; instead, I held the book to my chest, pausing for a moment before starting to sing the song, *I am free*. My voice wavered; I couldn't finish. I remained there, standing at the head of the unmarked grave, surrounded by winter's unmistakable silence, which echoed through the valley and all around me. Silence went through me. I never felt such loneliness.

On my ride back, I berated myself for not asking my father about his life, instead of some distant cousin, whom I'd never met. What do I care about Kilakeena? I had so many questions that would now go unanswered—questions about his life, his family, and his childhood; questions about my life, my childhood, and the way we lived.

For some reason I pictured my first pair of moccasins—holding out one foot for my father to see. *Waay'll, waay'll, four years old. This must mean you're big enough to go fishing with me,* my father had lightly complimented me. Pride swelled in my young heart.

My mind stayed in the past as I envisioned myself taking aim with the small blowgun at a frog. I blew the dart, my father moved, and the frog jumped away. *C'mon, son.* I followed my father through tall grass and watched his fishing cage swing with each step, hip high, through the reeds. One small moccasin after another, I followed my father.

That happy image drifted away and was supplanted by another. An abandoned Indian village. Empty Cherokee homesteads, places that should have been loud with laughter were eerily silent. Children's play-things lay discarded in the dirt, empty corn grinders remained out front. Inside, dusty blankets lay strewn about and spiders' webs crisscrossed from baskets to beds. Food supplies lay scattered on tables. This was a ghostly scene.

I won't remember it, I thought; I'll force the image to disappear. I'll count my numbers one, two, three—*sagwa, tadly, soly*. The image persisted, where were the people? *Ghosts*, someone commented. No, I'll count my numbers one through ten—*sagwa, tadly, soly, nicky, hisky, sulalty, talcoy, sunaly, sontnalg, scohee*, and again.[3]

And at last I saw Nickojack, in my mind's eye, teaching numbers to me. My Cherokee friends stood bare-chested and waited patiently for me. Freed from my lessons, I wrestled with friends from Cherokee families.[4] In my mind I felt the sun shining; I felt warm days filled with activities. I learned to use a blowgun, shoot a bow and arrow, wrestle with companions, and play in the river. We swam naked, sisters and brothers, cousins and friends. I learned my Cherokee numbers, one through ten—*sagwa, tadly, soly, nicky, hisky, sulalty, talcoy, sunaly, sontnalg scohee.*

I'd been so happy in that village with my friends, growing up with them. Three and a half years of living the Indian way. The happiest time of my life,[5] I thought. But after that we moved to a ghost village. We always seemed to be moving from one silent abandoned Cherokee village to the next, every year, a new ghost home. The thought of it made me shiver. I'll count the image away—*sagwa, tadly, soly, nicky, hisky, sulalty, talcoy, sunaly, sontnalg scohee.*

Why, I wondered. Why did he make us move away? I hated that we moved. I hated the ghost places. He could've explained that before he died. Instead, he harped on some distant cousin named Kilakaeena. What do I care about Kilakeena?

NOTES

[1] This is an exact quote taken from the Silas Mercer Beasley Jr. Story as collected by Shackelford Sims (1978).

[2] Although Silas sees this as superstition, it is highly likely that the Cherokee taught their children this as much out of consideration for others.

[3] This is the spelling provided by Silas, Jr. in his first article published in the *Lawrence Democrat* and cited in Shackelford Sims (1978). Correct Cherokee spellings can be found at 'Counting in Cherokee' (2020).

[4] The list of childhood neighbors—Thompson, Sunday, Davey, and Nickojack families—is taken directly from the Silas Mercer Beasley Jr. story as collected by Shackelford Sims (1978). The spelling of Nickojack is more commonly seen as Nickajack. The Cherokee spelling is *Nikutse'ge.* The census of 1835 lists *Nickojack, Nickejack and Nickajack.* According to the 1835 census, Nickejack's family—10 full bloods; Sunday's family—8 full bloods and so on.

[5] See Shackelford Sims (1978).

CHAPTER 13

SPARKS IN A NATION

The Night of December 20, 1865

The generous Mister Dodd had also left a sack at the gravesite, filled with a loaf of bread, an apple cobbler and a piece of meat—dried venison. Later that evening, I tried to share it with my family, but none were well enough to eat. My brother William however, mustered the strength to talk. I didn't have the heart to tell him that father had passed. William, like the others, had slept through my father's dying moments. Instead, I let him talk.

"I know how Elias betrayed the family." His voice startled me as it came out of the shadows of night.

"What's that?" I must admit I wasn't sure if I wanted to talk with William. He was an odd one, never expecting anyone to stay angry at him for long.

"Kilakeena Elias Boudinot. I know how he betrayed us, all of us." It didn't matter whether I wanted to talk to William or not; he continued the story and as I said, I let him.

"I saw him once when I was a boy. I was ten years old, perhaps. Kilakeena traveled to a well-populated village in the Snowbird Mountains to meet with members of the Bird Clan. We traveled there to see him, hear him."

"I saw him once, also," Julia whispered.

"What?" I asked surprised.

"Yes, when I was a little girl, I saw him at a gala given in his honor in Charleston."

"But you never mentioned this before," I questioned her.

"I didn't know that Kilakeena Elias Boudinot was your cousin," she explained.

"My mother's cousin," I corrected her.

"Yes, well anyway, I was very young, maybe four-years-old. I recall sitting on the staircase of an elaborate home in Charleston, my face pressed against the stair rails, attempting to get a better view of Kilakeena. Everyone had come to the gala to see the handsome Cherokee Indian and his new bride Harriet Gold. I watched as the Indian requested a dance with my mother:

"*May I have this dance, Madam?* Kilakeena requested with a bit of a bow. *I'd be honored,* my mother blushed. He twirled her about the room just as he did every other swooning woman as I watched, perched on the stairs. And when he finished dancing with my mother, she caught sight of me.

"*Julia, you should be in bed, like the other children. Your father and I will wake you when it's time to go home.*

"*Just a few more minutes?* I had pleaded.

"*Perhaps, one dance before the child goes to sleep,* Kilakeena advocated on my behalf. Thrilled at the prospect, I put my hands together as if saying a prayer.

"*Please, Mother*, I begged.

"*Oh, all right. As long as Mr. Boudinot is sure it's no trouble.*

"*Trouble,* he countered, "*of course not. It would be my pleasure.* I bounded down the stairs and Mr. Kilakeena Elias Boudinot took me by the hand.

"*My daughter, Julia,* my mother introduced me.

"*I'm Mr. Boudinot.*"

"*You're a real Indian, aren't you?* I had asked with excitement.

"*I am,* he confirmed, lifting me onto his toes so that I would glide as he waltzed me around the room, but before the dance was over he had lifted me into the air, my nightgown billowing out and twirling as if it were a ballroom gown." Julia sighed softly.

"Then I watched, covertly, from the staircase again, having sneaked back down after being sent to bed. I gawked; I suppose I should say, as he danced with his bride the lovely Harriet. Her honey-colored hair tied up with ribbons and a few ringlets fell about her face. They stared into each other's eyes," Julia's words swooned, remembering a magical moment.

"So you met the man," I blurted abruptly.

"Yes," Julia countered curtly. "But William, please, beg my pardon, I interrupted you. You were saying that you saw him in a village."

"A Cherokee village," I reminded him where he had left off.

"Yes, of course. Well, keep in mind that we didn't live in the village. Our cabin was on the outer ridge, but close enough that we could see our neighbor's cabin and a few others." As William spoke these words, I felt a strange pang of emotion, not sure if it was jealousy or regret, I hoped it would subside. Homesickness, perhaps. "I well remember the cabin," William continued.

"We spent winters in the cabin, only the coldest part of winter, the woods were our home most of the time. But in the winter we sat by the fireplace and listened to stories, while smoke and scattered sparks rose steadily up the flue of the chimney. The blaze offered warmth that extended well beyond the hearth. The fire's amber glow highlighted the log and daub walls and brought a certain artistic presence to our otherwise rustic home. Papa had built the cabin and mother had decorated it, so to speak, with dried bundles of sage, sweet-grass, onions, and turnips, which hung from the rafters. Their spicy herbal fragrances seasoned the air. I remember the scent of mint giving way to the potent rich aromas of wild onions. I love the smell of wild onions, don't you?" William didn't wait for an answer.

"Even the shadows were amusing in a scary sort of way. The fire's light always seemed to cast an enlarged and eerie image of the roots and vegetables. When the flames stretched and dipped and stretched again, the shadow of the dried herbs would dance against the wall, which was wonderfully scary when papa told us a ghost tale or mother talked of monsters, like Stone Man."[1]

At the word, ghost, the image of an abandoned village came to mind. I shook it away, thinking then that I should tell William about our father's death, but I didn't; instead, I let him yap on and on.

"Golden tones washed over our old cabin giving a visual warmth to the red blankets that were tossed over our pallets. Ochre-colored baskets sat at the foot of our beds. They held our clothes, pottery tools, buckskin, beads, and short blowguns. Papa's long blowgun stood against the wall. The baskets were dyed with blood-root and yellow-root, in geometric patterns; they were double-weave baskets.[2]

Our pallets were lined with furs. The coziness of the cabin made it easy to forget that outside of our windowless-abode, winter lived with icy intensity. I miss that cabin, our first cabin, where we grew up," he whispered. He sounded as if they'd lived there for many years. William took in a breath and then let it go; his nostalgia disappeared. I felt cheated.

"I remember the distance between the cabins, too," he added before pausing.

"How's that?"

"I'll get to that. First, let me tell you about Kilakeena Elias Boudinot. I'd never seen a more handsome man in my life. Wouldn't you agree, Julia?"

My wife didn't answer.

"Julia?"

"She's fallen back to sleep," I told William in a whisper. Probably dreaming about a *real Indian*, I thought with disdain. "She can tell you later. His beauty was the envy of any man and some women for that matter," my brother added. I didn't smile.

My brother continued, "We men are just as vain as the ladies, especially Cherokee men. Oh, how they prize their beauty. But mixed bloods, now I'd have to argue that we're the prettiest men of all. That's why my wife married me," my brother boasted playfully but with aplomb and a laugh that ended in a coughing spell. I now, softened my feelings toward William. His cough, which caused him to seize up, then sent him forward gasping for air. It continued, wracking his body for more than a couple of minutes. I sat forward, not knowing what I could do and waited with some concern. This fit eventually subsided, which is when my brother's words took a bleak turn.

"Silas, I know Cherokee men who have killed themselves after seeing the disfigurement brought on them by small pox. Have you looked at me in daylight? Am I going to horrify my wife?"

"Oh, William," I said.

"To think I make it through a war without losing a limb or an eye only to have my face mutilated by pock marks. I can feel one developing above my lip," worry filled the edges of his voice. "I'm an ugly sight, aren't I?" He choked on these words, holding back tears.

"Not everyone suffers such defacement," I tried to assure him, but my words were hollow as I had no evidence to support my claim. Plus, the pustules were beginning to swell and multiply on his face. He sniffed frequently and rubbed at the puss-filled sores, which seeped a yellow substance that dripped onto his lips. He licked his lips. He'd have pox down his throat by morning; I was sure of it."You can be sure that Kilakeena never faced the pox. His face was perfect," William wiped puss from the corner of his mouth.

"I remember him standing in the center of the long-house and the rest of us sitting on tiered seats. He spoke about how much progress the Cherokee were making.

"New Echota settlements have become progressive. The people there have two-story houses, a wood mill, a smithy shop, a general store, and a newspaper office where I print the 'Cherokee Phoenix,' the newspaper, Kilakeena added holding up a copy of the Cherokee/ English newspaper for all of us to see. *The men have plows and the women have spinning wheels and looms. They make their own clothes out of calico cloth.* He listed these accomplishments with pride.

"We hadn't seen New Echota in some years because the Governor of Georgia had outlawed Cherokee festivals and Chief Ross feared that they might arrest the leaders of the Nation, if everyone came together. If that happened, Cherokee men wouldn't stand still. If our warriors attacked the Whites, then the Georgia militia and federal troops would come and kill us. It would be a massacre, especially, if we were all at one place, like the festival. So when Kilakeena turned to all of us and said, *The Chief doesn't agree with me, but I believe that we should hold the festivals again; we should stand up to the Whites. And Scaleeloskee and Ridge agree with me,* we were surprised.

"Everyone missed the festivals, I longed for them with a glutton's appetite," he confessed.

"Stews cooked over open fires. Corn bread aroma in the air. Storytellers gathered children together. Women gossiped and passed out treats—strawberries and peaches. Dancers proudly donned their finest regalia and strutted like peacocks among the crowded encampments. Trading blankets, which were filled with knives, shells, skins, furs, silver jewelry, iron pots and kettles, colorful calico cloth, and trinkets

91

of every kind, framed the perimeter of the festival grounds. And our relatives, especially from the Deer Clan, arrived anxious to greet us.

"Anyway, Kilakeena was a skillful orator. No Lincoln mind you, but he was articulate. All the people listened with awe when he spoke.

"Papa and Two-Turtles listened to the whole speech when Kilakeena came to the village in the Snowbird Mountains. Mother sat with Tsiskwa'gwa and her sisters, Suna'wa Udsi' and Nannie. We, children, were allowed to listen this time, too. Usually we played outside while the men met in the longhouse or the women met in the asi. I remember some of his exact words." William shifted his weight and then told us what he recalled, "First, he told us that this is what he told the White people in Boston:

"What is an Indian? Is he not formed of the same materials with yourself? For, of one blood, God created all the nations that dwell on the face of the earth. You here behold an Indian, my kindred are Indians, and my fathers sleeping in the wilderness grave—they too were Indians.

"Kilakeena's words must have elevated his White audiences to a height of moral perpetuity. After all, he had played on their collective guilt in order to get their money," my brother commented. "He had a strong finish.

"There are, with regard to the Cherokee and other tribes, two alternatives; they must either become civilized and happy, or sharing the fate of many kindred nations, become extinct ... they will, they must rise. Yes, under such protection, and with such assistance, the Indian must rise like the Phoenix, after having wallowed for ages in ignorance and barbarity. But should this Government withdraw its care, and the American people their aid, then, to use the words of a writer, 'they will go the way that so many tribes have gone before them; ... They will vanish like a vapour from the face of the earth, their very history will be lost in forgetfulness, and the places that now know them will know them no more.'[3] I ask you, shall red men live, or shall they be swept from the earth? They hang upon your mercy as to a garment. Will you push them from you, or will you save them? Let humanity answer.[4]

"I have begged them and now I am begging you. Take up civilization with all your energy, in all your ways, and be saved, not only by the white man's religion, by the white man's ways. Become more civilized, Christianized, stay away from whiskey, and above all, he begged, *Sign no treaties!"* At that my brother laughed, a sardonic laugh, which turned into a spasm. I felt a chill over me.

"Who was planning to sign a treaty?"

"The U.S. government sent agents, with free whiskey, to help Indians make treaties. By giving up a parcel here and a parcel there, the U.S. planned to peck away at the land like a flock of chickens, until nothing was left for the Cherokee," William grimly predicted the outcome.

I wondered if William realized that father, a White man, was dead and buried this very day. I saw his burial unfold in my mind's eye. I pictured the grave, the hole in the ground with the blanket lining. I wondered who had dug my father's grave. Mister Dodd is too old, too frail to have achieved it on his own, especially in such a short time. Who had taken such care laying out the blanket in the base of the grave? And who had folded the other blanket like a pillow? William continued to speak.

"So Kilakeena, Scaleeloskee, and Ridge traveled from their home with the Deer Clan through the countryside to see the members of the different clans—the Paint Clan, the Blue Clan, the Potato Clan, the Long Hair Clan, the Wolf Clan and our Bird Clan. They carried the word of Chief Ross—*Sign no treaties!* The War Women and the Peace Women, including Tsiskwa'gwa met at the *asi* and determined, and later proclaimed, that to sign a treaty would be punishable by death—a traitorous act to be followed by execution. Blood Law, they called it. No exceptions!

"Things went from bad to worse over the next few years. At Beaver Dam, the Georgians ran Cherokee off their land in the dead of winter, without giving them a single blanket. Outraged, the Chief sent for Ridge and gave orders to attack, but not to kill. Ridge took a group of young men to Beaver Dam to protect our land. They put on war paint like in the old days and whooped and hollered and brought fear into the hearts of those White squatters."

"Was Kilakeena with them?" I asked.

"No, but his younger brother Stand was there," William reported.

"Anyway, the squatters ran to the Governor who sent troops, but by the time they arrived, only four Cherokee warriors remained who had stayed the night to drink the squatters' whiskey. The guardsmen brutally beat them and put them on horses, hands tied behind their backs. One Cherokee, Chewoyee, kept falling off his horse. On the third fall, the soldiers left him on the path for dead; his skull had been fractured.[5]

"Two escaped to tell the tale and a third was taken to the Georgia jail," Thomas chimed.

"Thomas, how are you feeling? I asked, but he didn't answer.

"Thomas?" Still no answer. William picked up the thread of the narrative and continued.

"The Chief sent Kilakeena to Washington to meet with lawyers who, it turned out, were able to argue in the Supreme Court that Georgia's treatment of the Cherokee was unreasonable. In the meantime, they arrested another Cherokee man, Tassels, claiming that he had murdered his own friend while under the influence of whiskey. Chief Ross sent word again to Kilakeena who went to the federal courts. Again the Supreme Court ruled that the State of Georgia had no jurisdiction over the Cherokee. The Supreme Court Justices demanded that the Governor of Georgia release Tassels, and come to Washington to explain his actions. Instead, …"

"Called to Washington so he could explain; instead, the Governor hanged Tassels in the rain," Thomas rhymed.

"Thomas, are you all right?"

"And Andrew Jackson to this day, says *aw, too bad* and smiles away," Thomas sang.

"Thomas?"

"And Andrew Jackson to this day, says *aw, too bad* and smiles away."

"Thomas!" My voice flared.

"He's delirious, Silas. Let him be," William told me.

"But he's right about Jackson, isn't he?" I questioned with disgust.

"Jackson!" My brother matched my disgust with equal vehemence, spitting the name and adding, "Somebody should've killed him at Horseshoe Bend."

"And what about Kilakeena? What happened to him?"

NOTES

[1] See Mooney (1891, 1900/1992) for the story of Stone man.
[2] The double basket weave is unique to the Cherokee. Children on the Qualla Boundary are taught which plants make which dyes to be used in basket making, something I learned while visiting the Qualla Boundary (Clair, 2003).
[3] The embedded quote is taken from the works of Washington Irving and is part of Kilakeena's speech.
[4] I have been as faithful as possible to the actual words written and delivered by Kilakeena Elias Boudinot, but I have presented an abbreviated version. The speech, "Address to the Whites" is drawn from Perdue's reprint and insights (Perdue, 1983).
[5] Wilkins (1986).

TENSION STOKES THE FLAME

Later the Night of December 20, 1865

"I'll tell you what happened," my brother Reuben spoke up. "Right after you check the perimeter, soldier."

"I'm not a soldier," I quipped.

"You don't have to remind *us*," my brother William retorted.

"What's that supposed to mean?"

"You know what it means, Silas. You should've shot those bastards when you had the chance," William complained. I stood up and slung my rifle over my shoulder. Stepping lightly, I passed over my sister, Nan. She rolled as I stepped, tripping me.

"Be careful," Reuben cautioned. I didn't answer him. I unlatched the door.

"Don't forget to check behind the cabin," William added.

"I'm not an idiot."

"Never said you were."

"Didn't have to."

"Hush up, you two. You sound worse than Thomas and Malachi ever did," Reuben intervened.

I walked the perimeter; dusk had long past surrounded the cabin. I searched the hills for a sign of a campfire and saw nothing. Maybe William was right, I thought. Maybe I should've shot those no good bastards. If I'd shot them I wouldn't have to listen to William or walk about in the cold. Shallow considerations, I knew, but the thoughts passed through my mind just the same. In seriousness, I knew that my family remained in jeopardy, in part, because those two varmints roamed free and they roamed free because I let them go, not once, but twice. Blast it, what am I doing, thinking this way, then that way.

I trudged around that cabin half a dozen times with the same thoughts circling in my head. Then to break my cycle, if not my torment, I checked on my mare. She was close enough to field grass to be fine for another day, but I broke open a container of oats just the same. I gave her a handful. "Good girl," I told her, stroking her mane with my free hand. She whinnied. I stroked her again. Eventually, she calmed down, and so did I. I gathered some of the tinder that I'd tossed aside the night before when putting out the roof-fire and brought it into the cabin.

I neither spoke nor looked at my brothers as I entered the room. I tended the fire and returned to my place at the table, my rifle at my side. Neither one of them had mentioned my father's absence. Couldn't they see that he was gone? Couldn't they feel the gaping hole left in this family? We sat in silence for some time.

"Silas?" Reuben sought my attention. "Are you all right?"

"Fine."

"If you get sleepy, let me know. I'll help keep you awake."

"You could finish telling him the story about Kilakeena," William spoke up.

"I don't need any stories."

"Suit yourself," William dropped the subject.

"Did you know that mother and father were arrested?" Reuben queried to no one in particular, but I'm sure it was directed toward me.

"But Kilakeena was arrested first, wasn't he?" William asked as if he didn't know.

"Yeah, but before that Jackson called for the Cherokee Removal as part of the Indian Removal Act. Outraged by this turn of events, Chief Ross traveled to Washington,[1] but before he left, he instructed Kilakeena to write articles for the newspaper in Cherokee and English, telling the people what had happened and to stay on their land."

I listened and realized that my father had just been getting to this part of the story when I had heard a noise outside. He'd been saying something about the Indian Removal Act. I wanted to know what my father had intended to tell me.

"Go on," I encouraged.

"Kilakeena did what the Chief asked and for doing so he was arrested." Reuben's voice wasn't much stronger than William's voice but he seemed dedicated to telling me the story, probably more concerned about keeping me awake. He groaned as he propped himself up against the wall.

"Soldiers arrived at Kilakeena and Harriet's house in New Echota. A knock came at their door.

"*Colonel Nelson requests your presence*, a soldier told Kilakeena as he opened the door.

"*I've had that honor once before; I prefer not to see the Colonel*, Kilakeena Elias replied.

"*We have our orders*, the soldier replied. And with that a dozen soldiers dismounted and pointed their bayonets at Kilakeena. *You're under arrest*, the soldier in charge added.

"*By what right do you arrest my husband*, Harriet demanded, pushing her way in front of Kilakeena.

"*Colonel's orders, ma'am.* The soldiers set Harriet aside, surrounded Kilakeena, and marched him to the Colonel's headquarters. Once there, Colonel Nelson accused Kilakeena of writing blasphemous articles that portrayed the Georgia Guard negatively.

"*What is this vulgar trash that you call journalism?* The Colonel waved the flimsy *Cherokee Phoenix*, newspaper in Kilakeena's face.

"*How dare you write such stories about the Georgia Guard. You are nothing but an ignorant Indian!*

"*I never claimed otherwise*, Kilakeena countered, straight-faced. The Colonel scoffed.

"*Surely, you can't possibly be responsible for the articles written in this paper*, the Colonel altered the course of his argument, while pointing an accusatory finger at Kilakeena. *No Indian could write so well*, he declared. *Which one of the missionaries actually wrote these articles?*

"*Is it Worcester?* he demanded to know. *Is it Worcester who is writing these articles?* Kilakeena remained silent.

"*The missionaries are trying to convert you, so that they can get you to sign over the gold mines for their own use*, Colonel Nelson told Kilakeena. "*They'll only bring destruction upon you*, the Colonel yelled. *You are not the real editor. Those articles are acts of treason in my assessment and your unwillingness to give up the real authors will not fare well for you. Speak man, or I shall fall upon you and beat you myself, here and now.* Kilakeena refused to speak.

"I will have you flogged within an inch of your life if you do not speak. Kilakeena did not speak.[2]

"Get him out of my sight, the Colonel commanded to his guards. The guards threw him out of the office and left him to his own resources to walk back home.

"And so it was that Kilakeena was relieved of his arrest without a single lash across his back. Kilakeena told his friends and relatives that he wasn't sure what deterred the Colonel from having him whipped. I think the Colonel realized he didn't need a Cherokee martyr on his hands," Reuben concluded.

"By early June, the Guard carried out its earlier threat that if the missionaries didn't sign the loyalty oath, then they would be imprisoned. The Georgia Guard, under orders from Governor Gilmer, once again arrested the good missionaries who refused to lie down like weak dogs before injustice." In spite of the anger which inflamed Reuben's story, he grew tired. He slid sideways, but caught himself in time to lean upon his elbow. He continued the story in a softer voice.

"Once again, the soldiers arrived in New Echota, drew their rifles, and pointed their bayonets. Helpless before the guardsmen, the Cherokee people stood horrified as they watched the missionaries, Buttrick, Worcester, and Burrick, as well as John Wheeler, Kilakeena's brother-in-law and assistant on the press, each in turn, being chained about the neck with metal shackles and tethered to the back of a horse-drawn cart.

"He's a man of the cloth, Worcester's wife wailed as she tried to free her husband from the chains. Kilakeena's brother, Stand, pulled Worcester's wife back, fearing the soldiers might accidentally hurt her with their bayonets.

"Jesus, help us, Harriet beseeched heaven as she reached her hands upward toward the sky, attempting to save the missionaries.

"This is against all rights found in the constitution, Kilakeena argued. *I'll find a way to free you,* he called out to his friend Worcester, a tall man with eternally unruly hair and a placid face.

"Jesus will look after me, Worcester declared, *but a lawyer wouldn't hurt,* he added with a smile toward his wife.

"*Give us your shoes,* a soldier demanded of the men. Chained about the necks, they sat, removed their shoes and handed them over to the soldiers.

"*Walk,* the soldier demanded. Each man, barefoot, began the long march, over fifty miles.

"They collapsed under their bloody feet on several occasions and thus were dragged by the chains. Thus, they entered the prison, their torment began in earnest.[3]

"Under these conditions many signed the loyalty contract and were released. However, two missionaries, Worcester and Butler remained steadfast in their refusal to swear allegiance to Governor Gilmore and the State of Georgia." My brother paused as if the story had reached its conclusion.

"But I thought you said mother and father were arrested?" I spoke up.

"Lots of people were arrested for not signing a loyalty oath to the State of Georgia ..." Reuben's voice trailed away.

"But we didn't live in Georgia then, did we?" I asked.

"No, we were living where North Carolina is today," William inserted.

"Then why were our parents arrested? Did North Carolina have a loyalty oath, too?"

"No, they were arrested later, for something else," Reuben added without explaining. "Silas, my head hurts somethin' fierce."

"I'll finish the story," William offered, as I got up and took water to Reuben.

"Kilakeena returned to Washington to obtain a lawyer for Worcester while Chief Ross and another group of lawyers worked on another case—*The Cherokee Nation v. the State of Georgia.* Chief Ross, being seven-eighths White, blended in with the lawyers. His pale skin, curly hair, and English fluency, hardly characteristics of what Julia would call a *real Indian,* served him well in the courtroom; nevertheless, something went wrong. But Reuben really knows more about it than I do," William apologized. Reuben had finished sipping a ladle of water; he picked up where William left off.

"Chief Ross's case came to trial first in 1831. Chief Justice John Marshall presided. At the end, he gave a lengthy speech that dragged on and on. The courtroom was full of interested people from Henry Clay to Davy Crockett who listened as the old judge spoke: *As much as I abhor what the State of Georgia has done, I must in the end declare that the case cannot be heard before the Supreme Court.*"

"Why?" I asked.

"Good question. One that everyone in the audience, including Scaleeloskee and Kilakeena, wanted answered. The judge explained that the lawyers had declared that the Cherokee Nation a *foreign nation*, when in fact the Cherokee Nation is a *domestic and dependent* nation not a *foreign nation*."

"So, what does that mean?"

"It means that the Chief Justice was trying to find a loop-hole to help us. If we were a domestic, dependent nation, then the United States would be responsible for protecting us from Georgia."

"He was sending Jackson a message," Reuben added.

"What happened to Kilakeena's case?" I asked.

"You mean the missionaries? Yes, well, the following year the Court ruled without hesitation that the State of Georgia had no right to incarcerate Reverend Worcester and that Georgia had no right to interfere with the Cherokee Nation."

"When word reached New Echota, the people began to celebrate. Chief Ross returned to the homeland. Kilakeena and Scaleeloskee prepared to leave Washington, as well; but, just before their departure, they heard a rumor that Jackson had decided to ignore the Supreme Court decision." My brother's voice was growing weak at the conclusion.

Astonished, I asked, "How could he? The President can't do that," and then I wondered, "Was the rumor true?" My protest and queries provided the impetus for more stories, which I'm sure would've continued immediately, except the baby started to cry.

"Julia," I beckoned. "Can you feed the baby?" She murmured something. I went to her side.

"Julia," I crouched down beside her and helped her unbutton her blouse. By the firelight I could see the rash across her chest. The baby cried. I laid her in the crook of Julia's arm. My wife turned on her side and let her breast set next to the baby's waiting mouth. She managed to work a few drops of milk from her breast. I tried to help support the baby's head.

"She's hot, Silas. Terribly hot." Julia looked to me with concern. I fetched the water again and sprinkled a bit of it on my baby's face. Then I blew a cool breeze across our infant's head. I brushed Julia's hair from her face and then brought water to her lips. Within moments though, Julia looked to me for relief.

"That's all I can do, Silas," said with a trembling voice. Then she surrendered to her fatigue, falling back onto her blanket. The baby lay quiet in her arm. I soaked a piece of cloth in water and placed it on the baby's lips. I watched her suckle, weakly. I stayed with them. My older brothers grew quiet. They'd done their job—keeping me awake; it was nearly dawn. William snored and Reuben groaned in his sleep. I thought, their stories had indeed served their purpose, but as for me, I still didn't know why my father blamed Kilakeena for his having to sit sentry at the face of a cave or what Kilakeena had to do with my mother's twisted gait.

Although those questions plagued me, I did feel relatively secure that those Confederates would stay away. So I let myself sleep. Drifting into a dream, I left my own questions and my brothers' story behind.

NOTES

[1] Chief Ross made numerous trips to Washington D.C. and enlisted the help of such famous people as Davy Crocket and Henry Clay. Chief Ross was nick-named Cooweescoowee which is the Cherokee word for a rare migratory bird seen occasionally in Cherokee Territory (Mooney, 1891, 1900/1992).

[2] Boudinot's rendition of this story was printed in the *Cherokee Phoenix* and reprinted in Perdue's (1983) collection.

[3] The story of the missionaries' brutal arrest was printed in the *Cherokee Phoenix* and is summarized in Wilkins (1986, pp. 226–227).

CHAPTER 15

NEGOTIATIONS

Late during the Night of December 20, 1865

I awoke to a foul odor—smells of sour breath and sweat soaked blankets. Sickness seemed everywhere around me. Telltale traces of urine lingered in the stale surroundings of the closed cabin. And something else within my midst. Covering my nose and mouth, I raised myself up on one elbow and looked over Julia's side to see the baby. Turning the blanket down, I saw the source of the other stench that I had smelled—feces. The baby lay in a puddle of diarrhea. I prayed dysentery wasn't our next obstacle to face. I gathered myself up and found a towel in the kitchen. I cleaned my baby girl and then the area under which she had laid. I tossed the foul towel outside for now. I walked quietly around the sleeping figures, covering those who had thrown their blankets off. The cabin was cold. I stoked the fire and added a few more branches. Eventually, I came to rest back in the chair by the table. I lit the coal oil lamp.

"Blazes, Reuben! You scared me."

Reuben was sitting straight up against the wall, his eyes frozen in a forward stare. I thought he was dead, until he turned his head with a quick jerk and then tried to stand up.

"You need some help?" I offered. He nodded. I assisted him to his feet and took him outside to relieve himself. When we returned to the cabin, he asked me if I wanted to hear the rest of the story. I nodded.

"Can I join you at the table?" he asked. "I think I feel a bit better." I pulled out the other chair.

"So, even though we'd won the court cases, Andrew Jackson didn't care," Reuben said, settling into the chair next to me, a blanket about his shoulders. He launched into the story as if we'd never stopped.

"Kilakeena was a young man, with a young man's sense of righteousness; he, along with his cousin Scaleeloskee, went to the White House and demanded to see the president. Although, led down one corridor after another eventually they stood eye-to-eye, face-to-face with Andrew Jackson.

"*I've heard a rumor*, Kilakeena posed, *that you do not intend to respect the decision of the Supreme Court. Are you questioning John Marshall's wisdom?*

"*Are you questioning mine?* Andrew Jackson retorted.

"*Yes,*" Kilakeena said firmly.

"*John Marshall has rendered his decision, now let him enforce it.*"[1] Jackson defiantly and dismissively turned away from Kilakeena.

"*Are you saying that you won't come to the aid of the Cherokee people who suffer, even as we speak, at the hands of the Georgia Guard? They beat our women, arrest our men, hanged George Tassels, squat on our land, refuse us rights in their courts, set one woman's cabin afire while she and her children were still inside! And you will not lift a finger?*

"*I'm saying that you should pack your belongings and move west. You've wasted your money on lawyers. They've fleeced you.*

"*Wasted our money? Are you saying that we shouldn't have fought in the courts?* Kilakeena asked with angry disbelief.

"*It's moot point,* Jackson replied.

"*We've done everything you've asked and more. We're civilized, we're Christians, and we're educated. What more could you want?*

"*I want you to move west,* is all he said.

"*After all my father has done for you,* Scaleeloskee spoke up. *He fought for you at the Battle of Horseshoe Bend; you betrayed him then, just as you betray him now. Have you no sense of loyalty?*

"*I regret that this is the way things must be,* Jackson's final words were spoken without sympathy as he ran a hand through his thin, white wisps of hair, *but I have no intention of protecting the Cherokee people.*

"Scaleeloskee fumed with anger; Kilakeena dropped his head in despair. The two cousins returned to the Nation with the disheartening news. While Scaleeloskee held hope that the President-elect Van Buren would see the world with different eyes, Kilakeena resigned himself to the miserable fate described by Jackson—removal to a reservation in the West. And in the meantime, his friend, Worcester remained in jail.

"When Chief Ross heard what had happened, his anger exploded; he returned to Washington. Despite his every effort, Washington politicians turned a deaf ear and Van Buren came into office upholding the Indian Removal Policy. Support for the Cherokee began to slip away. Still the Chief wouldn't give up hope. He just needed time and a plan.

"An idea came to him, which he shared with his friend Major Ridge one day.

"*Ridge, what if we negotiated a special form of citizenship; where we maintain our Cherokee rituals, but swear our allegiance to the United Sates?*

"*Never!* Ridge proclaimed.

"*Why? This may be our only chance.*

"*A chance for what? To live under the rule of the Georgia Governor? Are you mad? Have spirits taken over your mind?*

"*My madness may be what saves our lives.*

"*Better to move west than become citizens of Georgia. What kind of Cherokee would even suggest such a thing?* Major Ridge censured Ross and then stormed away leaving the Chief behind. Chief Ross made one more declaration as Ridge walked out the door, *If we do not live as Cherokee in Georgia, then I will move the tribe to Mexico!*

"Ridge traveled immediately to Kilakeena's home and repeated the Chief's ideas—citizenship or Mexico and his own words—Better to move west than become citizens of Georgia! He told Kilakeena, *Write that in the newspaper!*

"So, Kilakeena did. Of course, when the Chief saw it, he became furious, yelling: *This is the talk of traitors! Cowards, who would split the nation!* The Chief rallied support; as did Ridge. Alliances developed. Those who would stand with the Chief and negotiate citizenship or those who would stand with Ridge, Kilakeena, and Scaleeloskee.

"Escorted by several warriors, the Chief rode to New Echota, dismounted his horse and strode into the office of the *Cherokee Phoenix*, a small, one-room cabin, with printing press and desks. Newspapers hung from clothesline, wet ink drying on the line. Wheeler, Kilakeena's assistant, looked up from where he stood by the press, setting the type. Kilkaeena turned from his job, laboring over translations. Each looked at the Chief whose eyes blazed.

"*You are no longer in charge of the press! Get out!*

"The Chief's warriors surrounded Kilakeena; and then, forced him and Wheeler to leave. They kept guard over the press, until another printer could be found. The Chief set the new editor the task to print a paper that named Kilakeena a traitor.

"When Kilakeena's brother Stand heard this, he turned on the Chief. Stand may have been younger than Kilakeena, but of the two, Stand was the larger and the stronger. He was born a warrior, like his Uncle Ridge, and had a temper that was not easily assuaged. He gathered the men and …"

"Are you telling Silas about how Stand stole the press, which weighed tons?" William's voice came from the shadows with renewed energy. "So that the Chief couldn't print any more newspapers."

"Stole it? How did he move a press?" I asked. "It must have weighed a ton."

"It did! He got help from the Georgia Guard," my older brother John chimed in. He had awakened, too. I'd seen his form shifting restlessly about earlier, but hadn't been sure that he was awake and listening.

"The Georgia Guard? His own enemy? That makes no sense," I questioned with disbelief.

"Yes, he also hid the tiles that made the bilingual paper possible, syllabary tiles and English alphabet tiles. So that even if Chief Ross procured another press he wouldn't have the tiles, so he still couldn't publish another newspaper."[2]

"Made of iron, he couldn't have destroyed them. Did he hide them?"

"No one knows for sure."[3]

"Perhaps, Malachi can tell us more since he joined Stand Watie's regiment," John suggested.

"Did you hear from Malachi before we left Georgia?" I questioned John.

"The last letter I received from Malachi was nearly four months ago. He wrote, that they were fighting in Oklahoma, but added that they were headed to Arkansas in the near future. I tell you, the fighting between Stand Watie and Chief Ross is another story altogether."

"Sort of," Reuben added.

"What do you mean? Is the feud still going on?" I asked Reuben. "*Waay'll*," he pronounced the word 'well' the way my father used to say it. I thought of my father and then I wondered about Malachi, my youngest brother, who was off fighting with Stand Watie. I yearned to see him and a lump in my throat caught as I thought of my father wanting to see Malachi before he died.

"Yes, the lines were drawn; that's for sure. Chief Ross called Kilakeena a traitor and Ridge called Chief Ross naïve and ignorant. Ridge, Scaleeloskee, and Kilakeena formed a coalition that planned to sign away the Cherokee territory. Ridge proclaimed himself the voice of the Cherokee people and went to Washington to negotiate a treaty."

"But the Blood Law," I queried.

"Indeed," William highlighted my point, but his voice sounded weak again.

Reuben continued, "Yes, to sign a treaty was punishable by death."

"And President Van Buren faced the mild wrath of liberals in the north, so when Ridge arrived he sent Ridge back saying, *The treaty must be signed in New Echota, where the Cherokee people can come if they want to show any adverse feelings toward it. But if they don't come, I will take it as a sign that the Cherokee people agree to all provisions within the Treaty.*

"When Chief Ross heard this, he told the people not to go, not to give this treaty any credibility. The people listened to their Chief; their silence sealed their fate," my brother concluded.

NOTES

[1] See Josphy Jr. (1994).
[2] See Wilkins (1986).
[3] Based on information provided by Gary Greene of the New Echota Historical Site, the syllabary tiles were found on a recent archeological dig where the Boudinot's water well would have been.

CHAPTER 16

THE BEAR MAN STORY

The Night of December 20, 1865

A solemn silence surrounded us in the cabin. I sat with my rifle next to me now and let my brother's concluding remarks echo in my mind, *their silence sealed their fate.* No one spoke another word, until I broached the subject again.

"William?" I wanted to ask him what happened next. If all this negotiating had taken place in 1832 or 1833 before I was born, then why hadn't I grown up in Mexico or in the land just across the Mississippi River?

"William, what happened in 1833?" I asked, but he didn't answer me. I was born in 1834 and although my mother credits me for having the best recollection of any of her twelve children there are things about this that I couldn't be expected to remember; I was either not yet born or simply too young.

"William?" Again the answer was silence. He had fallen asleep as had the others. Reuben had returned to his spot on the floor. And the others slept restlessly.

Straining my memory, I thought back on my childhood. I could remember my first pair of moccasins. I received those when I was four–years-old. My memories came in images. I saw myself eating with my younger brothers and sisters, sharing the one meal a day. Sitting around a common pan filled with scrambled eggs or a large basket filled with salad greens and roots. I kept trying to picture it all.

I recalled the Cherokee village that we lived in for several years. I recollected my friends' faces. Again, I felt a wave of loneliness wash over me. I pictured us returning from a religious revival some ten miles, or more, away. When we came back, my mother told us, *Never speak badly of Indians.* What brought that on I am not sure; neighbors, a Cherokee couple, had cared for our house while we were gone and the woman generously cleaned some of my mother's dirty skillets. Perhaps, it was that. However, the only time I did hear bad words about Indians is when we were in the presence of White folks, like at that revival meeting. At any rate, she called us to her side so that she could teach us a Christian song. I remember standing at her knee and gazing at the tears that filled her eyes while she sang the song, *Oh! How Happy Are They, Who Their Savior Obey.*[1] I never knew if she was crying because she'd found Jesus or lost something else. I thought about these things while I sat sentry in this godforsaken cabin.

And then I remembered a conversation that took place on my fourteenth birthday, my father took me aside and told me, *Son, it's time for you to start wearing the white man's shoes.* That was the first time I wondered whether I was White or Cherokee. I didn't want him to take my moccasins away.

"Reuben?" No answer came out of the darkness. I was wondering about the fact that Chief Ross was only one-eighth Cherokee. What makes somebody Cherokee? What makes them *a real Indian*? "John?" Again no answer followed. Everyone slept except for me.

"Silas?" my mother's voice reached out in the darkness. "You should sleep." Instead, I asked, "Was Papa a White man? I mean thoroughly, through and through?"

"Your father is like the bear man. Do you know the story of the bear man?" she asked me. I breathed deeply before answering her.

"No." I pursed my lips to fight back tears. I still hadn't told her about my father, at least not so I was sure that she understood.

"Tsiskwa'gwa's husband told us this story. Your father liked it.

"Once some time ago, a man went hunting in the mountains and came across a black bear, which he wounded with an arrow. The bear turned and started to run the other way, and the hunter followed, shooting one arrow after another into it without bringing it down. Now, this was a medicine bear. It could talk and it knew the thoughts of people without their saying a word. At last, the bear stopped and pulled the arrows out of his side and gave them to the man, saying, *It's of no use for you to shoot at me, for you can't kill me. Come to my house and live with me.* The hunter thought to himself, *He may kill me*, but the bear read his thoughts and said, *No, I won't hurt you.* The man thought again, *How can I get anything to eat?* But the bear knew his thoughts again, and added, *There'll be plenty.* So the hunter went with the bear.

"They went on until they came to a hole in the side of the mountain. *This isn't where I live, but there is going to be a council here and we'll see what they do,* the bear explained. They went into the cave. It was full of bears—old bears, young bears, and cubs, white bears, black bears, and brown bears—and a large white bear was the chief—Chief White Bear. They sat down in the corner, but soon the bears scented the hunter and one asked, *What smells so bad?* Chief White Bear reprimanded him, *Don't talk so; it is only a stranger come to see us. Let him alone.* The Chief told them to get back to the issues at hand.

"Food grew scarce in the mountains and the council needed to decide what to do about it. So far, they had sent out messenger scouts in search of food. While the members of the council were talking, two bear-messengers came in and reported that they had found a country in the low grounds where there were so many chestnuts and acorns that they stood knee-deep in the food. The council members announced their pleasure and readied themselves for a dance.

"When the dance and council were over, they began to go home, except for Chief White Bear, who lived there. At last, the hunter and the bear went out together.

"They didn't stop until they came to another cave. *This is where I live,* the bear told him and they went in. By this time the hunter was very hungry and was wondering how he could get something to eat. The bear knew his thoughts. He rubbed his stomach with his forepaws, like so, and instantly, he had both paws full of chestnuts and gave them to the man. The bear rubbed his stomach again, like so, and gave the man both paws full of huckleberries. The bear rubbed again, like so, and his paws filled with blackberries, which he also gave to the man. The bear rubbed himself yet another time, like so, and had his paws full of acorns, but the man could not eat them because his belly was full.

"The hunter lived in the cave with the bear all winter, until long hair like that of the bear began to grow all over his body and he began to act like a bear; yet he still walked like a man. One day in early spring the bear provided a portent to him, *Your people in the settlement are getting ready for a grand hunt in these mountains, and they'll come to this cave and kill me and take these clothes from me—* he meant his skin—*but they won't hurt you; instead, they'll take you home with them.* The bear knew what the people were doing in the settlement just as he always knew what the man was thinking.

Some days passed and the bear repeated, *This is the day that Topknots[2] will come to kill me, but the Split-noses will come first and find us. When they have killed me, they will drag me outside the cave and take off my clothes and cut me in pieces. You must cover the blood with leaves, and, when they are taking you away, look back after you have gone apiece and you will see something.*

"Soon they heard the hunters coming, and then the dogs found the cave and began to bark. The hunters came and looked inside and saw the bear and killed him with their arrows. Then they dragged him outside, skinned the body, and cut it in quarters to carry home. The dogs kept on barking until the hunters thought there must be another bear in the cave. They looked in again and saw the man way at the farther end. At first they thought it was another bear on account of his long hair, but they soon saw it was the hunter who had been lost the year before. So they went in and brought him out. Then each hunter took a load of the bear meat and they started home, bringing the man and the skin and meat with them. Before they left, the man piled leaves over the spot where they had cut up the bear, and when they had gone a way, he looked behind and saw the bear rise up out of the leaves, shake himself, and go back into the woods.

"When they came near the settlement the man told the hunters that he must be quarantined without anything to eat or drink for seven days and nights, until the bear nature had left him and he became like a man again. So they shut him up alone in a house and tried to keep very still about it, but the news got out and his wife heard of it. She came for her husband, but the people wouldn't let her near him; but she came every day and begged so hard that at last after four or five days they let her have him. She took him home with her, but in a short time he died, because he still had a bear's nature and couldn't live like a man. And that is all I know about the bear-man.[3]

"As for your father, he lived among the Cherokee," my mother concluded.

I knew what she meant. I thought about how people grow accustom to other people's ways of being in the world.

"Do you think people always change?" I was thinking about how uncomfortable the White man's shoes were that I donned at the age of fourteen. Hard brittle leather scraped and rubbed against my heels and toes leaving bleeding blisters and sores. Several years later, I made a new kind of shoe that combined the softness of the moccasin with the sturdiness of the leather. I gave my father a pair and he judged them to be an improvement over the White man's shoes.[4]

"Do you think we always adapt?" I questioned her.

"When I was a young girl, a wise woman named *Tsiskwa'gwa* told me that when White men were new to this country they often asked Indians to be their guides. There is a story of three such White men who asked the Cherokee men to guide them down a river in their canoes and across an unfamiliar land. Having reached the land, they disembarked. As they moved down a path in search of a place to camp for the night, they encountered a rattlesnake. The White men rushed back to their canoes. The Indians followed to see what they were doing. The White men grabbed their rifles and darted back to the place of the snake. They pointed their muskets, but the Indians ran forward and told them to cease. The men put down their guns reluctantly. Then the Indians encircled the snake and pulled out their pouches of tobacco. They blew the smoke toward the snake whom they called *grandfather*. In a short while the rattlesnake relaxed and fell into a deep sleep. Then all crossed the path in safety.

"Tsiskwa'gwa also told me that within one generation the Indian men no longer smoked with their *grandfather, the rattlesnake*; instead, Cherokee men raised their rifles against him and shot."[5] My mother paused at the end of her story. I nodded, but she couldn't see me in the darkness.

"If you came across a snake what would you do, Silas?" my mother put the question to me like a test. But I already knew the answer. While I lived in the caves, I encountered a rattlesnake. It was my first year in hiding. I had found a more than suitable cave, near water, with excellent protection. This cave was like a deep pocket. I slept well until one morning when I awakened abruptly to the sound of a rattler. I reached for my gun and using the butt end I came down hard and fast on that snake's tail. It slithered away. I remember thinking at the time, I would miss the warmth of that cave and the lush foliage that surrounded it, but where there is one snake, there are usually more. And once you've hit a snake, he's not likely to forgive you.[6]

I thought of my mother's question again. Then I wondered whether I had behaved like a White man or an Indian, or someone betwixt and between. Julia certainly never thought of me as a Cherokee; to her, only Kilakeena was a *real Indian*.

My mother and I both fell asleep for a while, but we continued our conversation before dawn as she and I awoke. I felt a bit better after having slumbered. I thought, perhaps, she felt better, too. After checking on the others, I asked my mother a question: "What happened in the Cherokee Nation in 1833?"

"The people saw the flaming sky," she told me. "Everyone saw the streaking lights across the night sky.[7] They ran to Nannye-hi and asked her if she knew what it meant.

"*It is a very bad omen,* she told them.

"*Concerning what?* one man asked.

"*The stars threaten to come out of the sky if the Cherokee people sign a treaty and leave their homeland.* The Chief agreed; he told the people, *Listen to Nannye-hi, stay on the land, sow the seeds and harvest the crops come fall.*

"The fall gave way to winter that brought no treaties and no soldiers. Everything was quiet. The most exciting event happened on March 18, 1834—you were born." I imagined that she smiled at this thought. "We planted again that spring and harvested again that autumn without incident.

"Not until December 29, 1835 did any significant acts takes place concerning the homeland. It happened at Kilakeena and Harriet's house in New Echota. Your father's friend, my uncle Two-Turtles witnessed it all. He went as a messenger to report back to Chief Ross. When I heard the news of what had happened at Kilakeena's home, I sang and I prayed:

"Do hi yi, O'ht ge hest ti, do hi yi—good-bye, happy day, good-bye,"

Hikayu'l-Une'ga, Oh Ancient White
Hikayu'l-Une'ga, Oh Ancient White
O Kanti, O Selu, sk'salata'titege'sti,
Oh Kanati, Oh Selu, support me continually,
sa ka'ni ginu't'ti nige'su"na. Sge!
That I may never become blue, Listen!

"I sang this prayer, the song of the hunter.[8] It asks the spirit of peace to bring the hunter strength in times of trouble. I knew that trouble was on the way."

NOTES

[1]   Taken directly from the Silas Mercer Beasley Jr. Story (Shackelford Sims, 1978).
[2]   Many Cherokee men of the time styled their hair into a knot on the top of their heads.
[3]   The Bear-Man story is drawn from Mooney's (1891, 1900/1992) collection. Quarantine was frequently used among the Cherokee as a medical practice.
[4]   See Shackelford Sims (1978).
[5]   See Mooney (1891, 1900/1992).
[6]   See S.M. Beasley Story (Shackelford Sims, 1978).
[7]   Extraordinary meteor showers and meteor storms have been reported in 1833, 1866 and in 2001. In 2001, a spectacular display was called the Leonid Meteor Storm. I watched with my daughter Calle; it was amazing!
[8]   The Hunter's song can be found in Mooney (1891, 1900/1992).

MY COUSIN BETRAYED ME

Late Night of December 20, 1865 and on into the Morning

My mother tried to recall every detail of the story that Two-Turtles had told her. I listened with equal care:

"A nervous anticipation chilled the air, speaking of the climate in my cousin Kilakeena's home on December 29, 1835. Unnecessary preparation did nothing to calm the cold sweats and squirming stomachs of the adults. Two-Turtles had watched them fidget. He described it, saying that Harriet kept after the children, moving from one project to the next. She directed them to help her with this or that until each had a chore—dusting, sweeping, wiping glasses, cleaning ashes from the hearth, or slicing bread. Mrs. Worcester darned socks that had already been darned. She went upstairs and downstairs looking for different yarn, or a better needle, or a different pair of socks. Sometimes, she returned with a completely different stack of mending. Reverend Worcester wrote in his journal, but broke the tip of his quill more than once. He twisted and wrung his hands each time. Elias made extra trips to the woodshed to bring in dry firewood. The parlor wood-box sat filled beyond capacity. Elias seemed oblivious to this fact as he made further trips for dry timber."

"I thought Reverend Worcester was in prison," I interrupted.

"They released him when Kilakeena promised to sign the treaty," my mother explained before continuing. *Ah, I thought, Worcester was his friend who suffered much for the Cherokee. This must have played into Kilakeena's decision to sign a treaty.* My mother continued the story.

"The first knock at the door sent a jolt through Harriet's body. Her muscles tensed. She froze in place. The knock came again. Kilakeena answered the door, finding Ridge and Scaleeloskee at the doorway.[1] Their presence brought a sense of relief to Elias, but Harriet remained twisted and tense.

"Twenty men in all, representing the Treaty Party, eventually arrived at my cousin's home on the evening of December 29, 1835. Christmas had been spared by a few days at Harriet's request on behalf of the children and so that she might pray for intervention. Elias beseeched no one. Not Jesus, not God the Father, not even Commissioner Schermerhorn.

"John F. Schermerhorn arrived last. He came with General Carroll and an entourage of soldiers. His smug expression annoyed everyone. Schermerhorn, in his usual tactless manner, dismissed the soberness of the gathering with a repugnant remark:

"*Believe me, your ancestors are dead*, he said callously to one Cherokee elder and then added, *They won't know the difference.* To another he added, *So Chief, as long as you're leaving, do you have any horses or farm equipment you want to donate to the service of the Christian community?* Appalled by the remarks, Harriet excused herself. Two-Turtles witnessed everything in silence and committed it to memory as instructed by Chief Ross.

"Schermerhorn raised the paper before him, adjusted his spectacles, and proceeded to read:

"*WHEREAS the Cherokee are anxious to make some arrangements with the government of the United States whereby the difficulties they have experienced by residents within the settled parts of the United States under the jurisdiction and laws, ...*"[2] My mother tried to recall the words exactly, but interrupted herself, saying, "It was a lie, a sham. We weren't anxious to make a treaty." I could think of no appropriate response; I shook my head.

"The Devil's horn[3] continued to say things like, *And whereas the said commissioners did appoint and notify a general council of the Nation to Convene at New Echota on the 29th day December 1835; and informed them that ... those who did not come they should conclude gave their assent.*

"Chief Ross told us to stay away," my mother added defensively."Schermerhorn cleared his throat and continued to read: *ARTICLE 1: The Cherokee Nation hereby cede, relinquish, and convey to the United States all the lands owned, claimed, or possessed by them east of the Mississippi river, ...*

"At the words—cede, relinquish, and convey, my cousin, Kilakeena Elias Boudinot glanced at the others. Two-Turtles looked around, as well. Some of the elders had tears in their eyes. Elias would not look around the room again.

"*ARTICLE 2*: … Schermerhorn's voice boomed through the meeting room, promising territory in Arkansas and a perpetual outlet west and trading for salt and other goods. *ARTICLE 3: The United States would always have the right to make and establish posts in any part of the Cherokee Nation. ARTICLE 4: The Osage would have to move.* Already they were breaking their own treaty with the Osage in order to sign a treaty with us. It's hard to imagine that Kilakeena trusted them. What was he thinking?" my mother asked in dismay. "*ARTICLE 5* promised that our new lands would never become part of a state in the United States. How do they explain Arkansas?"

"How many Articles were there?" I asked.

"Twelve," she skipped then to Article Eight.

ARTICLE 8: The United States agrees, … to remove the Cherokee to their new homes, … that sufficient number of steamboats and baggage wagons shall be furnished to remove them comfortably," my mother paused. "Comfortably!" To remove them comfortably," she scoffed. She announced the next Article.

"*ARTICLE 9*: Promised fair assessment and reimbursements; *Article 10* … *ARTICLE 11*: Claimed that we agreed to let our treaty money be invested by the President of the United States as part of a general fund for our Nation's needs. Finally, *ARTICLE 12*: Allowed those who wanted to become citizens to do so, but that wasn't true either. They wouldn't even let your father stay."

"But we did stay, didn't we?"

"Schermerhorn finished reading the Articles; he puffed up his fat face, sucked in his lower lip and let it pop out with a chirping noise. *Welp, that about does it.* Commissioner Schermerhorn lowered the paper to the table. He dipped the pen into the inkwell and held it out for the first to sign. No one moved.

"*Well, what are you waiting for?* Schermerhorn asked impatiently with a complete lack of empathy or sympathy. His earlier words had been pompous and stinging. His crude and unfeeling style did nothing to ease the pain with which the members of the Treaty Party approached their task. An elder began to cry. Tears trailed down his weathered face.

"Twenty Cherokee men stood as the representatives of the Treaty Party, none of whom moved toward the parchment or the plumed pen that Schermerhorn extended to them. General Carroll looked around nervously and then turned to Schermerhorn, concerned.

"At last, Major Ridge, dressed in epaulets and full uniform, given to him by Andrew Jackson, turned to his hesitant companions, took a deep breath, and addressed the contingent:

I am one of the native sons of these wild woods. I have hunted the deer and the turkey here, more than fifty years. We come by this land from the living God. They take this land from us by the writ of deception. From the time of the British, their numbers have grown so far beyond our own that resistance to them is futile. We cannot remain here in safety and comfort. I know that we love the graves of our fathers. I know that we all hear the voices of the ancestors on the wind. The tears that flow down the cheeks of the strong are the tears for the homeland lost. We will never forget our homeland. But we cannot stay here. An unbending necessity tells us that to stay here is certain death for the Cherokee Nation and the children of future generations. There is but one path to safety, Major Ridge reached for the pen, dipped it into the inkwell, and marked his X on the parchment. Then he bravely turned to face his companions adding, *I have signed my death warrant and fully expect to die for it.*[4]

"Scaleeloskee took his father's arm. Then he slid his hand downward and gently released the pen from his father's fingers. Scaleeloskee signed in English, John Ridge, beside his father's X. My cousin came forward next.

"Kilakeena turned to see the faces of the men before him. He looked compassionately into their eyes. He caught sight of his own father, Oowattie and his brother, Stand Watie, who came to support him. And finally, Kilakeena addressed the gathering: *I know I take my life in my hand, as our fathers have also done. We will make and sign this treaty ... We can die, but the great Cherokee Nation will be saved. They will not be annihilated; they can live. Oh, what is a man worth*

*who will not dare to die for his people? Who is there here who would
not perish, if this great nation may be saved?*[5]

"Having spoken these words, Kilakeena Elias Boudinot turned
and took the pen from his cousin, Scaleeloskee and added his name to
the list of those who would commit the Nation to the Treaty of New
Echota. No one spoke again that evening. Instead, each man, in turn,
simply took pen to paper and added his mark to the treaty. And so
the deed was done. My cousin had betrayed me." My mother's words
seemed final.

We sat in the dark much as we had the first night that we came
to this cabin. She sat crossed-legged, with a blanket wrapped about
her, and rocked back and forth from her place on the floor. I watched
her figure enter the light and recede into the shadows. The chiaroscuro
left a haunting image in my mind of my mother disappearing into the
darkness. It felt ominous and foreboding.

"So, I am related to a traitor," I announced in disgust. My
mother took offense at my words, even though she had suggested it
was so. "Do you dismiss that you are related to me?" she questioned.
Indeed, she was not the traitor, she stayed on her homeland. Her
reproach and continuing silence hurt me. I was grateful when Reuben
interrupted this scene.

"And then the soldiers came, by the thousands, more than one
for every man, woman, and Cherokee child. They built forts, stockades
and ..."

"And they counted the people," my mother interjected. Then
she added, "They counted our rifles and they counted my children."

I felt relief at the sound of my mother's voice joining us again.
I feared the darkness of her story might leave her silent for a long time.
I rose from my place at the table and took her the water bucket. My
movements awakened others. I had already heard my brothers stirring
again, but now they were fully awake. As I was caring for my mother,
I wanted to change the direction of the conversation, I asked, "Where
was Kilakeena while the forts were being built?"

It was John who answered with a biting tone. "He stayed with
his wife Harriet until ..."

"I know what happened to Harriet," Julia piped in.

"How could you?" I asked. I loathed the fact that she knew more than I about my own people.

"It was in the all the papers," she noted as a matter of fact. "Kilakeena wrote about it and my mother read the article over and over, aloud to us, as if it were a story, a fairytale."

"A fairytale? How could anyone describe this as a fairytale?" I flared at her. Julia brooded for a moment or two and remained silent until Lydia soothed her spirit.

"So your mother read to you from the newspaper that printed Harriet's story?"[6]

"Yes," is all she said. Julia needed more coaxing.

"Tell us," Nan added. Silence still followed.

"Please," Lydia added.

"Oh, all right," Julia conceded. "The story begins with Elias saying, *She's waiting to see each of you,* as he directed the company inside his home in New Echota. Kilakeena's brother Stand stood in the parlor accompanied by his friend Fields, and the Reverend and Mrs. Worcester." Julia continued.

"Harriet expressed her fears, her doubts, her hopes. She asked what is heaven. Elias held her hand gently and stroked each finger. *Harriet, my sweet Harriet, we cannot know what heaven is before we experience it. For its glory is beyond that of our living imaginations,* Kilakeena Elias told her.[7]

"*No man shall see God and live,*"[8] Harriet responded and closed her eyes. Elias continued to hold her hand. She spoke as if from far away.

"Elias wiped Harriet's forehead and offered her a sip of water. He held her in his arms and placed the glass to her cracked lips.

"After leaning back on the pillows, she recovered her calm saying, *my darkness is gone, now. How sweet will be the Conqueror's song when God lifts me to His bosom.*[9]

"Harriet smiled and then her body once again convulsed. She gasped for a bit of air and collapsed into the cotton coverlets. Elias eased her back onto the pillows.

"*All is well,* she told him. *Heaven is within my grasp.*"Harriet's moist eyes searched and saw something beyond her husband. She stretched forward. Her eyes became transfixed. Suddenly, she slumped backward. Her body drooped. Her words ceased. Her breath came no more.

"Elias stared at the weak and frail form, lifeless, before him. He blinked back tears and took a deep breath, *I should have spent more time with you,* he whispered, *I should have loved you more.* The handsome Cherokee Indian lowered her eyelids and touched her hand one last time before leaving her side," Julia concluded the story of Harriet's death.

"My mother and her friends spoke of Harriet as the Cherokee princess, the white woman who married Kilakeena the most handsome Cherokee brave and went into an exotic land to save the souls of Indian children." Julia's voice drifted off.

Is that what my wife wanted, I wondered. *Had she expected to come to an exotic land, to be treated like a Cherokee princess, who would save the precious heathen children? First, she would have to save me. Did she love me or the idea of me?* I wondered.

"And what became of Kilakeena?" Lydia asked.

"He married someone else and moved west. Such a coward," William concluded abruptly. The word, coward, struck like a hot poker against my skin, reminding me of that night, nearly five years ago, when William had called me a coward for being a conscientious objector.

"Has Malachi come yet?" my mother wondered aloud, changing the subject.

"Not yet," I told her.

"Your father will want to see him," she added. A lump as big as a rock developed in my throat.

"Mother," I was about to tell her and my brothers and sisters of father's death, but Reuben interrupted me.

"Silas, I hear something. Horses, maybe," he added with concern.

NOTES

[1] I have taken literary license here. According to Gary Greene of the New Echota Historical Site, Scaleeloskee (John Ridge) was not in attendance at the signing of the treaty. He affixed his name to it at a later date.

[2] The *Articles of the Treaty of New Echota* have been re-published in the *Cherokee Observer* (vol. 6, no. 1. November, 1998, pp. 4 & 12).

3   Schermerhorn's nickname, Devil's horns, is mentioned by Wilkins (1986).

4   The opening of Ridge's speech is taken from an earlier speech that Ridge may have presented on December 22, 1835 and which is reported in Wilkins (1986, pp. 286–287). The final sentence is what Ridge supposedly said at the signing (see Wilkins, 1986 p. 289). Ridge did not speak English and liberties may have been taken with translations over the years. Nor was Ridge necessarily the first to sign the treaty.

5   Kilakeena Elias Boudinot's famous speech can be found in Josephy Jr. (1994, p. 329). Kilakeena mentions Tom Forman one of Chief Ross's close supporters.

6   On August 16, 1836, Kilakeena Elias Boudinot committed these recollections to paper and sent them in the form of a letter to Harriet's parents. The letter/story "The Death of Harriet Gold Boudinot" was originally printed in *The New York Observer* (New York, NY) on November 26, 1836. It was later reprinted in the *Journal of Cherokee Studies* (Spring, 1979, pp. 102–107). I am grateful to Purdue University's Humanities and Social Science library for obtaining a copy of the article (*Journal of Cherokee Studies*' version) from the Vanderbilt University Library.

7   "The Death," p. 105.

8   "The Death," p. 105.

9   These words were spoken on August 14, 1836 after a fitful night of convulsions ("The Death," p. 106).

MY DARKEST HOUR

The Morning of December 21, 1865

Morning had arrived without warning. Either asleep or enthralled by the story of my mother's cousin, Kilakeena and his late wife Harriet, we hadn't taken notice. I heard the horses' hooves now also, as well as the rattle of a carriage. A knock came at the cabin door in short order.

I opened it to find a well-dressed man of middle years. Balding a bit on top and spectacles pinching his nose, otherwise he was lean and handsome. Wearing a dapper suit and carrying a bag, I figured out who he was just as he was saying so.

"I'm Dr. Harder. I've been sent to see to some small pox patients."

I opened the door wider and gave him view of the cabin. He took a handkerchief from his pocket and held it over his nose and mouth. I left the door ajar for a bit of air and daylight to grant him a better look. I introduced myself and led him to the extra chair by the table. He sat down with his bag on the floor next to him.

Leaning over, he opened the satchel and extracted a pair of tweezers. Then he went to my wife and pulled back the blanket from around her face using the tweezers instead of his own hand. I followed him with my eyes as he made his rounds.

"Measles," he pronounced, covering her up again. Turning next to my son, Willie, he again pulled the coverlet back in the same manner and announced, this time, "Small pox." He looked at each in turn. Only Nan fought his inspection; she tugged her blanket back from him and held it tight.

"All, but that one, have small pox," he determined pointing to my wife Julia. "She has the measles." He returned to the chair. Then turning to Willie, he asked, "Can you get up from your pallet and walk to me, boy?"

"Yes, sir." Willie, my four-year-old boy, raised himself up and meekly walked to the doctor, who stared at him without touching him, glancing here and there.

"Does your head hurt?"

"Yes, sir."

"Are your eyes feeling dry?"

"Yes, sir."

"Does your skin itch?"

"Yes, sir."

"How old are you, lad?"

Willie held up four fingers.

"Have you ever seen a monkey?" Willie asked the doctor.

"No, I don't believe I have," the doctor replied.

"They live in the jungles of Tennessee," Willie added.

"No, boy; there are no monkeys in Tennessee."

"You may lie back down, boy," the doctor added.

"Papa, tell him."

"Lie down," Doctor Harder repeated.

"Do as the doctor says, Willie."

The doctor pulled several small bottles from his bag and made a medicine by mixing them. Then he took the concoction to Willie. I watched silently.

"Sit up, boy," he commanded. "Here, take this." He spooned the medicine into Willie's open mouth. After completing this ministration, he returned the medicine bottles to his bag and sealed his satchel, before turning to me.

"Would you join me outside?" he asked. His face grim. He started for the door. I followed him outside. There he provided his dire prognosis.

"I think all the others will pull through," he predicted, "but I'm afraid that you'll lose your boy. He'll be dead by morning." His words assaulted me in such a way that I couldn't speak. Then he mounted his buggy and drove off without another word.

I returned to the cabin and took special care to keep an eye on Willie. He slept restlessly, moaning much as before. Morning pressed into a worrisome afternoon for me. By late evening, Willie had been asleep for several hours.

"Willie," I coaxed. "How are you feeling?" But my child didn't answer me.

"Willie," I tried again, brushing his blonde bangs away from his eyes. He opened his eyes and looked at me. His lips parted. No words ushered forth.

I wanted him to speak so desperately, that as I simultaneously felt his body go limp in my arms, I begged him to speak.

"No, Willie. No!" I cried. "Talk to me, Willie," I gently crushed his fragile figure to my chest. Then pulling him away, I searched his face. His eyes remained open staring vacantly. "Please, Willie."

"You can't die! You mustn't. Do you hear me, boy!" I alternated between demands and sweet implorations, until I realized the futility of my cries. Willie lay dead in my arms. Eventually, I lowered his eyelids with the smooth motion of my hand. Cradling my only son in my arms, I carried him to the chair and rocked him.

This is the doctor's doing. What vile concoction had he given my son? What despicable experiment had he performed? The only one of us he gave medicine to is now dead. "Oh, Willie, my Willie. What has this doctor done to you?"

Contortions of anger and anguish flooded over me; waves of loss and emptiness followed. I felt each emotion, one after the other, until they boiled in a cauldron of hatred that seared through me.

I imagined a gleaming silver dagger in my hand meant for the doctor. I would have stabbed him, and stabbed him, and stabbed him, a thousand times, had I thought it would bring my Willie back to me. By what right had he taken my son's life? I moaned like a madman in the darkness of that cabin. I held the limp little body in my arms through the night. Wailing curse words, at times, whimpering pleas for a different outcome, at other times. My brothers remained silent through my grieving. They had no idea how to comfort me. What words can bring a child back to life? There are none.

"My Willie, oh my Willie."

Eventually, I set Willie down in his accustomed place, next to Julia and made my way outside the cabin. I realized that I could've buried Willie in the Dodd family cemetery, but it just felt too far away. So I took the shovel from the buckboard and dug the grave myself, within view of the cabin. I tried to get Julia to come to his graveside, but upon understanding what had happened, her grieving took hold in a different way from my own. Wracked with sobs, she eventually fell into a deep sleep.

Alone, I prepared my boy for the grave. I laid him on the table, washed his face, and combed his hair.

"Where has my Willie gone?" I lamented as I pulled the comb through his blonde locks and then, "Didn't I tell you, you need a haircut, son." I swiped his bangs away from his eyes. "Oh, come back to me, Willie," I cried. I buttoned the top button on his jacket and smoothed his pant legs.

"I should have made shoes for you." I rubbed his bare feet. At the very least he should have had moccasins, I thought. I carried him to the grave, set him down and placed a blanket in the resting spot, just as I had seen at Mr. Dodd's cemetery for burying my father. I laid his tiny body in the hole, reached down, and placed his hands across his chest. I laid a second blanket over the top of him. "Oh, Willie."

I silently cursed the doctor as each shovelful of dirt hit Willie's body. When it was done, I fell to my knees and cursed myself.

The distortions that love and loss bear on time are nearly indescribable. I believe it took me most of the morning to bury Willie. I suspect I sat by his grave most of the afternoon. At some point, I felt a hand upon my shoulder. When I looked up, I discovered that it was my mother.

"A snowbird has fallen,"[1] she lamented.

I could only nod.

She raised me up and as she did so, her talisman fell from its place. She grabbed the black, feathery talisman and stuffed it down her blouse. We stood for a long while, in silence, by Willie's grave. After a time, she spoke again.

"I buried a baby in these mountains, too," she told me. I hadn't known that my mother had buried a baby in the mountains. It would seem there were a number of things I didn't know about my mother's life. Nor did I think I was ready to hear them at this particular moment. But I'd be forever grateful to her, for as sick as she was, she stayed with me. Even when her strength to stand gave out she leaned on my elbow and then lowered herself to the ground. Wrapped in a blanket against the mild winter wind, she sat facing west, away from the burial plot. I sat facing east, staring at Willie's grave. An ineffable grief hung over us; an indescribable stillness surrounded us.

"Find some wood to make a cross for Willie's grave," my mother eventually told me. I did as she suggested, gathering wood as well as hickory bark. We stripped the wood and rolled the inner-hickory bark on our thighs until it turned to malleable yet sturdy rope, and then I took two branches and whittled them with a knife so that their shape was smooth and straight. I carved Willie's name and the date, December 22, 1865, into the wood. I pushed it into the earth and pounded it with a rock. I brushed away a tear.

I took a deep breath and rejoined my mother, sitting at the foot of Willie's grave. I stared far away. My mother pulled her blanket snugly about her shoulders.

"Once a long time ago, …," my mother began and as I listened to her, I felt Willie's spirit drifting away. I missed him so. I wanted to grab his spirit to make him stay. And my father, I wanted my father back, as well. I thought that surely these have been my darkest days, but at that moment, I had no idea of the cursed events that were yet to come my way.

NOTE

[1] *A snowbird has fallen*, is an expression used by the Cherokee to disguise the loss of something great through the loss of something small. For example, the Cherokee would say the snowbird has fallen when an eagle had been killed (see Mails, 1996). The story of Willie's death can be found in Silas' original writings as collected by Shackelford Sims (1978).

PART 2

SNOWBIRDS

GREAT BUZZARD AND THE BELOVED WOMAN

A Long, Long Time Ago ... Willie's Grave—December 22, 1865

"Long, long ago," my mother began, "when the earth was all water and the birds and the animals lived in *Galun'lati*, beyond the arch, there was a problem—*Galun'lati* was becoming too crowded. The animals and birds who lived in this sky heaven were growing in number and they needed more room. They wondered what might exist under the water on earth; perhaps, they should explore it as a possible home. Like our men in council, they nearly talked the idea to death before anyone took action.[1]

"That's when *Dayuni'si*, Beaver's Grandchild, the Water-beetle, stepped forward and volunteered to explore the waters. Water-beetle darted over the surface of the water, but couldn't find a solid place to rest. She took in a great breath and dove to the bottom of the ocean. As Water-beetle surfaced gasping for air, the other creatures of *Galun'lati* saw the mud within her grasp. The mud began to grow until it became a great island in the sea. The island was fastened to the sky at the four cardinal directions and was positioned under the arch of the universe. This land became known as Turtle Island.

"In the beginning, Turtle Island was moist and muddy. It was far too soft to be a good home for the animals. They grew anxious and sent out different birds to fly over the mud in search of firmer ground. Each bird returned to *Galun'lati*, exhausted and discouraged. At last, they sent Great Buzzard to seek dry earth.

"Great Buzzard flew over immense oceans all around the world. By the time he reached *Tsaragi* country, he was growing weary and his wings began to flap and strike the earth. The wet earth gave way under the Great Buzzard's wings. Everywhere that Buzzard's wings touched the earth an enormous indentation formed a valley and everywhere that the bird's wings scooped the earth upward a mountain emerged.

When the creatures of *Galun'lati* saw this they became worried that the whole earth would be nothing but mountains and valleys if they didn't stop Great Buzzard. So, they called him back to heaven.

"When the mountains and valleys were dry and firm, the animals and birds and insects came down to inhabit it. They knew that bringing light would be their first task as the earth was very dark. So, they searched and found the sun and set her in motion to follow a track from east to west." My mother added, "And they raised Sister Sun higher until her highest height reached seven-hands-breadth into the sky.

"All of the living creatures were instructed to fast for seven days and to watch and keep awake for seven nights. All did well the first night, but by the second night some of the animals and birds and insects were falling asleep. By the third night many more fell into the land of dreams. By the seventh night, only a handful of animals remained awake. These animals include the owl, the panther, the raccoon and others that can stay awake at night. As for the trees, only the spruce, the pine, the holly, the laurel, the cedar and hemlock stayed awake through the seventh night. For them, the gift was granted that they would stay green all year and that they'd hold the strongest medicines.

"Then the light of the night was placed into the sky—Brother Moon who reflected his sister's bright beauty and life-granting warmth. Giving hope to those who had failed in their vigil, Moon helped them to see what they otherwise could not see in the darkness of night.

"People came after the plants and animals. Some say that when heaven became so crowded that people were pushing and shoving to get an elbow's worth of room, a woman who stood near the edge of *Galun'lati* was pushed out of heaven and fell to earth. She had her baby in her arms. On her fall downward, Great Buzzard saw her and swooped under her to catch her on his back; and then, he gave her an aerial view of the homeland and placed her gently on earth. When I was young, I often dreamt of flying on the back of the Great Buzzard.

"Perhaps, Willie's spirit is being carried on the bird's mammoth wings as we mourn his spirit." She offered me this comforting image before she added another thought, "Jesus takes the children."

At this point, tears rolled down my cheeks. I wiped them away. My mother felt my pain. "You are my son; your pain is my pain," my mother shared.

"The woman whom Great Buzzard floated to earth also had a son. The son grew into a man and the mother grew into an old woman who eventually passed on to the western land of ghosts, leaving her son alone on Turtle Island. This man's name was *Kana'ti*."[2]

I knew what my mother was saying to me. But I couldn't bear the thought that I might lose her to illness as well. "No," I whispered. But she ignored me and instead took up the story of the first son, *Kana'ti*. "*Kana'ti* was blessed with an abundance of food and many animals to hunt. In the beginning, he was very happy. He traveled about the land, visiting the animals and enjoying the berries. There was much to see and learn. But after a time, the man grew discontent. He wasn't happy with his existence. He was bored. In his unhappiness, he began to act very strangely. *Kana'ti* shot at the deer even when he wasn't hungry. He picked plants from the earth, but didn't use them. He threw stones at the bird's nest and he trampled the home of the ants. He killed living creatures without reason or need. "The animals were frightened of *Kana'ti*. They held a meeting to consider what to do about him. After many failed attempts of their own to develop a worthy plan, one of them suggested seeking the Great One's advice. They prayed to the Creator who listened to their prayers and answered their concerns.[3]

"One day as *Kana'ti* lay sleeping in the afternoon sun, the Creator let a plant grow up alongside of him. It was a beautiful plant with tall leaves and a feathery tassel on the top and above the tassel was a beautiful woman. *Kana'ti* awoke and could hardly believe the vision before him. Upon seeing this radiant woman, his gentleness was given back to him. He extended his hand for her to come down from the corn stalk. She did so, but not without bringing an ear of corn with her to remind her of where she came from, and to share it with *Kana'ti*.[4]

"She was a magical woman, the Spirit of Corn. People call her The Great Corn Mother, *Ginitsi Selu*. *Selu* and *Kana'ti* started a family which grew into a great Nation," my mother announced "*Yunwiya Nation*.[5]

"*Kana'ti* and *Selu* lived in the Cherokee homeland with their only child, whom we will call, Little Boy. The father of the boy, as we already know, was called *Kana'ti*, Lucky Hunter. The mother of the boy, we already know, was *Selu*, Corn Mother. What we don't know is how Little Boy made a discovery that would change their lives.

"*Kana'ti*, Lucky Hunter, would never fail to bring home a load of game whenever he returned from hunting. Selu would prepare the game by cutting it and washing the blood into the river. Little Boy played by the river every day. One day his mother thought she heard him playing with someone else. When the boy returned, his parents asked him who he was playing with. Their son told them that an older boy came out of the water and announced that he is Little Boy's elder brother. The parents realized immediately that the strange boy was born of the buck's blood that *Selu* had washed off into the river. "Each day that Little Boy went to the river's edge, the strange boy would appear and play with him, but he wouldn't stay around for adults to see him. One day, *Kana'ti* told his son to challenge the strange boy to a wrestling match. *When you have a firm hold on him, call out to us*, his father instructed. The boy did as he was told. He returned to the river and challenged the wild boy to a wrestling match and when he had a strong grasp of him, Little Boy called out for his parents to come. The strange boy struggled and yelled at his parents, *No! You don't want me. You threw me away*. Ignoring his pleas, the parents took him into their home in order to care for him; they named him, *I'nage-utasun'hi*, He-Who-Grew-Up-Wild. A brief time passed before the parents realized that *I'nage-utasun'hi* was not only wild and mischievous, but also magical.

"Both boys were impressed by the number of deer and turkeys that their father, *Kana'ti* would bring home. He-Who-Grew-Up-Wild told his younger brother that they should follow their father to discover where and how he managed to be such a lucky hunter. Within a few days, *Kana'ti* was off again to hunt. He took a bow and some feathers. The boys wondered what they were for. They followed *Kana'ti*, who entered a swampy area. Little Boy had difficulty traveling through the swamp. *I'nage-utasun'hi*, however, magically turned himself into a wispy bit of bird down and floated himself onto *Kana'ti's* shoulder.

From his father's shoulder, Wild Boy watched as *Kana'ti* collected reeds, fitted the feathers to their ends, and made sharp stones for the tips. Wild Boy wondered what possibilities these things held. As *Kana'ti* finished making his arrows, he headed away from the swamp.

"Wild Boy flew from *Kana'ti's* shoulder. He returned to his brother and after changing himself back into Wild Boy, he told his brother what his father had made. The boys continued to follow *Kana'ti* who traveled up the side of a mountain. When he reached the top of the mountain, *Kana'ti* pushed a huge boulder away from the front of a cave. Directly, a buck came running out of the cave and *Kana'ti* shot him with his bow and arrow. *Oho!* the boys exclaimed. They were excited to have learned *Kana'ti's* secret. *Kana'ti* kept all the animals that he hunted locked in a cave, so that all he had to do was push the big stone away and shoot the deer or the turkey or whatever ran out of the cave.

"A few days later, the boys repeated the journey without their parents' knowledge. First, they ventured off to the swamp where they gathered reeds, found feathers, sharpened stones and made arrows. When they were ready, the two brothers climbed the mountain to *Kana'ti's* cave. They pushed the boulder from the front of the cave and prepared to shoot the animals, but to their surprise the animals came bounding out at such a pace that they couldn't shoot them. Nor could they return the stone to its original place. The deer raced past the boys one after another. Then Wild Boy took aim at a buck. His arrow struck the deer in the tail and flipped it upward. His brother, Little Boy, followed his example and also shot a deer in the tail. Soon, the boys were striking all the deer with their arrows and curling up all the deer tails. That is why to this day, the deer tail curls up," my mother slipped into the role of a children's storyteller momentarily. I smiled weakly at the thought of it.

"But that's not all that happened. As the boys forget themselves in this mischievous pursuit, the other animals began to escape from *Kana'ti's* cave. The boys watched helplessly as droves of raccoons, rabbits, and all kinds of four-legged ones ran off into the woods. They also watched as flocks of birds flew into the open sky. There were so many flying creatures flapping their wings that *Kana'ti* heard the commotion and he knew that his boys were up to some mischief. "After traveling to the mountain, *Kana'ti* found his mischievous boys standing by the mouth of the empty cave and he told them, *Look what you've done! You used to be able to play all day because you didn't have to work for your food. I could simply bring it home, your mother would prepare and cook it, but now you'll have to hunt for your food. Life will be much harder. Kana'ti* was angry. He decided to teach the boys a lesson. After unleashing tiny vermin of all kinds and allowing them to bite his sons, he gave the boys a long lecture and sent them home to their mother.

"By the time the boys arrived home, they were tired, itchy, and hungry, but there wasn't any food. *Selu* took pity on her boys. Although there was no meat, she would get them something to eat. Carrying baskets with her, she went to the storehouse and when she returned the baskets were full of golden kernels. From these kernels she made a dish for her boys. Every day *Selu* went to the storehouse and every day she brought back baskets full of kernels that she cooked for her children.

"One day the boys became curious. Each wanted to know how their mother came upon this food. They followed her to the storehouse and they peeked inside. What they beheld scared them. *Selu* stood in the center of the room surrounded by baskets. She rubbed her ribs and under her arms and then from her body fell kernels of corn. The boys were terrified that their mother might be a witch. They scampered away and decided they must kill her. When she returned, she could tell by their expressions that they had watched her and she could tell that they planned to end her life as they knew it. But she too was magical. She told them that after her death, they should prepare the ground for planting by dragging her body seven times around in a circle on the land. Then the boys must keep vigil all night and in the morning corn would grow.

"And so the terrible deed was done. The boys killed their mother. *Selu* lay dead upon the earth. They dragged her body around, but only once and they didn't prepare the ground. They fell delinquent in their vigil from time to time. Corn grew by morning, but it only grew in some spots because the boys had failed to follow their mother's instructions."[6] My mother paused her storytelling. I was anxious to learn what *Kana'ti* would do when he discovered his wife murdered by his own sons. My mother stretched before continuing.

"When *Kana'ti* arrived home, he found his beloved *Selu* dead on the ground and his sons soundly asleep. Anger consumed him as he realized what had happened. He wailed, swearing revenge on his own sons, but as he lifted *Selu*'s limp body, he only wept with grief. His tears fell through the night until he saw a light on *Selu*'s face. Looking up to see the source of the light, *Kana'ti* spied the image of *Selu*'s visage on the moon. He realized then that both *Selu* and the moon looked down upon his tragic fate with pity. After burying his wife, he grabbed his sons and followed the track of the moon.

"By morning, they had reached the outer western edges of the *Yunwiya* Nation. There *Kana'ti* met men and women warriors of the Wolf Clan. He shoved his sons into their village, shouting, *Justice needs to be done!* The women encircled the boys so that *Kana'ti* could no longer see his sons. After *Kana'ti* told his story, he turned to the members of the Wolf Clan, saying, *the bravest and wisest, the most beautiful and most respected of women should decide if these boys will live or die. And from here forth, they will be called the Beloved Women.*" My mother stopped. She turned and looked at me, her back straight, her shoulders squared, her demeanor dignified, if not regal.

"I am one of those women; I am a Beloved Woman," my mother told me, "with the right to decide life or death. And I have made such a decision."

"Like *Nannye-hi*?"

"Like *Nannye-hi*," she answered.

"And you have made such a decision? Who?" I asked unable to envision my sweet mother condemning anyone to death. She looked deep into my eyes before turning her view away. "Who was it?" I persisted. Some time passed; my mother sat in memories. My mind searched the possibilities. And then.

"*Kilakeena?*" I asked somewhat shocked by the epiphany that had suddenly come my way.

"Because of the treaty?" I begged to know. I now lived her stories instead of mine. My current grief transferred to and through her

141

narratives. I needed these stories to survive my own grief. "Tell me," I demanded.

"The soldiers came."

"For the removal?"

"Before the removal."

"What happened?"

NOTES

[1] While attending the Native Voices conferences at Columbia College, South Carolina, I listened to a group of women discuss issues of importance. Representatives from the Catawba, the Peedee and the Cherokee were in attendance. Wanda Warren, Karen Montoyne, Lilly Little Water, and others spoke of serious issues, but were not afraid to add a bit of levity—one woman joked about how men talk the issues to death while women take action.

[2] The origin story comes from Mooney (1891, 1900/1992). However, the Cherokee do not include the woman who fell from heaven that part is based on Iroquois legend.

[3] The legend of *Kana'ti* and *Selu* can be found in Mooney (1891, 1900/1992). The Cherokee spoke of the Great White, an all-encompassing spirit of possibility and peace, but not a "Creator."

[4] See Awiakta's (1993) version of *"Kana'ti* and *Selu."*

[5] *Yunwiya* means real people or humans (see footnote 59 in Mooney, 1891, 1900/1992). A history of how the *Yunwiya* came to be called Cherokee (Tsaragi) can also be found in Mooney's book.

[6] For this version of *Kana'ti and Selu* see Mooney (1891, 1900/1992, pp. 242–249). Mooney collected this and other stories from several Cherokee storytellers among them, Swimmer, who used the Cherokee syllabary, which was invented by Sequoyah, to document the stories.

THE TURBULENT TIMES

Remembering May, 1836

"Stomping horse hoofs beat the ground. Steeds whinnied from the harsh jerking of the reins. Clouds of dust fogged the area. We watched as the men on horseback made a semi-circle around us. Your father had been hoeing in the garden, your brothers had been playing with a stick and ball; you, just two years old, sat beside me; I stood with my bag of wild onions preparing to take them to the river. We froze like deer in our places, except your father who dropped the hoe moved toward his rifle. He also quickly noted the number of riders, twelve. All federal soldiers, save one, who dressed in civilian clothes and whose jowls flapped as he addressed us.

"*At last, a place where I can speak English*, the Commissioner said looking at your father, *What's a white man doin' in these parts, anyway?* Your father remained silent, studying Shermerhorn's face, which sagged with late-middle age and the extra fat of a man who worked without sweating.

"*You do speak English, don't you?* the Commissioner demanded to know. His piercing eyes narrowed.

"*I do,* your father said curtly, *but I'm the one who should be asking the questions. Who are you? And what do you want?* Your father let his eyes roam from one soldier to the next, checking their readiness to take aim. He now held his own rifle securely by his side."*I've come on important business,* Schermerhorn told us as he reached inside his leather saddlebag. Your father remained cautious. *I have papers to show you.*

"*What papers?* your father asked curtly. I took the opportunity to scoot you children into the cabin.

"*I have in my possession the Treaty of New Echota. It was signed on December 29, 1835. I've been sent by the President of the United States to gather the signatures of the mountain Cherokee who were unable to travel to New Echota to sign the treaty due to inclement weather. We're sure that you'd like to add your names,* here he looked at me, *to the growing list of Cherokee who will receive a bountiful compensation for their lands in exchange for land west of the Mississippi River. The treaty invokes you to remove yourselves from the east and establish yourselves in the west. The United States government will help you build schools, churches, homes, and roads. Furthermore, the federal government will help you move. This treaty has been signed by some of your most prestigious leaders including Major Ridge, John Ridge, and Elias Boudinot,* Schermerhorn announced.

"My stomach churned at the mere mention of what Kilakeena had done. Schermerhorn, the civilian commissioner, continued. *You should turn in all your belongings to the government. They'll be carefully inventoried and returned to you in your new home in the west.* Schermerhorn paused and then added, *you need to translate that and repeat it to your woman.* He had used an irreverent word in place of woman. I bristled at the insult. Your father turned to see the distressed and angry expression on my face.

"*She won't sign,* he told them.

"*That's for her to say, not you,* Schermerhorn retorted bitterly.

"I shook my head and finally said, *I will not sign.*

"Schermerhorn sat back in the saddle and let a sigh fill the air, as though he had heard this repeatedly. Then he turned, raising his eyebrows to the captain who sat high on the horse next to him. The captain dismounted and signaled to two of his soldiers to join him. He waved them into the cabin as he stood face to face with your father. The lieutenant colonel remained locked in a stare with your father. "The soldiers shoved me aside and entered our cabin. Looking first at you children before surveying the belongings; their eyes moved slowly about from one side of the cabin to the other. Then they over-turned baskets, flipped blankets and furs, tipped over our pallets and scurried you children from one side of the cabin to the other as they inspected our home and furnishings. They looked in the corners, behind the door, and over the mantle. This is how they took inventory.

"Then the lieutenant colonel and his two soldiers mounted their steeds, rejoining Schermerhorn and the other soldiers.

"*Well?* Schermerhorn questioned.

"*A half dozen half-breeds, that's what we have here,* the soldier reported in a loud clear tone, but then he leaned over and whispered something else to the captain. Schermerhorn looked in your father's direction and then to me.

"*You're only making this harder on yourselves,* Schermerhorn declared with disgust. He shook his head, pulled the reins of his horse and turned to leave. We watched the departure.

"*A long trip for nothing,* I mused. *They wasted their time and energy riding here, thinking they would persuade me to sign that treaty.*

"*No,* your father told me, *that's not the only reason they came.* I didn't understand, at least not at first. *Reuben! William!* Your brothers darted from the cabin and ran to your father. *Listen carefully. The soldiers were here for a bad reason. When they were in the cabin did they look at our rifles?* he asked your brothers. Both boys nodded. *We must warn our family and friends. The soldiers must not know how many rifles a family owns.*

"They had counted our rifles, and I realized something else, they had also counted my children. But I knew then that your father was sending the boys to warn our neighbors. I ran to the cabin, snatched a jar of honey and brought two gathering bags outside. Your father instructed your older brothers.

"*I know that it's your uncles who should say when you're ready to be hunters or warriors, but today I say that you're ready to be warrior/ messengers.*[1] *William run to the home of your grandparents and tell them to hide all but one rifle. Reuben, you must run to Nickojack and Sweetwater and deliver the same message. I'll ride to Tsiskwa'gwa's family and then onto Tsali and others,* he spoke with hurried breath.

"*It's a long way,* he continued. *Your thighs will ache and burn. Your stomach may feel as if it is ready to eat itself, but you must keep a constant pace. Don't stop to eat. Don't stop to rest. Don't run too fast, but don't go too slowly. Your lungs will feel tight, but keep going, it's important!* he emphasized." My mother took a quick breath and continued the story.

"I dipped my fingers into the honey jar and presented the sweet, sticky nectar, saying, *Reuben, come here.* I slipped my fingers into

Reuben's mouth. He licked the honey. I did the same for William. Your brothers obeyed without a word, they felt the gravity of the situation. You, Silas, were too young to understand.

"*It's light,* I told your brothers, speaking of the gathering bag. *I've placed a bit of skwali root inside. If the soldiers stop you, then tell them you are gathering food for your family.* I turned to William and handed him the other bag. *Chew the skwali from time to time, but don't stop to eat. The skwali will take your hunger away and give you the energy that you need.*[2] Then I told your brothers how to keep their rhythm.

"*Keep the bear song in your head, Tsa'gi, Tsa'gi, hwi'lahi; Tsa'gi, tsa'gi, hwi'lahi. Ge'i, ge'i, hwi'lahi; Ge'i, ge'i, hwi'lahi. Hear the steady beat of the drums in your head.* I gave them the tempo, only I changed the lyric, one word—*hunter,* to *soldiers. When you hear the soldiers coming upstream, upstream, down the river you must go; When you hear the soldiers coming downstream, downstream, up the river you must go.*"[3]

"*Go now!* your father yelled.

"*Speak Tsaragi to your neighbors*, I called after them as each dashed off in different directions. The gathering bags bounced lightly against each boy's hip. Your father mounted his horse and rode off at a gallop toward *Tsiskwa'gwa*'s home.

"I ran to the cabin and removed the extra rifle that hung over the mantle. Swinging its strap over my shoulder, I then grabbed another gathering bag and slung it over my other shoulder. I placed your sister Mary, just a baby, inside it. I lifted you onto my hip and instructed John to watch Joseph. I threw an old blanket over my shoulder so as to cover the rifle, and moved as fast as anyone could while encumbered by two infants and a rifle."

"So I helped you hide the extra rifle?" I asked my mother as she paused during her story telling.

"So to speak," she said, probably thinking I was more trouble than help. But my comment made her smile just the same.

"Where did we hide it?" I asked.

"In Bear Mountain cave."

"Then what happened?"

"We returned home."

"No, I mean about the soldiers and Schermerhorn, and ..." I paused. "And Kilakeena?"

"Not much for several months."

"Not much?"

"Not until August. During the hot summer days, the dying days, when we had more strangers come in one day than we'd had in a year."

NOTES

[1] In Cherokee tradition it was common for the uncle to make decisions about when a boy was ready to go hunting or to war, not the father.

[2] *Skwali* was used to treat coughs or in large doses to stimulate vomiting when necessary. Its popularity has waxed and waned over the centuries. Europeans bought it from the Cherokee, but it fell into "entire neglect" by the early 1900s (Mooney, 1891, 1900/1992, p. 326). Contemporary Cherokee authorities suggest that heart leaf was used to stop bleeding (see Hamel & Chiltoskey, 1975). It could have been used to decrease the appetite and stimulate energy via its ephedrine content. Ephedrine, taken in large doses, may be dangerous (lecture by Dr. Brenda Stein, 2002, on early herb and health); it was taken off the market in the United States in 2004.

[3] The bear song can be found in Mooney (1891, 1900/1992).

CHAPTER 21

BEHIND THE PRISON WALL

Remembering August 1836

"It happened on a calm morning. The air felt fresh, bright. I noticed that the campfire had burned out, which had blazed the night before when *Nikutse'ge*[1] and Sweetwater had arrived for a visit. The fire had given us light as we'd stayed awake late into the night, talking politics, mostly, but by dawn only cold ashes remained to meet the morning's light.

"I woke first. The children slept, as did our guests. Your father snored, rolled over, and snuggled under his blanket as I stepped around him. I *went to water.*[2] Alone.

"After bathing and praying, I returned by way of the mountain path. I expected to find the scene around our cabin much the same as I had left it; but to my surprise, as I entered the clearing, I discovered the tranquility had been interrupted. I heard voices and saw several men and women, whom I didn't know, talking to your father and our neighbor, Nikutse'ge. Sweetwater, wrapped in a blanket, stayed a distance from these strangers.

"Dressed in white shirts and dark jackets and pants, the strangers looked like preachers. I had met a preacher, once. He had attended the Feast of the Turning Leaves in New Echota as a guest of Chief *Tsan* Ross.[3] I kept my distance, assessed the scene with caution, and then slowly approached your father.

"*This, here, is Reverend Jones*, your father told me.

"*It's a pleasure to meet you, ma'am,* the preacher nodded. I nodded suspiciously.

"*We've come*, he waved a hand to introduce his companions, *to share the word of the Lord with you. Jesus, our Savior, has much to offer. We are beholden to Him who led us to your homestead*, the preacher spoke fluidly. His words flowed on while his women folk and

149

assistants nodded their praises with loud responses, *Amen. Yes. Praise the Lord!*

"*Bushyhead,* the preacher called to his colleague. *This is my companion. His name is Jesse Bushyhead and he is a Cherokee Minister to the Cherokee people. His people. Your people,* the white preacher added, looking at me. Bushyhead nodded. Reverend Jones continued.[4]

"*Bushyhead can translate my words to you.* He looked at me and then to Nikutse'ge and Sweetwater as he spoke. *I want to tell you all about the good works of the Lord,* the preacher thumped the bible he held within his hand. I wondered if this man only wanted to have *his* words translated so that he should be the mouth and everyone else the ears. I have both ears and a mouth, I thought, but remained silent.[5] White men can be very arrogant. Anger stirred in my empty stomach. I had children to feed. I turned and started to walk away as the preacher's words droned in the background, *The Lord wants you...*

"A sudden veil of quiet fell over the group. I turned back around to see why the preacher's words had ceased so abruptly. Your father was hushing the preacher by signaling with his finger to his lips. Then he turned to Nikutse'ge, who nodded. Yes, they both had heard the horses' hooves and now so did I. Your father readied his rifle. Nikutse'ge reached for his musket, which leaned against a near-by birch tree. Sweetwater and I saw the concern in your father's eyes; we moved toward the children. The preacher and his companions seemed confused; until, they turned to look behind them.

"Reverend Jones and Bushyhead quickly rallied to the aid of your father and Nikutse'ge. There they stood defiantly, together, against the approaching soldiers.

"The once brisk, fresh, morning air became clouded with dust and dirt and the smell of soldiers and horses. A regiment of cavalry appeared before us. Joseph and John clung to my skirt; Reuben and William joined your father. Sweetwater moved toward me and reached out for you, Silas, so that you wouldn't run in the way of the mounted steeds. She also held Mary in her arms; Martha remained asleep in the cabin.

"*We have orders to collect all the fire arms owned by the Cherokee. The rifles will be inventoried and returned to you after you complete your move west,*" the lieutenant colonel announced as he sat high in his saddle.

"Your father spoke next: *The missionaries have no rifles and I'm a white man, not a Cherokee. I'll keep my rifles and ask you and your soldiers to be on your way.* His voice never wavered.

"*I have my orders,* the lieutenant colonel repeated firmly. As they were locked in argument, I entered the cabin, scooped up Martha, and then watched from the doorway.

"*And your orders were to disarm the Cherokee. I am not a Cherokee,*" your father repeated.

"The lieutenant colonel motioned for two of his soldiers to dismount. They did so and then accosted Nikutse'ge, one of them, yanking his rifle from his grip. Nikutse'ge put up only a short struggle due to being so badly outnumbered. He backed a step away with fierce resentment and seething anger that showed on his face. Soldiers pushed their way into our lodge. They came out with one rifle.

"*Here, sir,* they showed their superior.

"*This man should have three rifles, the one he's holding and two more. Look again,* he commanded his soldiers. The soldiers upended the cots, kicked over the baskets, and turned over each hide and blanket to no avail.

"*I know that you have a third rifle. Where is it?* the lieutenant colonel demanded.

"*I repeat, it is you who are in violation here, sir.* Your father spat the word, *sir. I am a white man. You have no right to confiscate my rifles.* Your father's words boiled on his tongue. One of the soldiers raised the butt end of his musket and came toward your father, ready to strike.

"*No, wait,* I cried out. *I gave the third rifle away,* I lied to him. "*I'll hear no more stories. Arrest her,* the lieutenant colonel commanded, pointing at me. The soldiers lunged toward me and each grabbed me by an arm, jostling the baby I held. Your father stormed toward the soldiers. Violently, he threw one away from me and then the other. I slipped, caught myself, and made my way to Sweetwater. I handed the baby to her and then shoved the two of them toward the cabin. Quickly, I gathered the other little ones and pushed you all into the cabin. By the time I turned around, all of the soldiers had dismounted; they held the Reverend and his assistants and their wives. One of the women screamed.

Your father struggled against the grip of several cavalrymen, as did Nikutse'ge. Outnumbered, he and Nikutse'ge were subdued within moments, their hands tied behind their backs; their faces ground into the dirt. Blood trickled from your father's nose. Then the soldiers turned toward me. My heart pounded. One of the soldiers grabbed my hands, pulled me forward, and tied my wrists, one to the other. As quickly as this storm ensued, it ended. The soldiers surrounded us—bound captives. The struggle over, the dirt settled about us. The lieutenant colonel looked at your father.

"*Well, Mister White Man, you're now under arrest for aiding and abetting a Cherokee as well as resisting arrest.* He mounted his horse. *Bring them along,* he ordered as he turned the reins of his horse's bridle and started toward the fort.

"No one spoke as we endured the long walk to the fort. Your father let his anger burn inside his chest. I suspect it took his mind off the pain emanating from his forehead. A huge lump surfaced on his brow and blood still trickled from his nose. Nikutse'ge looked to your father from time to time, but your father wouldn't even glance around. He stared straight ahead. I had trouble keeping up, but so did the other two women, the White preacher's wife and Bushyhead's wife. I took some comfort in the fact that the soldiers left Sweetwater behind. I knew that she would care for you children.

"When we arrived at the fort, a sergeant removed the ropes from my wrists and brusquely shoved me into a stockade with the others. It was there that Bushyhead and Jones told us their primary reason for having come to visit us, which was to tell us to hide our rifles from the soldiers, but we had done that earlier or at least I had hidden one rifle.[6] And now we were arrested for it.

"Your father, then thanked Jones and Bushyhead and their wives for the attempt to warn us even if it was too late. Bushyhead apologized and Jones asked us to pray with them. Your father said, this wasn't their fault. He looked to me for my assessment, I answered him. *Doh-HYU-hnoh—This is true.*[7] *It's not their fault, and I thought to myself, it is Kilakeena's fault.*"

My mother stopped her story on this note and looked far away. I had the hindsight of nearly thirty years, I thought, perhaps, it was not Kilakeena's fault; rather, it was Andrew Jackson who should be blamed.

We sat quietly by Willie's grave.

NOTES

1. Nikutse'ge pronounced Nickojack

2. The expression *going to water or taken to water* generally indicates more than bathing. *Going to water* suggests that the individual is going alone to call upon the spirits; *taken to water* may indicate that a spiritual mentor is taking someone to water. For example, the religious leader would take the ball players before a major game to be scratched and then submerged seven times under water. Warriors, storytellers, the sick, those in need of help from the spirits, and others may invoke the practice of *going to water* (see Mooney, 1891, 1900/1992, p. 389).

3. Tsan pronounced John.

4. Evans Jones and Jesse Bushyhead supported Cherokee resistance. They preached Chief John Ross's request that the Cherokee people resist the treaty and stay the course. They also advocated Christianity. David Foreman, was Jones' assistant. Bushyhead was a friend to Chief Ross and an active preacher among the Cherokee (see McLoughlin, 1984; also see Ehle, 1988).

5. White Christian missionaries were surprised to find that the Cherokee were not docile people. Cherokee resistance to Christianity was a constant struggle for the missionaries (see McLoughlin, 1984).

6. General Wool demanded that the Cherokee turn in their rifles. When they refused to do so, he blamed the missionaries, especially Jones and Bushyhead. According to Jones, General Wool arrested "four Indian men and two of their wives, one white man married to a native and myself [Jones]" (McLoughlin, 1984, p. 322). Wool released all but Jones and his assistant whom he tried to engage to bring in the Cherokees' rifles. Jones suggested to the elders that the Cherokee turn in their rifles voluntarily, but with the covert plan for them to hide some of their guns and give the oldest guns to the soldiers.

7. *Doh-HYU-hnoh—This is true*, is a Cherokee compliment given to speakers whose rhetoric is so persuasive that it rises above the other opinions or interpretations (see Klausner, 1993, p. 11). Truth was not considered a fact. For example, when asked to swear to tell the truth in a court of law, a Cree Indian said, "I'm not sure I can tell the truth … I can only tell what I know" (see Clifford, 1984, p. 8).

EVEN WHITE MEN CAN SEE

Remembering August 1836

Each of us, directed by bayonet into the courtyard of the fort where daily activities were underway, glanced about. Soldiers moved with buckets in hand, some cared for horses, a few cleaned their rifles, others worked shirtless building a large stockade. We were directed to a mess tent. Flies buzzed about the tables where many a soldier had previously set his plate.

"*We're not hungry,* your father said, refusing the food.

Reverend Jones insisted, "*Just take us to see General Wool.*"

"*Suit yourself,* the soldier said, turning around. *Follow me.*

"He led us to the door of the general's office. Just as we arrived, we were pushed aside. We watched a young major enter the general's office. *Wait here,* our escort commanded. And as we did, we found ourselves privy to every word the general spoke to the major via an open window.

"*Renegade Cherokees?* General Wool repeated with a sarcastic tone. *Renegade Cherokees. Hmmph. let's see now, we have two missionaries, their assistant, their wives, one Cherokee man, one white man and his Cherokee wife who cannot weigh more than ninety pounds with a heavy hide on her back. These are the renegade Indians that Jackson has sent me to round up? This is ridiculous,*" General Wool lamented with disgust. We peered through the window and watched as the general rubbed his brow. The soldier guarding us was noncommittal in his duty and equally curious, so we all stayed within hearing distance and took turns at the window.

"*Actually, this is beyond ridiculous. It's inane. And quite possibly, insane,* he added.

"*But they wouldn't give up their last rifle, General,*" the major defended his actions.

155

"*One rifle! One rifle! Do you think they will stage a grand assault with one rifle?* General Wool demanded of the officer.

"*I'm not sure, sir.*

"*You're not sure! For Christ's sake Major any idiot can see the man was only hiding one rifle so that he could hunt and feed his family. I cannot believe that Jackson has sent me to gather up these sheep for him.* The general stood and strode across the room to the window, near enough for us to see him. He looked out at us. The officer remained motionless and silent.

"*We need to release them. But not Jones. Bring Jones in. I think he might be useful,* General Wool decided.[1] The major turned toward the door. We all stepped away from the window. *Wait,* the general commanded. The major stopped. The general continued, *I have composed a letter. I think you should hear it.* Perhaps he thought we should hear it too," my mother added.

"General Wool began to read:

To: The Honorable Lewis Cass, Secretary of War
From: General Wool
Dear Sir,
The duty I have to perform is far from pleasant, only made tolerable with the hope that I may stay cruelty and injustice, and assist the wretched and deluded beings called Cherokees, who are only the prey of the most profligate and most vicious of white men ... The whole scene, since I have been in this country, has been nothing but a heart-rending one, and such a one as I would be glad to be rid of as soon as circumstances will permit. If I could, and I could not do them a greater kindness, I would remove every Indian tomorrow, beyond the reach of the white men, who like vultures, are watching, ready to pounce upon their prey, and strip them of everything they have or expect to have from the government ... Nineteen-twentieths, if not 99 out of every hundred, will go penniless to the west.[2]

General Wool looked at his officer. *You do know what the plan is, don't you?* he asked the young man. *After we confiscate the rifles we are supposed let them plant their fields. That way, after they are rounded up, the soldiers can harvest the food and use it to feed the imprisoned Cherokee. More soldiers are on their way. This is a plan unworthy of an officer and a gentleman.* The general's shoulders slumped. *Whites will surely swoop down on the Cherokee homesteads and steal the chickens and dogs, the blankets and baskets, the pottery and the cattle, the mills and the peacocks, the buckboards and the horses, the houses and the land, and anything and everything the Cherokee value.*

"*What greedy scheme are we a part of?* he still read from his letter. *More than a contributor, I am a co-conspirator. I should think that the poor wretched Cherokee people should be kind to call me a dog.*

"Within a moment the door opened and the major left.The general came out to speak with us.

"*As you've heard, the federal government has a removal plan in effect. I have just written a letter to Secretary of State asking him to cease this miserable plan. You have my word that I will do whatever I can to help you.* Then he dismissed us as if we were his soldiers."*Jones,* he turned to the missionary. *Stay, will you? We need to speak.*"

NOTES

[1]   Jones left the mountain region so as not to be conscripted into the service of the General to the deficit of the Cherokee (McLoughlin, 1984, pp. 322–323).

[2]   General Wool's letter was written on September 10, 1836 (Ehle, 1988, p. 302).

UPHILL, UPHILL

Recalling the Summer of 1838 ...
While Still Sitting at the Foot of Willie's Grave

"We were released; we returned to our cabin. Life went on much as it had before," my mother continued her story as we sat again by Willie's grave, after having walked and talked. "Of course, we had less meat since your father couldn't hunt without a rifle."

"Couldn't you use the one that you'd hidden?" I asked.

"We vowed not to use that rifle. I wouldn't even tell your father where I had hidden it. Only you and I knew the secret of where that cache lay," she smiled at me. I retuned the smile.

"We farmed, grew more vegetables, and gathered more roots and nuts. Your father fished more often. We sang, we prayed, and we played. We, that is you and I, secretly stored dried fish, nuts, and roots in the cave. I told no one where it was. Sometimes I took blankets to our hiding place. Your father and I talked politics when we met with our neighbors. Other than that we lived in the usual manner until one dreadful day in the summer of 1838.

"I tended to the field that day, steering stray morning glories away from the melons and carefully side-stepping ripe strawberries, the beans had nearly reached the corn plants. I dug my fingers deep into the soil around the base of the stalks, loosening the dry dirt and making space for fish remains to act as fertilizer. I remember thinking that we needed rain.

"Silas, you were four-years-old and Mary was three, and Martha just a baby. You and Mary played on the path that led from the house to the field under the supervision of your aunt, *Su'nawa Udsi'*—Little Hawk. She tickled you. I remember you squealed with delight, and both tempted and taunted your aunt by calling her what your father called her—*Sunny, Sunny, Susie, Susie, you can't reach me.* You begged to be caught. I recall a peel of laughter and giggles that sprinkled through the air, as periwinkle is sprinkled along the edge of the forest. Your Aunt Sunny stretched toward you with tickling fingers." My mother enjoyed the memory.

"I was the same age as Willie," I noted. And my sorrow returned. It gushed over me and through me. I wanted to cry out in pain. I wanted to wail, but instead I swallowed it like bitter bile and held it down for my family's sake. They slept in the cabin.

"Yes," my mother agreed. Then she returned to her story.

"*You must listen to your mother when she calls you;* your Aunt *Su'nawa Udsi* playfully chided you.[1]

"It was at that moment that I heard a noise. *Hush*, I whispered forcefully. Everyone stood still. Yes, there it was again. I clearly heard the sound of the seven-coo bird—*Kukukukukukukew*—with a slight variation in its imitation. I answered with like response. Turning to your aunt I reached for the baby in her arms.

"*Go tell Silas to come quickly.* Without a word, my sister darted off in the direction of the river where your father had taken your older brothers, Reuben, William, John and Joseph, to fish for mountain trout.

"I held Martha in my arms as I scanned the woods. Just then Two-Turtles stepped out from behind a tree and motioned to me.

"*Come uncle*, I beckoned him forward. He was the one who had signaled me with a bird call.

"He led his horse behind him, swung the reins around a tree limb, and came to my side, where he placed a hand upon my shoulder. I matched his warm greeting. Your baby sister squirmed within my embrace. You hid behind my skirt, as did Mary. *Something is wrong*, I thought, well before he told me. I backed up a bit to search his eyes for an answer. He avoided my gaze and instead looked approvingly at the baby.

"*Another beautiful baby. You've grown to be quite a woman, Sallie. And the mother of how many now?*" he asked.

"Seven. This is Martha. *She'll be a full year next month. Silas and I have named her for one of Silas' relatives again, but ...*" Two-Turtles interrupted me.

"*But she looks like ...,*" he paused before saying it, "*she looks like Kilakeena.*" He glanced into the baby's eyes. I nodded. Martha, more than any of our other children, looked like Kilakeena. The child's soft black hair and doe-shaped eyes unmistakably matched Kilakeena's when he was a child. The undeniable resemblance coupled with the infant's semblance of innocence provoked a tension for Two-Turtles, I think. He turned his gaze away from the baby. Then he noticed you."Oho, *our young Silas Jr., are you well?*" Two-Turtles asked you, but you hid shyly and didn't respond. I stroked your light brown hair that was streaked with sunshine, "Go ahead; tell your uncle," I encouraged you as you, Silas, had something to be proud of that day.

"*These are my first moccasins,*" you announced with pride. "*Oho! Then you must be four summers old,*" Two-Turtles responded with a smile.

"*I am. My mother made these for me,*" you added. "My father took me fishing yesterday because if I am old enough to have moccasins, then I am old enough to go fishing. But they're hot in the summer," you took off your moccasins and placed them into Two-Turtles' outstretched palm for his inspection, after which you darted off to meet your brothers and father on the path.

"I filled a gourd with water from the bucket and offered it to Two-Turtles. He nodded in appreciation.

"*You need food,*" I added. Turning to enter the house, he grabbed me by the sleeve.

"*I have to talk to you and Silas,*" he urged.

"*I've already sent for Silas. He'll be here soon,* I calmed him, and only then did he release my sleeve. I entered the house and made a dish of corn meal and greens and brought it to him. He sat under the shade of an elm tree and ate in silence. Hunger showed in his gaunt cheeks, which undulated with each chew.

"*I'm sorry we haven't more,*" I apologized for the scanty amount "*But Silas will be back with fish.*" I knew the thought of trout sizzling over a sage and hickory fire would be appealing to Two-Turtles, but he only nodded lightly.

"After a short time, we heard Silas Sr. and the boys making their way through the brush. Your father, who led the way, pulled an especially thick branch of hemlock aside and held it back for them. Your older brothers tumbled through the pine and raccoon-berry bushes and toward their Uncle Two-Turtles.

"*Uncle Two-Turtles! Uncle Two-Turtles!* the boys shouted. Always thrilled to see him, they lunged in his direction and fell into his hug that became a quick game of wrestling.

I interrupted my mother's story; saying, "I don't remember Uncle Two-Turtles." She sighed in response. "Each time Two-Turtles came to visit he taught your older brothers more about fishing and hunting. On past occasions, he helped them improve their blowgun techniques and taught them to string a bow and shoot an arrow. You were too young to do these things; you wouldn't remember Two-Turtles." I wanted to ask what happened to Uncle Two-Turtles, but decided not to interrupt again as my mother began her story anew.

"Anyway, Two-Turtles greeted your brothers and sisters with as much enthusiasm as he could muster, but his heart was heavy with some news. I became more and more concerned. Your father recognized this right away.

"He shushed you boys. "*Put your things away. Then take this trap and clean the cage. Put the fish in that bucket of water.*" Your brothers carried the cage, which sparkled full of mountain trout that had fallen prey to the temptation of black walnut bait—a simple trick that Two-Turtles had taught your father long ago when they had been traveling companions.

"*You look tired, tsogali-my friend*, your father told Two-Turtles.

"*I grow wearier each day*, Two-Turtles answered.

"*What now?* your father asked him. Two-Turtles breathed deeply.

"*What is it?* your father asked again.

"*The removal has begun*, Two-Turtles looked squarely into your father's eyes.

"*Chief Ross sends a message. Submit to the soldiers without incident. Don't surrender early, but don't fight or run when the soldiers come, either. He asks his people to go peacefully.* Two-Turtles hung his head, briefly. Then he looked into his friend's eyes again and continued.

"*I've been spreading this message as quickly as possible. Thousands upon thousands of soldiers are already rounding up Cherokee and taking them to stockades.*[2] *I saw two boys, about the age of Reuben and William, maybe, Joseph's age. They panicked when they saw the soldiers and ran. The soldiers tracked them down and carried them off. Just boys. Crying for their mother. At another homestead I gave the message to an old woman, a clan mother. She accepted the message. I heard the soldiers coming and she sent me to hide in her storehouse so that I could continue to relay the Chief's message to the people. I watched as she calmly stood in front of a dozen soldiers with bayonets pointed at her. She asked to take her baskets and they wouldn't let her. They told her that everything would be inventoried and given back to her after she moved to the land beyond the great Father River. I saw the fear in her eyes and the bravery in her heart. She asked the soldiers if she could feed her chickens before she left. They agreed.*

"*Walking slowly to the front post where the feedbag hung over a nail, she stopped to look at it all one last time—her house, her fields, her baskets. She retrieved the bag, turned and flicked corn kernels to the ground where the chickens gathered by her feet. After she finished, she carefully rehung the feed bag, as if she would return.*"[3] Two-Turtles couldn't continue. His head drooped. He covered his face with his hands.

"Your father remained speechless, stunned; he put his hand on Two-Turtles' shoulder.

"*It's worse where the Georgia Guard is involved. My eyes have seen things that my lips tremble and beg not to tell. My heart is on the ground as I think it will happen to you very soon,* Two-Turtles' voice cracked.

"*No, that's where you're wrong, my friend. It won't happen to us. You forget that I'm a white man. Although at times I would like to forget that fact, the truth is that I am white. They can't remove me. My wife and children will stay with me,* your father explained to his worried friend.

"*Oho, Silas,* Two-Turtles said with sincere surprise. *Is that what you think? Oho, Silas! It's not so. They're rounding up any and all white men they find. The Federal Troops call them the 'special friends of the Cherokee Nation.' The Georgia Guard calls them 'Injun lovers.' No, Silas, white men aren't left to live on the land. Ridge's daughter*

163

married a white man—a soldier no less. They have him in a stockade!⁴ He'll be removed. Silas you're not safe. Your family isn't safe. The chief asks that you surrender peacefully with your family."Never! I will never submit to such treatment. My family won't be marched off to a stockade like prisoners, or worse yet, like cattle. These are my children! This is my wife!

"Your father turned his back to Two-Turtles and strode toward the ridge. There he viewed a wide stretch of rolling Smokey Mountains. As his eyes scanned the panoramic view, he caught a glimpse of something on the trail in the distance. It took him a moment to recognize the dark blur over the ridge—a battery of soldiers. He froze for only a second, and then quickly yelled to us. *"Run! RUN! The SOLDIERS are COMING! The SOLDIERS are COMING!"* He gathered Mary in his arms. I strapped Martha to my chest with a shawl and darted toward the house to gather what I could, but your father caught me by the arm.

"No, there's no time! Go to the caves, the ones beyond Bear Creek. You know the one I mean, right? He asked in a hurried and desperate tone. I nodded. Somehow he knew the hiding place, though I had never told him which cave I had picked.

He turned me around. We could hear the soldiers, like distant thunder rumbling along the edge of the hills and up through the valley. Soldiers! Trampling on horseback! And on foot! They approached from three sides. But the path grew daunting. More of the soldiers dismounted and led their horses through the thickets.

"RUN! Silas yelled to you children again. You all scurried toward the hillside.

"Two-Turtles freed his own pony and then he untied our horses. He gave them a strong swat that headed them away from the cavalry. Perhaps, he could find them later, but at least this way the soldiers wouldn't get the horses. He swooped you upward into his arms and set the pace into the hills. Su'nawa' Udsi took Joseph by the hand. Reuben, William and John followed your father.

"I ran while glancing every which way to assure that each of you children headed toward the hillside. I felt as if I couldn't breathe. My heart raced and my head pounded. I ran uphill with labored breath and a baby bouncing against my ribs. I held fast to young saplings, but for only a moment as I caught my breath and steadied my footing. Then I used the tree to push off and start again. Your father ran ahead of me, as did Two-Turtles. I could see my younger sister and Joseph scurrying up the hill. All accounted for, but I needed to move faster. I knew that we had to make it to the top of the ridge and over it in order to be out of sight. Over the slope, I thought, we'd be safe.

"I ran! I felt the sweat pour down my neck under my hair. I could hear my heart pounding and my chest felt as though it would burst. I heard you yell, *No!*

"*My moccasins! My moccasins!* you exclaimed as you jumped from Two-Turtles' arms. You ran down the hill toward the soldiers. I was the only one who had the opportunity to catch you. I lunged sideways! I stopped you. But then I couldn't stop myself.

"I felt the baby bang against my side as I lost my balance and slipped. I slid against the dry dirt and leaves. Downward. I rolled to my side, protecting the baby with one arm; I stretched to catch a sapling in order to stop my descent. My hand slipped. It scraped against the bark; branches ripped my face. I slid faster down the mountainside. I couldn't see. With a sudden jolt, my foot crunched against a rock. It stopped me. Pain seared through my foot and ankle. I grimaced, winced away the dizziness that followed and looked up. Two-Turtles had raced after you and had you safe within his grip. "Your father had reached the top of the ridge where he stopped, turned, and saw that I had fallen. He looked beyond me. I turned. The soldiers were coming.

"*Go,* I yelled to him. *Go!*"

NOTES

[1] The practice of having the children call both their mother and her sisters by the name/title of mother is common to many Native American people. This is because they often shared the child-rearing responsibility; each woman deserved respect from the children (Moore, 1997).

[2] New Echota Historical Site docents report that approximately 16,000 soldiers were involved in the removal.

[3] Wilkins (1986).

[4] Wilkins (1986).

UPSTREAM, UPSTREAM

Recalling the Summer of 1838

"Sunuwa' Udsi', your father called. She turned to see him pointing down the hill at the baby and me. Two-Turtles put you down and turned you toward your aunt. He sent you scurrying along the ridge toward her. Your father saw me struggling to regain my footing. He passed Mary to Su'nawa' Udsi', who then had all the small children except for Martha, the baby.

"*Upstream, upstream!* Two-Turtles instructed tersely. *Sunuwa' Udsi'* and the children disappeared over the ridge.

"I stood up, but fell. My ankle crumpled under me. I tried again, in vain. I looked up at your father. He quickly made his way back down to me. Gliding and sliding from one sapling to the next, his feet turned sideways, moving swiftly, he reached me. Two-Turtles followed.

"I unknotted the shawl that held Martha to my side. Too startled to cry, she stayed silent as I handed her over to your father. Then he helped me onto Two-Turtles' back; I wrapped my legs around his waist and my arms around his neck. He quickly climbed uphill. We could hear the soldiers' horses scuffling, snorting and whinnying. "Two-Turtles hid us behind a wide Standing One. He motioned with a wave of his hand for your father to go on. He went thirty feet or so, and hid behind a grandfather elm tree. We watched. Waited. Silently, he motioned for Two-Turtles to ascend. Like deer, we moved through the forest, angling our paths, moving from one tree to another for cover. If I hadn't hurt my ankle, if only I could've moved faster, I thought.

"*Halt!* The lieutenant's voice boomed. We froze. I held tight to Two-Turtle's neck. We all looked to where the command had come from.

"*Drop it,* he ordered one of his soldiers. A private held your father's fishing cage in his hand. More than a dozen mountain trout sparkled in the afternoon sun.

"*Sir, I just didn't think such a fine meal should go to waste,* the private explained.

"*We're not scavengers,* Smith told him in an angry tone. *Drop it!*

"*They've probably run off into the hills, sir. Do you want us to go after them? They couldn't have gotten far.*

"*No, I've had enough of this for one day.*[1] *Let's circle back and meet with the other regiments. General Scott wants a head count for each day. We need to do that and feed the ones we have. We'll come after these Indians tomorrow.*

"*You there,* Smith turned to a group of privates. *Stay overnight at this homestead in case those Indians decide to return. You too, sergeant.*

"*Yes, sir.*

"Then the sergeant added with deference in his voice, *Sir, I have no overnight provisions, no rations, sir.* He made this comment while glancing at our fresh trout.

"*Yes, oh, all right,* Smith conceded. He yanked the reins of the horse's bridle, causing the horse to whinny, as he led the rest of the men back down the trail toward the Cherokee Agency and the holding pens.

"We watched as the soldiers mounted their steeds. The remaining infantrymen gathered some wood and started a fire to cook the trout. They helped themselves to our belongings. Your father watched as the soldiers broke his fishing cage to extract his catch, gut the trout, and toss it into an iron skillet they had taken from our cabin. We watched as they drank from our gourds and used our utensils. I think that your father must've felt fire in his chest. He gripped the baby tighter.

"Martha let out a whimper. Two-Turtles waved him on. We were close to the ridge and the soldiers were distracted. Two-Turtles followed with me still on his back. We made it over the ridge, down the slope, and into the cool creek waters. There, Two-Turtles glanced down as he took a step into the creek. He saw that my ankle had swollen already. He lowered me, saying, *Soak it*. I submerged my aching ankle and foot into the water. He steadied me. Your father joined us, dipped his hand into the water and let the infant suckle his finger.

"*Can you handle it from here?* Two-Turtles asked your father. He nodded.

"*I need to warn our friends, as many as I can. Tsiskwa'gwa, Tsali and the others*. Turning to me, he spoke of my family.

"*Your mother's home is far; it's probably too late to warn them,*" he both appraised and apologized.

"*Most of my family left*. He looked surprised. "They went west; they *followed Kilakeena. I'll tell you more later,*" I promised. *Go then, please hurry. Maybe you can reach Tsiskwa'gwa and the others in time. Please, tell Nikutse'ge and Sweetwater, also,*" I begged my uncle as I leaned on your father's arm. Two-Turtles nodded and darted off.

"Your father and I made our way upstream. My foot and ankle throbbed even within the cool waters and I could barely put weight on it. Balancing myself with only one good foot on the rocky riverbed slowed our escape, but the soldiers were not inclined to follow. We waded downstream, far beyond the bend and past hollow's cove. Carrying Martha and steadying me took a good deal of your father's strength and agility, but he didn't think about the task at hand. I think he thought only of the injustice of it all. The muscles of his shoulders and arms tightened; his hand made an involuntary fist.

"At last we saw the parting of the high grasses and cattail where Su'nawa' and the children had made their transition to land. From the embankment, we made our way along a deer trail that took us close to the caves that overlooked Bear Creek. The trail circled upward, curving around the mountain. I hobbled laboriously. It was dark by the time we joined Su'nawa' and the children.

"Exhaustion gave way to sleep in short order. I nursed Martha and then let Mary suckle at my breast, as well. You curled up next to me. We four slept together. Your father kept watch by the opening of the cave. Sitting with his knees pulled up and his arms crossed over them, he let his head drop back against the cave wall and dozed intermittently. But his arms jerked from time to time and his hands groped for the rifle that didn't exist within his grasp. Su'nawa' slept with the older boys around her. The night passed without intrusion.

NOTE

1   General Wool and General Scott resigned their commissions rather than take part in the cruelties of the Cherokee Removal (Ehle, 1988).

BELOVED WOMAN, WAR WOMAN

Recalling the Events of the Summer of 1838

I sat listening with a grateful heart as I knew my mother was sharing this to keep my mind off of my loss, my Willie. She was answering the question that I had begged of her on the first night in the cabin. How had she come to walk with a limp? I was beginning to understand why she had kept the story from me. And I was beginning to understand why she was telling me now. She continued.

"In the early morning, I shot awake from a touch at my shoulder, she said. My forearm automatically jerked up with a rush, not quite the snap of a whip, but effective nonetheless if you wanted to scare someone off. But it wasn't my intention to startle my own son. Joseph knelt beside me, a frightened child. I looked into his face, evidently your seven-year-old brother wasn't sure whether to flee or freeze, but I quickly took his hand

"*You frightened me, Joseph.*

"*You frightened me,* he returned. His hands trembled, "*Are you cold?*

"*I'm hungry.*

"*I know.* I dropped back downward onto the hard ground. Too weak to sit up, I sank back and closed my eyes. Something itched; I reached for my face. Caked on blood stuck to my forehead and cheek where the branches had scratched me. I rolled over to face Joseph. *Aaaah!* I moaned. A searing pain shot through my ankle and then settled into a throb.

"Martha, the baby by my side, let out a cry. I did my best to lull her. I loosened my dirt-covered blouse and nuzzled her cheek against my breast. But as she began to suck, I was overwhelmed by thirst. As if I were on the dying lands of the western deserts, I whispered to Su'nawa' through parched lips, *Su'nawa', water.*

"*Sallie, what is it?*" My sister Su'nawa' made her way over to me. She looked at my dirty, scraped face and touched my cheek.

"*Your skin feels warm.*

"*Silas,* Su'nawa' said, waking your dozing father. *My sister needs water and the children need food.*

Your father looked through weary blood-shot eyes at me and children. Then he scanned the cave. No trickling spring water. No mushrooms, just barren, dry rock. He put his head into his hands. Su'nuwa' and I waited.

"*How will we get water?* I wondered. *How will we eat? Your father couldn't hunt; the sound of a rifle would bring the soldiers. Even if he had a bow and arrow, the smell of a fire would reach the soldiers' greedy nostrils. Water! What of water? My throat was so parched I could hardly swallow. I couldn't nurse the crying infant. Water! But I wouldn't be able to walk to the stream. How would we carry water from the stream to the cave? No bucket. No gourds. No canteen. What of the children? Surely, they could walk, but the soldiers would be everywhere today. No, it wouldn't be safe for any of them to go down the mountainside to Bear Creek. We have nothing to carry water. Nothing. No beds, no blankets, no food, no gourds, skillets, or rifle, not even a bucket or a cup! Suddenly, I remembered the rifle, hidden in the back of the cave, but what good would it do us? What we need is water. And there were a few supplies that I had squirreled away, but not enough for more than a few days. It was too soon to break into survival supplies. And I hadn't thought to store water.*

"*Silas?* Su'nawa' persisted.

"*I'm thinking,* he snapped at her. *What would you have me do? Carry it back in my hands?* Like me, he had been thinking the same things. Like me, he had no solutions, only questions and concerns."Su'nawa' fell silent. Not out of fear, I'm sure; she didn't frighten so easily. No, although his anger was misplaced, his questions posed practical concerns. She waited patiently for a time, but too much time passed. The baby whined and Joseph now tugged at Su'nawa's sleeve."*Silas?* she queried again more emphatically. He didn't respond. She rose. Spying Reuben's blow gun, she took it up in her hands."*I already thought of that. There are no darts.*

"*Then I'll make some.* She unsheathed the knife that hung from her hip belt and left the cave.

"Your father made his way to my side. *Tell me, Sallie, what plants or roots grow here that I can bring to you and the children to eat?* I thought for a moment. *Yun-oo-gi-s-ti. What bears eat—Yun-oo-gi-s-ti. Berries are ripe. The dried ones are near the top of the branches. Look low and under the leaves for the plump ones. Look along the deer trail that we followed here yesterday. Wild roses are edible and still blooming now. See if the honey locust tree is ready to give up its seed pods. The flesh that lines the seeds should be ready for eating. Look for wild potato roots, too.* I described several plants to your father. Then I pulled him closer to me and whispered."*This is where I hid our rifle. Look in the back of the cave, wrapped in a blanket.* This news made your father smile.

"*I knew there was more than one reason why I married you,* he kissed me on the forehead.

"Your father recovered the rifle from deep within the crevices in the back of the dark cave. He gave the rifle to me, for now, but in the future it was your father who would sit crossed-legged at the entrance of the cave with our rifle across his lap, keeping vigil, night after night, like a sentry. He took Reuben with him to find food. I propped myself up against the curving wall of the cave. You children sat around me.

"*We won't be gone long and we won't go far,* your father assured me before he left. With those words, I realized that he had been afraid to leave us alone for fear the soldiers would find us. True to his word, he returned long before Su'nawa', but by late afternoon both were exchanging the benefits of their efforts.

"Su'nawa' had been unable to make the darts as readily as she'd hoped. Fastening the thistle to the point with morning glory stem didn't hold as well as sinew would have. Besides, the child's blowgun was half the size or less than an adult blowgun. It'd never have achieved the power to force the dart through the thick hide of an animal's skin. She gave up after several tries, she told us. Instead, she set her mind on taking the life of a squirrel.

"Armed with several rocks, Su'nawa' waited near a pignut hickory tree, where, true to their nature, the squirrel surely did venture.

But as she glanced up toward the top of the tree, she discovered a fat raccoon snoozing in the crook of two branches. She wasted no time. She quickly gathered several more rocks and flung one at the raccoon. The first hit woke the animal and startled it. The raccoon decided to seek new sleeping quarters. As the raccoon made its way down the trunk of the tree, Su'nawa' hailed the other rocks at it until it dropped unconscious to the ground. Su'nawa' approached it with caution and then gave it one last crack to the skull. She beckoned the night animal spirits and called out.

"Oho! Spirits of the nocturnal animals look what has happened. Someone has killed your brother, probably a white man, for the white men have driven my people away from their homes and into the caves. The white men don't care about the spirit of this animal. I tell you now that I care. I will use this animal to save the lives of my people who are suffering in the caves. Your brother's spirit will become one with the spirit of my people and we shall overcome the atrocities of the white men.[1]

"Su'nawa' carried the raccoon to a spot by Bear Creek, not far from the cave. She strung the animal by the neck from a branch and skinned it by slicing through the fur and skin from the neck to its legs. She pulled hard; stripped it and set the fur aside. Next, she gutted the organs, ate the small red slippery parts immediately to give her the spirit of this animal—one that would be able to stay awake at night to help guard the cave. Then she sliced the esophagus, gently, removed it and the stomach, and the intestines, keeping each intact. These organs, she handled with care. She set them aside. Then she washed the blood from the fur and skin, before returning her attention to the stomach.

"She dipped the stomach lining into the river and thoroughly cleansed it of its contents—mostly half-digested vegetation. Then she saturated the stomach lining with cool water, filling the hollow organ, like a spongy canteen. After tying off the intestines and the esophagus, she set the newly made water sponge on the outstretched hide.

"Su'nawa' turned her attention to the bones. First, she stripped the meat and then broke the bones at the joints and pulled the tendons away. She saved the sinew to be used in the making of a bowstring. She splintered the bones with rock to make darts to go with the blowgun.

The larger bones she planned to crack later and suck the marrow for nourishment. She saved smaller bones to be utilized in sewing, as splinters make excellent needles. She hated to discard the meat, but like Silas, she knew that a fire would attract attention, even sundried jerky might draw vultures and with them soldiers. So Su'nawa' stabbed the earth with the blade of her knife digging a hole in which to bury the head of the raccoon and but before buried the meat decided to save it just in case. She brought the washed meat in the folds of the gathering bag that she had taken, just in case the soldiers left and we might be able to prepare and cook the meat later. All of this she had done before rejoining us in the cave.

"I was impressed by my sister's resourcefulness and ashamed that your father had snapped at her earlier, he might have been thinking the same, when he called you children. *Children.* You all perked up and listened to your father as you sucked the bones of the raccoon.

"*Children, do you know that in times of peace, the Cherokee run their government according to the white ways, the ways of peace?* he asked you. Most of you were too busy eating to answer; only Joseph asked a question.

"*Like white people you mean?*

"*No, like white ways. White means peace among the Cherokee,* your father explained. Su'nawa' and I listened closely. Perhaps, to make sure your father got it right, but also out of curiosity to hear him be the one to explain the Cherokee ways.

"*During the white times,* he explained, *the peace times, the Chiefs and the elders make all the decisions along with the Beloved Women and the Clan Mothers. I think if these were times of peace, your mother would be named a Beloved Woman, a Peace Woman, a Pretty Woman of the Clan.* Your father looked into my eyes as he spoke these words. I lowered my eyes.

"*And children, did you know that in times of war, a War Chief is named to replace the previously reigning chief and the Beloved Woman, Peace Woman, steps down to give her place to the War Woman. If these were times of war, I believe that your Aunt Su'nawa' would be honored as the War Woman,* your father looked toward Su'nawa'. She nodded in appreciation.

"*Papa, I just want you to answer one question,* you told him and then asked, *can we go home now?*

"*No,* he answered. My mother paused in her storytelling.

I felt compelled to ask her, "When did we go home?"

"Not for a long, long time, and not home, not exactly," she spoke with a deep sadness in her voice. I heard it as we sat by Willie's grave. I worried about my brothers and sisters, my wife and daughters, but I couldn't bring myself to leave Willie's side. I felt now that even if I had been able to take my family home today, it would never be home again because Willie wouldn't be with us. Perhaps my mother was reliving a similar sadness and permanent loss.

"I cried, didn't I?" I asked my mother. "Knowing we couldn't go home."

"Yes."

"I remember the cave, now," and as I recalled this I reflected on the reason for my crying. "I didn't cry because I was hungry or scared, or just because I wanted to go home; it was more specific," I told my mother.

"What?"

"My moccasins," I confessed. "I didn't have them with me. They were gone forever." She touched my shoulder gently as if to comfort the child from long ago as well as the man who sat beside her today.

"Your limp," I paused, having to draw the apology from deep within me. My mother turned to look at me. "It was my fault."

"No. It was Kilakeena's fault. He signed the Treaty."

NOTE

[1] Following the cruel colonization by the Spanish Conquistadors, whenever the Cherokee needed to kill an eagle for spiritual or ritualistic reasons, they blamed the death of the eagle on the Spaniards who they claimed had forced their hand (Mails, 1996).

THE BRAVEST CONFEDERATE I EVER KNEW

December 22, 1865

Before I could ask my mother the questions that now sat at the edge of my mind, we were interrupted by the creaking noise of the cabin door opening. We both looked up to see who was coming out. Nan stood in the doorway. She squinted against the brightness and then looked about slowly. She didn't seem to see us sitting by Willie's grave. She made no attempt to leave the porch; she simply stood there. I raised myself up and then bent over, reaching under my mother's arms to assist her up. She pulled her blanket tightly about herself. We walked, she limped, to the front porch.

"Nan, are you all right?" She didn't answer me. I went to her.

"Wait here," I told her. I took my mother inside the cabin and helped her to floor.

I returned to the porch and took Nan by the arm to a place near the cabin so she could urinate. But she stood without taking her usual posture. After a time, I turned her around and took her back inside.

I returned to my duties—adding kindling and stoking the fire, checking on my kindred patients, and dispensing water to the few who were barely awake. William shoved the water away.

"Are the pox down your throat?" I asked him.

"Where've you been?" his tone was gruff.

"With mother."

"Doing what?"

"Sitting," I didn't finish my thought aloud, ... *by Willie's grave.*

"Are you forgetting that these woods are filled with no-good wretches?"

"I haven't forgotten anything."

"I'll have some of that water now," he said. I took the bucket and the ladle and portioned a small amount of water. He leaned on one elbow and sipped with a grimace.

"Do you want some snow to suck on?" I suggested.

"And have you leave us unprotected again? You could at least have left the rifle with me if you were going to be gone so long." I didn't answer him. I drew away.

"Wait," his voice held a softer tone. "Another drink, please," he requested as his head dropped back against the floor. I waited for him to gain strength and lift his head, but he wasn't strong enough. So, I supported his head and held the ladle to his lips. When he was done, I let his head back down gently and started to turn away.

"What were you and mother talking about?"

"About when the soldiers came, about when we lived in the caves."

"And when we lived in the ghost villages afterward?" I remembered living in what my brothers and I called the "ghost villages."

"We were looking for the other Cherokee, for our relatives," I said.

"Is that what mother said?"

"Not in so many words. And not at all today."

"Silas, Silas, think, man. We didn't begin moving from one village to another until after our Uncle came to see father. Do you remember that?"

"Yes, but what does that have to do with anything?"

"Father didn't move us to one abandoned village after another to search for lost relatives. He moved us so that we could work the land, fix the old Cherokee homesteads, and sell them to white settlers."

"No, you're wrong."

"Am I?"

I wanted to wake my mother. I wanted to hear her say that my father would never have done such a thing, but something stopped me.

"He was an opportunist."

"He wasn't," I declared.

"He was, I tell you, and we were his conspirators."

"We were children," I reminded him with force.

"Till you were twenty-one?" he asked sarcastically. "Silas, face the truth. He made a profit on Cherokee land and he dragged mother and the rest of us along. We were a part of it."

"We weren't. You're mistaken," I told him.

"Really? Is that so? Tell me then, how did you get your promised lot of land, a horse, a rifle, and a bible on your twenty-first birthday? Open your eyes, man!"

I took my rifle. I headed for the door. I would hear no more of this, especially since our father was not there to explain his actions.

"Silas," my brother called after me as I slung the door open. "He was a white man, just like you!"

I banged the door shut, refusing to have any part of William. I headed down the path toward the river, but I veered off, realizing that the walk to the river and back was too short to satisfy the anger that was growing in my chest.

William was wrong, I thought. How could my father have sold the land to white men if I never saw a white man when I was growing up? William was wrong. He had to be wrong. But where did my father get the money for the horses and the rifles for each of his sons? It must've come from the sale of the harvest. But why move, why did we keep moving? We must've been searching for relatives, for friends after the removal. Or maybe he was afraid to settle down for too long in one place. Who would have accepted a family like ours? Some of us looked Indian, some white and others in-between. We never would've been accepted in a white settlement. Cherokee, maybe, but even then—

Screams interrupted my thoughts. Screeches. Howls. Something dreadful. I stopped in mid-thought. I jerked my head and cocked an ear toward the tortuous screeches of an animal; or was it a man? The noise was coming from the ravine up ahead. I swung my rifle off my shoulder and to my side as I darted through leaf-covered woods. Crisp branches breaking under foot. I angled toward the noise. The screams stopped, but a more sinister sound continued. A gnawing. A slurping. A rustling and scuffling.

I came over the low ridge of the ravine to see a pack of wolves feasting on a large animal. *No, on a man. My Lord!* I raised my Springfield and shot into the air. They scattered as I reloaded. I bit the cork from my powder pouch and held it in my teeth. I poured the black powder, then used the ramrod to jam it down the barrel, all the while never taking my eyes off the wolves, except to glance at the man who lay bleeding in the ravine. I took cautious steps, sideways down the hillside, while corking my powder bag and eyeing the woods. Within seconds, I stood by the side of a man whose stomach and entrails, ripped from the rest of his body, lay scattered, in part, by his side.

I glanced back up. A lone timber wolf stood at the top of the ravine. Lean and hungry, he bared his teeth. They dripped red with blood. I raised my rifle, but he turned and disappeared over the ridge. I felt a hand grip my ankle. I turned instinctively and pointed the barrel of the gun at the man's heart.

"Give me a bullet," he commanded between gritted teeth.

"What?"

"Don't stop to think. Shoot me!"

I stammered something. I'm not sure what. His eyes neither pled nor begged; they commanded me as if I was one of his soldiers. His uniform torn and bloodied gave away his rank—an officer in the Confederate army. His left hand continued to grip my ankle. His other arm lay gnawed and tangled in cloth; it dangled loosely over his jugular vein. He showed every sign of pain for just a second. The grimace was followed by a deep breath, which must have ended in a searing pain as he tightened his grip about my ankle.

"Let me loose, sir," I was still pointing my rifle at him. "Shoot me," he demanded, still holding tight. "Don't make a man beg." His eyes were clear and alert; he held me with his gaze. Never flinching, he squeezed my ankle tighter.

I floundered, flipping thoughts about in my head, trying to make sense of the fact that a man would beg for death instead of life. I wanted him to have entreated me with, *help me*; instead, the words, *Shoot me! Shoot me*, ushered forth. I heard the request again in my head. *Don't make me beg.*

"Shoot me," he commanded me; this startled me back to the bloodied mess of flesh before me.

"Look at me," he said as though that were reason enough. "Brother, can't you see?" He gripped my ankle tighter. My muzzle moved to his chest.

My mother's earlier words returned to me, *Brother Moon helps us to see what we otherwise could not see.*

I pursed my lips and took a breath. Never taking my eyes from the brave Confederate. As if I was standing at attention. He nodded. I pulled the trigger.

His heart exploded on impact. His blood sprayed my face. I flinched. His eyes met mine one last time and then his head jerked abruptly to the side. The blast echoed through the woods. I heard it over and over in the otherwise silent forest.

I backed away as I felt his hand slump, releasing my ankle from his grip. I looked down at his limp hand, and then back at his face. *Had this really happened?* Belief and disbelief. I shook my head. I backed up slowly barely able to leave his side. One slow step and then another, I tripped over a log, caught my balance and then sat on the lightly snow-covered log. I watched him, as if expecting him to move, to be alive again, and to speak. But he didn't move; he didn't speak. Nor did I make a sound.

I sat motionless on that log, dumbstruck for an indeterminable amount of time. I remained in my stupor until snowflakes began to flutter. They were large wet flakes that melted as they hit the warm blood that pooled around the dead man. I willed those snowflakes to become smaller and dryer so that instead of melting they began to cover the body in a blanket of white. I watched as nature claimed her prize.

I wished with all my heart at that moment that I had waited, at least long enough to say some kind word to this dying stranger. But what words? What words could capture his courage to ask for death with such bravery. What words justify his lot. And I, I had done nothing but finish the job that the wolves had started. I was no better than these predators. I had given this man nothing, not a good word, not a prayer, just a bullet through the heart. A heart that exploded into air. And so I ended his pain, but I could have waited. I should have waited, prayed with him or told him what a fine man he is, but I didn't know him. I didn't know what to say. I couldn't put his innards back in him, but I should have done something more.

I felt a sensation around my ankle as if his hand still gripped me there. I could've held his hand, I thought; instead of him gripping my ankle. But I didn't. I hadn't.

A snowflake landed on my eyelash, forcing me to blink, but not to cry. Forcing me to return to an awareness of my surroundings. Snow lightly covered me. I shook my hair and brushed my sleeves. Squinting, I looked to the sky and determined then that as pure and bountiful as the snowfall might be now, the flurries wouldn't keep up long enough to bury the body and protect it from the wolves. I stood ready to make my way up the side of the ravine and back to the cabin. This man deserved to be buried, I thought. I owed him that much. I needed a shovel.

I felt an unexplainable heaviness on my shoulders as I trudged back toward the cabin. Strangely enough, my brother's earlier words came to mind, *Silas, you might have to kill a man.* Prophetic in an ironic sort of way, the words made me shake my head. I never expected his words to come true, at least not in this way. Nor did I expect that one day my actions would make my own heart ache with regret for the life of a man whom I'd never before met. God help me, if I ever have to shoot a man again. Something was lost to me forever. I couldn't explain to myself the sorrow that I was feeling. But I knew then that it must be far easier to shoot a man in anger or revenge when the body and mind are prepared for such a thing than in a moment of quiet defeat, and for certain, far harder to stop oneself when anger rages through one's veins. It would seem that it is equally hard to pull the trigger in mercy; as it is, to not pull the trigger in anger or revenge.Snowflakes continued to fall. The cabin came into view. A serene scene replaced the images of a man ripped asunder.

ONLY TSALI KNOWS THE ANSWER

Recalling the Late Summer of 1838

I spoke to no one of the courageous confederate, except my mother. For her, only the briefest explanation crossed my lips, "A good man needed my help to go to heaven. A dark decision, difficult to make."

"I know about dark decisions," she shared and led me back again to sit by Willie's grave. She continued her family story of living in the caves.

"Silhouetted by the setting sun, a dark figure stood at the opening of the cave. Unrecognizable, at first, the shadowy form drew your father's attention immediately. He rose abruptly. Nearly knocking his head against the low ceiling of the cave, he caught himself just in time.

"*O' Siyo, tsogali,* his voice came softly so as not to wake the sleeping children.

"*Two-Turtles, my friend,* your father greeted him with relief. "*It's been nearly a month since you left us at Bear Creek. How are you?*

"*Two-Turtles?* I made my way toward them. *Two-Turtles,* I joyfully greeted him. We stepped just outside the mouth of the cave so as not to wake the children, and then, we sat leaning against the moss-covered rocks. The ground was cool in comparison to the muggy air of late summer that sweltered around us.

"*What news do you bring?* I asked anxiously. I couldn't see how drawn Two-Turtles' face looked under the light given to us from a sliver of moon, but I heard the weakness in his voice. Like a thin wisp of a spider's web torn from its connection.

"*Much has happened,* he spoke solemnly.

"*After leaving you, I went first to Nikutse'ge and Sweetwater. Like you, they chose to hide in the mountains. They left in plenty of time and are hidden safely. They would love to come to you, but the mountains are covered in an ivy of soldier blue.*

"After I warned them, I left quickly for Tsiskwa'gwa's home, but not quickly enough. When I came within view of her cabin, I could already see that the soldiers had arrived. Tsiskwa'gwa faced them alone. She didn't understand English, but I am sure she knew what they wanted. Like so many others, she fed her chickens quietly and calmly. I thought she would go passively like the others. But something strange unfolded. She went into her cabin and when she returned her face and arms and hair were covered in a blue paste. Then, with the soldiers waiting for her, she walked around to the side of the cabin, picked up an axe and split her beehive with a resounding crash. The commotion and angry buzz that followed sent the horses rearing and soldiers yelping and slapping themselves to get the bees off of their necks and faces.[1] One soldier became furious and leveled a hard blow to Tsiskwa'gwa's head. She dropped to the ground. I wanted to go to her aid, but instead my feet didn't move, his plaintive voice begged forgiveness. He hung his head for a moment; we waited.

"One of the soldiers dismounted, picked up Tsiskwa'gwa and threw her over another's horse. They rode off in haste. The swarm of bees in pursuit. Headed for the stockades I presume. The stockades are miserable. Our people will die there.

"What do you know of the people in the stockades?" I asked.*"I kept vigil near the stockades to see if I could learn any further news of Tsiskwa'gwa and her family and Tsali and his family, for I never found Tsali's family.*

"And? Tell me."

"I hid at a distance and watched. Each day the soldiers arrived with more Tsaragi. Sometimes, only one or two; other times, whole villages. One time, they arrived with motherless children, crying children. He shook his head.

"On the third day, they brought out the first dead Tsaragi—a child. The mother's weeping tore through my heart like a knife. The soldiers dug a pit and lowered the body. I felt compelled to keep vigil over the child's grave. Days passed. On the seventh day, a woman appeared outside the stockade walls, without guards. I couldn't guess why she had been released. She seemed to be coming straight toward me into the forest. I hid myself and waited until she was close enough

to hear a quiet call from the morning dove. I cooed to her. She turned her head in surprise. 'Please,' I implored her, 'Tell me how the others fare and how is it that you walk freely without soldiers at your side.'

"'My brother is a Shaman of the Blue Clan and he is terribly ill with the bloody lung. The coughs are wrenching his body and his skin grows grey in color. My brother beseeched the soldiers to allow me to collect healing herbs. They agreed.' She told me which herbs would heal her brother and I helped her to gather them. She told me that more deaths were sure to come because the soldiers were giving the people worthless food to eat. Every morning the people line up, she explained, and each one—man, woman, and child—receives a pound of flour and three strips of bacon. In the beginning, everyone refused to eat. But by the third day, the children complained of hunger and they tried to eat the food. The children choked on the powdered flour when they tried to eat it dry. We tried to mix it with water, she told me, but it only glues our hands together. Some have tried to toss the sticky flour into the boiling water or into frying skillets, but nothing seems to work. It is not like corn.'

"Each day the Shaman's sister searched for herbs to heal her brother, I helped her to gather greens and roots. We stuffed her dress with them so that she could feed more people.

"She told me at last that a War Woman stood and marched to the gates of the stockade. She called out in Tsaragi words, 'I would rather have a handful of corn than a pound of the white man's flour!' No one is sure who translated her words, but after that every Tsaragi received a cupful of corn in place of the flour," Two-Turtles told us.[2] We listened intently.

"I asked the woman if she knew anything of Tsiskwa'gwa and her family. She promised to ask around. She told me of many brave women. The numbers of detainees swell each day. There are thousands within this one compound. She described it to me.

"At the north end, ditches have been dug for the feces and urine. The Tsaragi crowd into the south end for sleeping. There are no blankets or pallets upon which to lie. The cookfires are positioned in the middle of the camp. The summer flies are large and troublesome during the day and the mosquitoes are relentless at night. Many children *have fevers. The men of medicine are trying to keep the sick cloistered in one corner, but the quarantine cannot be complete. The stockade is too crowded. Nor will the soldiers let the healers take the children to water. None have washed or prayed since they have been forced into the stockades. For some, it has been a full moon's turn. Women who have their moon time gather in one place, away from the food. They cry. The elders, the chiefs, and the medicine men try to mingle among the people, speaking words of encouragement and hope. But, each day more weep for loved ones they can't find or for those who are sick and dying. The place is filled with sorrow and sickness.*

"*One day, I watched the soldiers carry out three bodies—two children and one old man. I watched as the woman, whom I had helped to gather herbs, cried for her brother. She looked in my direction and her eyes said farewell, a farewell so final that I couldn't move and my heart ached.* Two-Turtles fell silent.

"Neither your father nor I spoke. We watched as the constellations moved across the sky. I searched for the *Seven Boys*, but couldn't see it. Blackness consumed its place. We remained quiet until the moon neared its sleeping spot in the west. And then my mother told me a different story.

"Our family was torn in different directions, my uncle Charles Reese. He decided that since the missionaries had bravely gone to jail for the Cherokee that he'd honor them by becoming a Christian. But when he went to be baptized the missionaries told him that he couldn't become a Christian because he has three wives. He told them that he couldn't leave two of his wives to go hungry. The missionaries wrote to their leaders in Boston, who sent their final word on the subject: Charles could keep only his first wife. Charles nodded when he received this proclamation and said, 'This is a good day; the spirits have smiled on me.' The curious missionaries asked him how this could be good news for him. He answered, 'Because I married these three sisters on the same day, at the same time.'[3] So, Charles and his three wives, and Susannah Reese, Oowatie, and their son, Kilakeena, and others, like Ridge and Scaleeloskee, left for the land beyond the Mississippi. I told Two-Turtles all of this as it had happened before the removal but I had not yet had a chance to tell him.

"*Did they leave with Elias's group, the Treaty Party?* Two-Turtles asked me.

"*I think so. They could see no good coming from staying here. The greedy, white men will destroy the ancient practices and the Tsaragi—full blood, half-bloods, quadroons, adopted—all would live in constant danger. The Tsaragi people would be better off to leave,* they said.

"W*hy did you and Silas stay? Two-Turtles asked me.*

"*I can't leave the homeland.* He nodded in agreement.

"That truth remains today," my mother told me and before returning to her story of the past, she added, "Silas, don't lead the family away from the homeland." I took this to heart, as she began the story of the removal once again.

"At that time, silence fell around our shoulders like a weighty shawl. We turned again to the stars, seeking consolation. I listened to hear the wind, or an owl, even a cricket, but nothing seemed to be speaking that night. I wished to hear the ancestors' voices. Maybe, if I remained very quiet, I thought, the words of the ancient ones would lift my spirit or at least bring me a sign of what has happened to Tsiskwa'gwa and the others," my mother continued.

"The stars passed slowly. The moon nearly gone when Two-Turtles said, "*I've more bad news.*" It seemed impossible that any worse news could exist. I shook my head.

"*It's about Tsali,* he began. I couldn't bear to hear that yet more suffering had unfolded. I braced myself against the words and the story that was about to unfold.

"*There are runners in the mountains right now. I met some of them covertly and told them that I would scout this area of the mountains while they search for Tsali and his sons along the northern edge of the Hiwassee River and the Little Tennessee. That way, I could protect you and your family and Nikutse'ge and Sweetwater from being discovered.* Your father and I didn't understand at first what my uncle was talking about—*What runners? Who are these runners?* But we held still and waited to learn more from Two-Turtles.

"*When the soldiers came for Tsali and his family they surrendered peacefully, but during the long hike back to the fort, Tsali's wife grew tired. She needed to rest. Neither she nor Tsali are young. A soldier became impatient with her and nudged her on with his rifle. As to be expected, Tsali took great offense at this treatment of his wife. He told the soldier to show some respect, but the soldiers don't speak Tsaragi. They shouted something back at Tsali and the words that neither one could understand acted like darts pelting their skin. When the soldier shoved Tsali's wife one more time, Tsali threw the soldier from his horse. Then his sons seized the other soldiers. They wrestled their guns away and somehow two of the soldiers were shot. Whether by Tsali or his sons, I don't know. Tsali and his three sons escaped into the woods, but his wife and daughters-in-law were taken to the stockade,* Two-Turtles paused. Too many questions swirled in my head for me to be able to ask a single one of them before he continued.

"*Lieutenant Colonel Smith, under the authority of General Scott, sent Cherokee runners, who had been in the stockades, to find Tsali and tell him that if he and his sons will surrender, the soldiers will discontinue the search for the other three hundred Tsaragi hiding in the mountains. After all, thousands already fill the stockades. He'll end the round up and begin the removal. He promised that no one will have to suffer any more; the ones in the stockades can move on to their new homeland if only Tsali and his sons will surrender,* Two-Turtles explained.

"*Do you know where they're hiding?* I asked Two-Turtles.

"*No, but there are many runners. They'll not only find Tsali, but every other Tsaragi who's hiding in these mountains,* Two-Turtles predicted.

"*But why would the runners turn in Tsali and others? Why wouldn't they just hide now in the mountains themselves?* asked Su'nawa' Udsi' who had awakened and joined us. She continued, *Why don't they run and hide? Why would they go back to the stockades?*

"*Because the soldiers are holding their mothers and grandmothers, their sisters, their wives and children, and their fathers and grandfathers. The soldiers threaten the ones they love. No, these young men will not run away,* Two-Turtles explained to your aunt. Then he turned to your father and asked, *Silas, will the soldiers keep their word? If Tsali turns himself in, do you think they will stop searching the mountains?*

"Your father shook his head before answering, *I don't know. It's possible that the Lieutenant is telling the truth. If the southern Cherokee were so easily coerced into the stockades and if they already have thousands pent up in the corrals, then it may be that the three hundred mountain Cherokee are nothing more than an annoying handful of Indians to them. Yes, they might leave us alone. But it's also possible that they're using the runners to find the hiding places of the mountain Cherokee and that they'll trail them, later. I just don't know. Tell me, Two-Turtles, what do you think Tsali should do?* Your father asked his old companion.

"Night passed into the edges of morning. Two-Turtles spoke softly in the dim light of dawn, *It doesn't really matter what I think, I suppose, only Tsali has the answer.*[4]

"Two-Turtles rose and turned to leave, but I caught him by the sleeve. With a nod, he accepted dried berries and a handful of nuts from me. A somber silence weighed heavily on each of us, each wondering what Tsali would decide.

"Perhaps a month passed, before Two-Turtles returned again. When he did, we found out what became of Tsali."

NOTES

[1] Blue pollen was made from the blue lark's claw plant and used to keep bees from stinging (Mooney, 1891, 1900/1992).
[2] This story comes from Ehle (1988).
[3] The story of Charles Reese's conversion in relation to his three wives is described in McLoughlin (1984, p. 205).
[4] Tsali's story can be found in several sources (see Ehle, 1988; Finger, 1984; Mooney, 1891, 1900/1992).

TSALI'S ANSWER

Recalling the Events of the Autumn of 1838

"In late August or perhaps it was early September," my mother began. "Two-Turtles returned again and relayed the fate of Tsali and his sons." Even the word, *sons,* triggered a sickening feeling in the pit of my stomach, my son, Willie, was no longer. I gripped my sides. My mother continued.

"Tsali told his sons, *I've decided to surrender, alone. I want you to stay here in the mountains and hide in the caves.* Each son, one after the other swore allegiance to his father, *I won't let you go alone. I'll stand beside you.* Even the youngest, who hadn't attacked the soldiers to protect his mother, pledged loyalty. Tsali begged his sons; *No, you must remain free. The soldiers may be lying,* he cautioned them, *It could be a trap. I should go alone.* But again his sons promised that, *If it's a trap, then we'll go to the stockade with you, together, as a family.*

"At daybreak, Tsali and his sons began their journey to the fort. Four Cherokee runners spotted them and quickly accosted them. Tsali told the runners that they were on their way to surrender. The runners flanked the group and escorted Tsali and his renegade sons toward the fort. Before reaching the Cherokee Agency, soldiers arrived on horseback.

"The soldiers' issued commands in English. Tsali understood none of it, as he spoke no English. Only the runners understood both. One soldier gave a command and several soldiers dismounted. They shoved Tsali and his sons into a tight group. An officer shouted another command. In response, a soldier grabbed the youngest of Tsali's sons and pushed him away from his father and older brothers. He fell to the ground. Another soldier grabbed him by the shirt and then held him back from his father and brothers. Taking a rifle from his saddlebag, one soldier forced it into the hands of one of the runners, *Shoot them,* he commanded. The Cherokee runner stood frozen by the thought of it. Soldiers thrust rifles into the hands of the other three runners and pushed them forward, until all four faced Tsali and his two older sons. Four additional soldiers dismounted their steeds and drew their rifles. Each soldier pushed the barrel of his rifle against the head of one of the Tsaragi runners. *Shoot them, or we'll shoot you,* came the command. The runners were terrified; their eyes bulged with fear.

"*Now!* The command crashed against their ears.

"The soldiers cocked their guns. The runners felt the hard, cold steel of the musket barrel against their skulls. Tsali suddenly understood what was happening. He cried out, but his words couldn't be heard over the commander.

"*SHOOT!* the commander yelled.

"The Tsaragi runners cocked their rifles.

"*DO IT! SHOOT THEM OR WE WILL SHOOT YOU!*

"The commander cocked his pistol. *NOW! h*e yelled as he fired a shot.

"The blasts split the air! Blood flew forward! Like thunder in a valley, the booming gunshots rocked the mountain cliffs and carried away the screams that came from father and sons. The youngest boy threw his hands over his face. He tried to cover his ears and his eyes at the same time. It was too late. He saw it all. His father's body dropped to the ground with his brothers' bodies—all slumped into a pile of death. A low, mournful moan rose from the boy's soul and ended in a stinging silence. At long last, a deep gasping noise rose into a wail and the boy cried out for his father as the soldiers dragged him away to the fort.[1]

"The tale was told to Two-Turtles by one of the runners who reported that Tsali's blood had sprayed across his face and blinded his eyes, which were already stinging with tears. He told Two-Turtles to call him, One-Who-Was-Speckled-With-The-Blood-Of-The-Brave, from this day forward.

"After spreading this news to those of us who were hiding in the mountain caves, Two-Turtles left again for the stockade. What he saw next left him with a quiet kind of madness for when he returned to us again, several months later, he couldn't speak."

NOTE

[1] Finger (1984) advanced the notion that the story may not be completely accurate and that Tsali may not have been as heroic as the account leads one to believe. However, most historians place a fair amount of faith in Mooney's heroic account of Tsali (see Mooney, 1975).

THUNDER AND LIGHTNING

Recalling the Winter–Spring of 1839

"Two-Turtles returned in the late winter of 1839. I remember the night that he crouched by the small fire in the center of the cave—his knees drawn up, his arms wrapped around his legs, his form rocking, slowly, back and forth. The warm red blanket slipped from his shoulders. He took no notice. He rocked and stared into the fire with eyes full of emptiness. Your father gathered up the blanket and wrapped it more securely about his friend's shoulders. Two-Turtles continued to stare at the embers. He made no sign that he recognized that your father sat beside him. He didn't speak. He hadn't spoken, not even when he arrived on the fallen crest of winter's cold winds—*Unoluhtana*.

"We'd gone months without word from Two-Turtles or anyone else. Venturing out of the caves, whether to find food or information was a dangerous undertaking. Hundreds of soldiers remained in the mountain region while thousands more carried out the removal. The cave was our only protection. But living in the cave meant that there was no corn, no chickens for eggs, no rations of herbs and vegetables. Your father had sneaked back to our cabin on two occasions and gathered a few necessities, but overall we had very little on which to survive.

"Eking out a meager existence from what we could find during the autumn months, left us with mostly nuts and dried berries to offer Two-Turtles when he returned in the last days of December. The lack of hospitality mattered not to Two-Turtles who took no more than a morsel of food a day. Nor had he spoken since he had returned to us. February turned into March and still Two-Turtles simply sat and rocked by day and slept restlessly by night. Your father marked off the days on the cave wall; I never understood why.

"I found Two-Turtles' silence to be deafening. It spoke of the unspeakable. It reverberated throughout the cave. It echoed. I wanted him to speak; and simultaneously, I feared what he might say. I spoke softly to him, but the tender Tsaragi words that begged him to sip the water died somewhere in the chilly air between us. He didn't seem to hear or see me. He rocked. Back and forth. Slowly. Rhythmically.

"One day, in late March, I placed a cup of brewed herbs near him and then moved away. Moderately encumbered by my latest pregnancy, I leaned forward and checked on the children. Stretching the fur coverlets across them, including you, Silas. I made sure that each of my seven children shared a portion of the blankets. Su'nawa Udsi' slept by the children. I looked appreciatively on my younger sister. She helped in so many ways. She gathered food; she watched the children; and most generously, she cared for Two-Turtles. Su'nawa spoon-fed him; she walked him to the edge of the cave so that he could relieve himself; and, she covered him when he was chilled. I, on the other hand, grew more impatient with his incessant rocking, his deafening silence. Hollow, I thought, the man once inside this shell has disappeared. Where is my uncle, I wondered? Who is this vacant being who rocks and rocks, I asked myself?

"Two-Turtles had carried the story of Tsali's fate to us in the early days of last August. His voice had trembled as he told us the details of Tsali's surrender to the soldiers. Now he knew of something even worse, I thought, but how could anything be worse than what had happened to Tsali. I looked at Two-Turtles, wondering, what has he witnessed this time that has struck him mute?

"My thoughts were interrupted by the distant lightning that seared the evening sky and the crack of thunder that followed like a cannon ball crashing through the sky. Lightning, re-awakened the darkness. Within moments, thunder crashed through the hillsides and rolled up through the valley. Two-Turtles jerked in response.

"*Tsiskwa'gwa!* Two-Turtles cried out.

"We all turned to face Two-Turtles. Lightning turned night into day and thunder rumbled like crashing boulders. Tsiskwa'gwa? Why was he saying my friend's name; I wanted to know.

"*Tsiskwa'gwa,* his tone mournful, pleading.

"I recognized the sound of his voice this time as a cry for someone gone—not lost, but dead. It was a cry to someone who will never answer, no matter how loud one wails or how sincerely one pleads. I heard it in the gasps of air that preceded the mournful lament. I heard it in the tremble of his voice. A knot formed in my stomach. A rock filled my throat. A black bile seemed to close in on me. My saliva tasted like dark thick blood.

"*Tsiskwa'gwa,* he repeated and it echoed in my ears.

"*No,* I declared. I shook my head in disbelief. *Not Tsiskwa'gwa,* but I knew it was too late. I could feel it. Tsiskwa'gwa's death is what had brought the silent madness upon Two-Turtles.

"*No,* I reasserted as if I could change the circumstance. If he didn't say it, maybe it wouldn't be true.

"*No! No! Not Tsiskwa'gwa,* I pleaded, grabbing Two-Turtles about the shoulders.

"*Don't say it, don't say it. Make it not so!* I yelled at him as I shook his shoulders. *Stop it!* I demanded. I hated his vacant stare and his endless rocking and his silence, his deafening, deadly silence. I hated the way he spoke Tsiskwa'gwa's name.

"*Stop it; stop it!* My words crashed against him and then ricocheted throughout the cave. Lightning pierced the night. Thunder pounded the ancient valley and shook the earth. I fell upon Two-Turtles with pounding fists. He didn't defend himself against my words or my flailing arms. The children began to cry. Su'nawa yelled at me; I didn't care. A storm raged inside of me just as surely as the first spring storm raged against the mountains and valleys of my homeland. I pounded my uncle with my fists. I hit his face, his arms, and his chest; until your father pulled me from Two-Turtles and thrust me to the ground.

"I slumped on the other side of the cave. My nostrils flared; my eyes narrowed. At that moment, I held Two-Turtles responsible for whatever had happened to Tsiskwa'gwa. I was mad with grief.

"Two-Turtles, at last, cleared his throat and began to speak."

THE TRAIL OF TEARS

Resurrecting the Trail of Tears 1839

"*I have witnessed sorrow,* Two-Turtles lamented.

"*Following Tsali's execution, I watched the forts where death lived among the people. I watched the people as they were brought in barefoot and nearly naked. They had been stripped of their possessions. The only things they carried into the camps were heavy hearts. The camps held evil ghosts that mingled with the blackness of the people's spirits and brought on much suffering and death. By August, the soldiers were burying six or seven bodies a day at Ross' Landing. The same was true at Gunter's Landing on the Tennassee River as well as at the Cherokee Agency on the Hiwassee. Every fort had Tsaragi bodies to bury. The Tsaragi elders begged the soldiers not to try and move the people across the mountains while they were so sick or during the dying days of summer. It was too hot.*

"*The people couldn't breathe without wheezing from the stinging heat. They couldn't eat without piercing pains clawing at their stomach and intestines. Dysentery. Children wretched and diarrhea was everywhere. [1] They begged to go to water. At last, the soldiers let some of them go to the winding river. So grateful to see Long Man that they cried as they prayed. I followed the people as they went to water. That is how I came upon most of my information about the camps. Hiding in the reeds, I made my way to them and they would give a description, an image of their misery and would beg me one after the other to find Chief Ross. They wanted to know when the suffering would end. Some spoke of their hatred for Kilakeena Elias Boudinot and the Treaty Party. They swore vengeance on Ridge and his son and others who signed the Treaty of New Echota, but most of the people were too weak to focus their energy on hatred or revenge. They either moaned with misery or cried for the dog spirits to come help them fight the disease.*

"I found Tsiskwa'gwa at the river one day. She was not well. Her face was drawn, her cheeks were sunken, her skin was sallow and gray; I almost didn't recognize her. She told me that the Cherokee were too proud to accept the food or clothes that the soldiers brought them in the beginning. Everyone fasted, but the children grew hungry and needed to eat. They cried to their mothers who eventually gave them the bacon and the flour, but the starch made them sick. He shook his head before continuing.

"As I told you earlier, one brave woman demanded corn for her people and Tsiskwa'gwa told me, it was the ghost of Selu herself who came into their camp. The children grew healthier once they had corn to nourish their bodies.[2]But then flies and mosquitoes came. The children grew more distressed. Two-Turtles leaned his head back, looked up at the rough ceiling of the cave, took a breath and continued.

"Tsiskwa'gwa asked if I had seen either of her two daughters? They are both pregnant, she informed me. I lowered my head, and told her, I haven't seen them. Then I asked her, Can't you find them in the camp? She explained, there are hundreds and hundreds of people in the camp and I rarely make it past more than a handful of sick Yunwi'ya without stopping to help or to rest. Plus, we were split up, she told me, adding that many of the mountain Tsaragi have been taken to other forts. I remember that Two-Turtles hesitated and averted his eyes, as he described her condition. *Tsiskwa'gwa raised her arms to stretch as she bathed in the river. Her armpits were covered in flaming red boils. Her arms had shriveled to thin twigs.*

"Tsiskwa'gwa told me that a few Tsaragi feigned conversion to the Christian religion so that they might go to water. The soldiers let new Christians go to the river with the preachers to be baptized, but I would rather live as an inflicted and diseased Tsaragi than a clean and healthy hypocrite, she said. That sounded like my beloved Tsiskwa'gwa.

"Then she asked about you, Two-Turtles shared, looking into my eyes. I breathed deeply. Tears welled in my eyes. I began to cry, softly.

"I told her that you were well-hidden and safe. Tsiskwa'gwa smiled weakly and then left the river so others might have their turn

bathing in the winding waters of the long man. Two-Turtles had paused at this point and for the first time in days, asked for water and wetted his dried, cracked lips.

"*The encampments were mobilized for removal at different times. The Hiwassee encampment was the last to leave. I followed at a distance. Soldiers loaded sick Tsaragi and the elderly onto wagons, a few others rode on horses, but most of the people walked. They passed the word along that a "talk" had been made between General Scott and the Tsaragi leaders. Chief Ross would lead the removal so the people would not be pushed too hard. Ross assigned different leaders to different groups. He took his group as early as possible along a western trail. Bushyhead and O-ga-na-ya and others coordinated the people on the Hiwassee.* I remembered Bushyhead, the Tsaragi man who had become a Christian preacher and gone to jail with us. He'd be kind to the people, I thought. Two-Turtles continued.

"*The people were told that if they tried to escape, the Tsaragi leader of their contingent would be held responsible. It didn't matter to some; a few ran away, anyway. But others wouldn't. Bushyhead talked many of your neighbors into surrendering to the soldiers. All stood firmly opposed to the treaty and the removal, but yielded on behalf of our Chief.*

"*Chief Ross tried to lead his group to the west by water. He tried to get Tsaragi people to ride on boats. But the boats were too big and scared the people and the waters were sometimes rough and the people were afraid because the boats were not like canoes. The water spirits, they said, must not be offended by placing such crushing boats on Long Man's back. They were afraid that serpents would reach up from the water and destroy the boats. Many young men and women ran to the mountains.*

"*Bushyhead's group, the one that Tsiskwa'gwa walked with, was organized last. Grateful that they could avoid traveling in the heat of summer, they left the Cherokee Agency in mid-September. I trailed them.*

"*They traveled less than ten miles a day. Some of the people were allowed to return to their homes and gather some belongings; others were not. Those who had clothing, food, or blankets always shared and often carried heavy packs on their back.* Two-Turtles stopped speaking again. The imagery in his mind wouldn't let the words flow. Eventually he continued, *"Consumed by whooping cough, the children seemed the most fragile and at risk of death. I saw a woman drop her load in order to carry a sick child. The child died in her arms and she carried his limp body throughout the day. She sang a wailing song that sent shivers down my back. When evening arrived a soldier took the boy's lifeless body and tossed it onto the death wagon, which was already piled high with dead Tsaragi children.*

"They buried the dead every three day. It would seem that provisions like food rations and fresh horses were to be supplied at previously designated points, but each time they reached their destination, the food had gone bad or the horses had been returned to the federal government. The meat was covered with fly larvae or worms and no one had sent word that the Tsaragi wanted corn. In desperation, the soldiers went with Tsaragi hunters to try and find deer or elk or wild turkey, but they returned without game. Too many Tsaragi had already been forced along this trail; they had hunted it bare.

"As the days passed, more young people deserted. More elders and more children died. Each day the death chants encircled the people. At every stop they buried more dead. Wagonloads.[3] *The women cried the wailing songs. The children cried. The men cried. Tears fell all along this trail.*[4] *They were on the trail for over seventy days when a mountain storm surprised them. It brought ice and snow during the night. Children shivered without blankets and mothers huddled together and tried to keep the children in the middle. The women became the shelters,* Two-Turtles spoke softly. *Soldiers built fires every few feet to stave off the chill, but it failed to warm the people.*[5]

"I was told later that when Ross's detachment met a similar storm, his followers suffered tremendously. The children were without moccasins and the soldiers didn't have enough blankets. Quatie, Ross's wife, gave her blanket to a child." Two-Turtles fell silent again; we waited.

"*Quatie died from the biting Northern Winds.*"[6] He told us and then his head dropped onto his arms. His black, matted hair hung like a tangled veil over his features. After a while, he slowly lifted his head.

"*Bushyhead's group also met a fierce winter storm,* he paused as if he was reliving the nightmare and couldn't speak again.

"*And?* I prompted him.

"*And,* he spoke at long last with a heavy sigh, *Tsiskwa'gwa*. I breathed deeply, bit my lip and held back the tears as I waited for the final pronouncement of her death.

NOTES

[1] The atrocities that took place within the camps, as well on the trail, are underdeveloped within the pages of this novel. One officer described himself as an "instrument of oppression" (see Nathaniel Smith's letter to General Scott in Ehle, 1988, pp. 342–343). Another soldier later wrote: "I fought through the civil war and have seen men shot to pieces and slaughtered by thousands, but the Cherokee removal was the cruelest work I ever knew" (Mooney, 1975, p. 124). "A deaf Cherokee, who was told to go left, turned right and was shot; people were forced to the stockades barefoot, in some cases, their homes were burned in front of them and women were beaten. An average sick report from one camp listed the following afflictions: Remittent fever, 11; diarrhea, 60; dysentery, 100; wounds, 25; measles, 63; whooping cough, 40; dead 6" (Ehle, 1988, p. 346).

[2] The claim that the Cherokee refused the food and clothes is supported by Ehle (1988). General Scott eventually provided rations of corn (see Ehle, 1988, p. 328).

[3] The Cherokee population at the time of the removal was approximately 16,000. Nearly 13,000 were marched west in the removal. Some estimates suggest that approximately 2,000 Cherokee died in the camps (see Wilkins, 1986). "Over 4,000 Cherokee died as the direct result of the removal," (Mooney, 1891, 1900/1992, p. 133). As John Burnett, U.S.A. Calvary wrote: "Murder is murder and somebody must answer, somebody must explain ... the four thousand silent graves that mark the trail of the Cherokee to their exile" (Ehle, 1988, p. 394).

[4] The Cherokee referred to the removal as "The Trail Where We Cried." It was later called the "Trail of Tears" (Ehle, 1988 and others).

[5] Reports also exist that suggest that soldiers tried to make the journey easier for the Cherokee, but to little avail (Ehle, 1988).

[6] Quatie Ross died of pneumonia near Little Rock (Wilkins, 1986, p. 327).

CHAPTER 31

TSISKWA'GWA

Reliving the end 1839

"*I found Tsiskwa'gwa on the trail,* he spoke softly and slowly. *She lay on the chilly earth, a blanket of snow beneath her body. Her onyx-colored hair spread out across the sharp white of the freshly fallen snow. Her hands, cracked and bleeding, clutched each other in a desperate attempt to keep her fingers warm. Her body trembled and her eyes stared forward.*

"*I held her in my arms and tried to breathe my warm breath onto her blue fingers,* his voice cracked. I gasped a small breath and tears rolled down my cheeks as I listened to him describe the awful scene.

"*She spoke to me before she died, saying the elders believe, we will recover from this, if not in seven years, then in seven generations.*[1] He took a deep breath and swallowed hard. *She said, we will return to the homeland. Great Buzzard will see to that.* Two-Turtles tore at his hair and then in a great sobbing wail he cried out her name. "*Tsiskwa'gwa! Tsiskwa'gwa! I should have rescued her the day the soldiers came to take her away,* he sobbed. We let him grieve. After a time, he composed himself with a deep breath and spoke again.

"*I watched as the soldiers placed the frigid lifeless form onto the death wagon. Tsiskwa'gwa's body lay next to that of a younger woman whose belly was swollen with child. The body was twisted; the face turned away from Tsiskwa'gwa's face, but as the wagon veered toward the west, I saw that it was one of Tsiskwa'gwa's daughters that lay beside her. The daughter's eyes held frozen tears.*

NOTE

[1] Stories vary as to the promise of recovery in seven generations.

205

BLOODY COVE

Recalling a Desperate Day and Night in the Spring of 1839

"Branches flicked across my face, slapping at my skin as I made my way down the slippery trail. My salty tears mixed with the sleet, one washing the other away, over and over again. My belly ached and my heart pounded as I ran awkwardly through the darkening forest. Hobbling from my ankle injury and cupping my forearm under my swollen breasts to support them. When I reached the bottom of the hill, I cradled my unborn baby by holding my protruding abdomen," my mother said. She was speaking more into the air than to me directly. The history was personal; the grief only now being shared. She continued her story as I sat lifeless by Willie's grave.

"I had wanted to be able to reach over to Two-Turtles and say, *Ayago li ga - Ehi s ti yu uda nv ta*—I understand the pain you feel, but I couldn't. Instead, I hated him. I hated him for bringing me the news of Tsiskwa'gwa's death. Of all the deaths. The end of the Nation. I ran from the cave despite the rains, despite the darkness. I didn't care that lightning flashed and thunder shouted angrily at me. I screamed right back.

"I ran with a limper's gait through the forest. Catching myself as I moved from tree to tree, from sapling to sapling, I refused to stand still. Tears rolled down my face. Rain washed them away. I slid in the slippery mud, regained my footing, and kept on going. Gusting bellows of wind raked through my hair and tangled it this way and that way. I couldn't see where I was anymore when suddenly my abdomen tightened like an iron cannon ball. I couldn't walk. The tightening seemed interminable. At last it released its grip. I took a few steps down the ravine; when suddenly, my ankle gave way. I slipped to the ground and slid deeper into the ravine, stones and mud flew like winged vermin. Stopping at last, I turned to get up again, but was seized with birthing pains; they came with great force. Like the claws and teeth of the cougar ripping me open, the contractions gnawed and slashed.

"Pain consumed me. Contractions came too close, one upon another. I couldn't breathe. I couldn't think. I only knew it was too early for this baby to come, but it was upon me. I could feel the infant's head pressing against me like a knife piercing me. Pushing with a force beyond my control, the pains raged against me. On all fours, I shoved my skirt upward, came up on my knees, arched my back, and let out a cry that echoed throughout the valley.

"A hot breath seared through my lungs. My body still frantic with almost constant birth spasms arched and twisted. I seethed and fell forward onto my hands and knees, the rain pelted at me. I gasped for air and then a second ripping and gripping push that caused my muscles to tighten and flare. Again the cry of birth and death intermingled and echoed throughout the mountains and valleys. I screamed with the force of the winds. The lightning lit the scene to reveal the baby's head. Thunder muffled my cries. The infant's shoulders twisted outward. I cried out again. Only the thunder answered me and only the rains met my face. There was no medicine woman to help me. There was no Tsiskwa'gwa to sing the birthing song. I wailed against the injustice; I cried for my loss. And then the last wrenching pain forced the infant girl out of me; she lay between my legs.

"I bit the cord, reached inside of me, and wrenched the after birth from inside with a final agonizing moan. Then I collapsed by the side of my infant. The child lay still. Rain fell on us.

"Eventually, I opened my eyes and reached out my hand slowly toward the infant. I touched the fingers, still curled into the palm. I longed to feel the baby wrap its fingers around mine, but the baby's hand fell limp.

"Rolling quickly to my side, I took my baby. I pressed the child to my heart.

"*No!* I screamed against the wind, against the thunder, against the lightning. *Not my baby, too.*

"I fell backward. I slid the infant upward and pressed her to my breast. Still, she lay lifeless. *Not my baby,* I whispered. A flash of lightning revealed a hollow on the mountainside. I dragged myself with the infant in my arm to the nook. There I nestled into the cove. Moments later, I lifted her head and looked down at the child who lay lifeless at my side.

"The rain pelted down around us; a river of blood streamed from between my legs. I kissed the baby tenderly before I lost consciousness."

SHE BELONGS TO THE MOUNTAINS

Remembering the Events of 1839

"Your father found me nestled in the alcove with the stillborn baby cradled to my breast. He tried to remove the infant from my arms; I struggled to keep the baby. Your father took my face in his hands forcing me to look directly into his eyes.

"*She's dead, Sallie. This baby is a child of the mountains,* he told me what I already knew. *Let me bury her here,* he said to me. Tears flooded down my cheeks as I gave up that baby.

"*I wanted to name her for Tsiskwa'gwa,* I gasped a breath to fight back more tears.

"Your father nodded as he took the listless form and left my side. But in a moment, I chose to follow him. He walked along the mud soaked trail until he found a sage bush and knelt beside it. Setting the stillborn infant under the bush, he began to dig with his fingers. The soft ground gave way to his digging. It was almost too soft. The wet damp earth surrendered its hold to your father willingly in large handfuls of wet earth. The mud walls that formed around the hole that he dug collapsed again and again. He tried to make some of the dirt stay in place by bracing it with twigs, but it was of no avail as the rain continued to fall.

"Your father unfastened his shirt, pulled it over his head and wrapped it around the baby, completely. Her face covered. Her tiny body concealed in the cotton folds. He laid her gently in the mud hole. Then he scooped up soil and placed it on the lifeless form. He patted the mud solidly over the baby and around her as if he were planting a seed. Then he covered the burial mound with brush and placed rocks on top so that the grave wouldn't wash away in the storm. He knelt by the side of the site. The rain diminished to a soft sprinkle. *It's a tiny grave*, he said solemnly, *a very tiny grave. A snowbird has fallen,* he whispered, *and with it the Great Eagle.*

"Distant lightning sprayed across the dark sky. Thunder crashed far away. Your father looked to the heavens. He shook his head with grief and then spoke in Cherokee, *U danh ti - u no le hi.* I didn't know that he knew this expression. *U danh ti -u no le hi, tsiskwa udsi - gentle winds, little bird.*

"Following this simple funeral, he took me into his arms and carried me as far as Pigeon River before stopping. There he laid me down to rest. Somewhere along the trail the rains had stopped. We slept through the night and much of the next morning. But when he awoke, he found that I was sick with a fever. He ripped the hem of my dress and soaked it in the cool stream; he laid it on my forehead, but the cool rag neither broke the fever nor brought much sanity to my words. Your father picked me up again in his arms. He set me down only to discover that he was covered in blood. It poured from between my legs. I tried to say something, but couldn't speak. As quickly as he could, he gathered me up again and with determination made his way for the cave."

BLOOD LAW

Remembering Mid-Summer 1839

"We have both buried a baby in these mountains," my mother concluded, as we kept watch over Willie's grave. We felt each other's loss. Eventually, she continued her story.

"I was sick for a very long time and your father and Su'nuwa' feared that I would die. But one day, you, Silas Jr. approached your father, climbed into his lap, stared at him with your sharp blue eyes and asked, *Will my mother sleep forever?*

"*No, I hope not,* your father told you. *I hope she'll awaken soon.* I heard your question; your voice awakened me. You were around Willie's age." My mother's voice rang with sweet longing. "And so I returned to the land of the living and left my dreams behind me.

"Each day after that, I grew stronger. The rains lifted and Su'nawa took you children to play at the river and practice the blowgun. She taught you games of chance and games of stick and ball. She cooked for us and reveled in the progress that I made. I appeared frail and looked much thinner than I ever had, she told me, but my spirit seemed stronger. Eventually, I became strong enough to go for walks with you children and gather roots and berries with Su'nawa.

One day, on our return from such a walk, Su'nawa took you children to the river to meet your father; he was fishing. I went back toward the cave to rest, but as I stepped through the foliage of the low hanging branches along the ridge that led to the cave, I was suddenly accosted by a Cherokee man. He appeared as though he had dropped from *Galunlati*—suddenly, without warning, standing before me.

"*Stay silent*, he commanded. I didn't move.
"*Are you Sallie Reese?*
"*I am.*
"*Cousin of Kilakeena?*

"*Yes.*"

"*O'Siyo.* He then greeted me, as he should have when he first encountered me.

"*O'Siyo*, I returned.

"*Are you also the friend of Tsi'skwagwa?*

"I *am,* I told him.

"*I am Tsi'skwagwa's son,* he announced, looking into my eyes. *Are you aware that my mother traveled to the ghost land?*

"I *am,* I lowered my voice and my head. *U danh ti – u no le hi –Gentle winds, tsogali—friend.*

"*There are no gentle winds for my mother or for anyone else among the Cherokee,* her son told me. *There is only bitter root to feed on.* I nodded.

"*Are you aware that Quatie is also dead?* he asked me.

"*The Chief's wife. Yes.*"

"And Nannye-hi?" he added. My eyes widened. *The remaining members of the Bird Clan have sent me to tell you that you have been named the Beloved Woman for the Bird Clan of the East. You will take my mother's place.* His words came with finality. Just the same, I shook my head.

"*No, I …* I refused the honor. I fumbled for the words; he stared at me, waiting. *I've never demonstrated the bravery of Nanny-hi nor Tsi'skwagwa. I cannot accept this title.*

"*The Chief said to tell you that this is not something that one chooses. This is something that one becomes.*

"*But there are others, older, wiser,* I offered. He ignored my comment.

"*The people are no longer united. Only the justice of revenge can restore balance and harmony. And only the Clan Mothers, the Beloved Women, can make the decision as to whether Blood Law shall be enforced.*

"*What?No.* I resisted as I began to understand him.

"*Chief Ross refuses to make the decision to execute or not to execute your cousin, Kilakeena and his uncle, Ridge and Kilakeena's cousin, Scaleeloskee John Ridge.*

"*Why does the Chief refuse this burden?* I asked. *It's his responsibility,* I added.

"*There are several reasons,* he skirted the issue.

"*I want to know them,* I demanded.

"*I may only know part of the story,*" he dodged.

"*Tell me what you do know.*

"*His nephew has been implicated in the Treaty Party.*

"*The Chief's nephew helped Kilakeena?*

"*Yes,* he said with surety.

"*And?*

"*The Chief has been a friend of Ridge's for many years.*

"*Does he think that I have not loved my cousin since I was a child?* My voice filled with disbelief and anger. *He thinks that I should decide Kilakeena's fate?*

"*Your voice won't be alone. There are seven clans.*

"*The clan mothers always speak with one voice,* I corrected him.

"*Not this time. The Chief says that each clan mother may send her decision.*

"*And then what?*

"*And then we will act in accordance.* I turned away from him; I had to absorb all that he had put before me. I walked the path; I paced. He watched in silence, waiting stoically for my decision.

"Memories of Kilakeena surged through my mind. I pictured how we swam together as children, in the river. How we ran together at festivals. I remembered him finding me in the caves and placing his arm around me, protecting me once long ago, when Andrew Jackson's men terrorized us. I thought of the day that he announced his conversion and told us his new name—Elias Boudinot. I recalled his return to the people at a later festival, when he described the missionaries as hypocrites and the white people liars because they didn't want him to marry Harriet Gold. And I remembered him turning away from our ways again, coaxed by Reverend Worcester. I pictured his sermonizing before the people, telling us to be more like the white people. I pictured in my mind's eye, his hand with feathered pen flowing across the final page of the Treaty of New Echota, signing away our land, our lives.

"I turned to face the young man, who stood waiting for my decision, and as I did I saw his resemblance to Tsi'skwagwa. The woman who had mentored me in the *asi* since the time I was twelve.

The woman who had caught my firstborn baby within her own strong hands. The woman who had taught me the secrets of herbal medicines and who had helped me become a woman.

"If I choose to enforce Blood Law, then Kilakeena will be executed. The Chief's sentiments were clear—a Beloved Woman isn't something that you choose; it's something that chooses you.

"At long last, I gave my decision. He nodded and then disappeared as quickly as he had come upon me. I went into the cave, where I fell into a deep sleep.

"Much later, your father woke me.

"*It's time to leave the cave,* he pronounced. I returned from my fitful dreams to a fitful reality and looked into my husband's eyes. He repeated his words, *It's time to leave the cave.* I nodded.

"*The children are waiting.* I looked to the mouth of the cave. I saw my children and Su'nuwa. Your father gathered the last of our things. He had his back to me, but I noticed him putting a turtle shell into his bag.

"*Where is Two-Turtles?* I asked. I had been so angry at him that I hadn't asked about my uncle.

"Your father looked away for a moment. He gathered his words carefully before speaking.

"*Two-Turtles is gone.*

"*Gone where?* I asked. A silence filled the air. When he had finished his packing he turned to me and spoke.

"*I found two turtle shells discarded in the mud outside of the cave.* He blames me, I thought.

"*I need to search for my family.* Your father nodded.

"*We will,* he promised. *We will.*

"*I want to go home,* I told him. He nodded again.

"I remember how your father crouched under the low ceiling of the cave and reached out a hand to me. I gathered up my blanket, wrapping all that had been around me. I followed your father out of the cave and never looked back."

THE SEVENTH GENERATION

Remembering Coming out of the Caves in 1839

"We traveled toward a western village. When we came within view, your father made us stand back in the camouflage of the forest, fearing that squatters would be waiting or worse yet, soldiers.

"*Wait here,* he had instructed.

"After watching from a distance for a while, he waved us down to join him. This village, unlike many others, which had been ransacked or taken over by white families, remained eerily unscathed. We stepped lightly through the dark lodge house where masks still hung from the poles. We walked carefully through the small *asi* where rocks remained in the center of the cold fire pit. You children followed cautiously as we adults moved through the sweat lodge where pallets sat along the sides of the walls and supported spiders' webs. We walked through our friends' homes, where dusty furs and blankets waited on the beds for the owners to return. We took note of the homes where gourds sat half-filled with parched corn, as if even the squirrels wouldn't disturb this scene. I raised a child's ball stick from its place on the ground outside one home. I stopped, looked at it, and replaced it. Somehow it felt wrong to disturb this place. I moved on, limping, without a word, until I stood in the center of the village and experienced the emptiness of it all.

"Your father joined me. He watched as I slowly scanned the village from east to south to west to north to east again. I turned in a full circle taking in the expanse of eerie silence—the interrupted lives, the absence of laughter, the abandoned existence, the village that stood like an empty shell.[1]

"*Here lives a silence that will echo for generations,* I reflected. Su'nawa heard my comment; she answered me.

"*Let the echo reach the seventh generation.*"[2]

"This is a sacred place," I told you children. *"If you listen with a good heart and a good mind, then you'll hear the ancestors' voices carried on the wind. Perhaps, one day, when you're older, I'll tell you their story, but for now, let us listen to the wind."*

"As hemlock pines gently swayed, you children listened to the wind; you listened to the voices of the ancestors; and, you heard the silence."

NOTES

[1] Silas Sr. and Sallie "lived mostly in abandoned Indian villages" (Shackelford Sims, 1978). They moved frequently. Their young son, Silas Jr., who later wrote his memoirs, recalled that, "At the first of my recollection we were living in the midst of a thick settlement of Cherokee Indians. I don't remember ever seeing a white man except one uncle. I never knew my father to live more than one year at a time in the same place except once where he stayed three years ... When we lived at that place, there were four families living almost in sight of us, namely: Nickojack, Davey, Thompson, and Sunday ... I well remember nineteen places that we lived at up to the time that I was twenty-one years of age" (Silas Beasley Jr., 1909, as cited in Shackelford Sims, 1978).

[2] All major decisions should be made with the seventh generation in mind, meaning that self-centered, short-sighted decisions that don't take into account how the results will affect future generations are capricious at best, and dangerous at worst. This rule of thumb is especially appropriate in ecological terms.

A BELOVED WOMAN IS BORN

December 22, 1865

I had told my mother of the dark decision that I had made when I had come upon the confederate soldier dying from wounds sustained by wolves; and now, she had told me of how she had made a dark decision concerning her cousin Kilakeena.

I knew my decision to shoot the officer was in the past, it couldn't be changed. But burying his body might bring me some solace. So, I helped my mother back to the cabin and planned to make preparations to dig another grave. Yet, when I returned to the cabin there were tasks to be done and a discovery made.

"What were those shots?" William asked.

"Nothing."

"It didn't sound like nothing. It sounded like two shots. And where have you been?"

"William, not now," I stopped him. As I turned from the fire to face him, I also glanced about the cabin. Something wasn't right. I looked at the sleeping forms again, quickly assessing where each had been. An empty space existed next to Julia where there should've been a sleeping figure.

"Nan. Where's Nan?" I asked. No one answered me.

"William, where is Nan?" I demanded. My mother awoke and lifted herself up on one arm. She glanced about and looked to me.

"William!"

"I don't know," he coughed phlegm and sniffled mucus.

I ran out of the cabin, stood on the front porch searching the woods. I saw no one. I circled round to the back, still no sight of her. Then I saw footprints. I followed the tracks that lead to the river.

"Nan," I yelled, but no one answered. I raced faster, my worry mounting with each step. Trees flew past my vision; I swung low branches out of my way. Snow fell more fiercely. Specks of white hit my face. I slid part way down the path, pebbles giving way under my feet. At last, I saw her, crouched by the river's edge. I slowed my pace.

"Oh, Nan," I whispered under my breath, relieved to see her. She couldn't have heard me from the distance at which we stood. Nevertheless, she stood and turned to face me. When she saw me, she smiled and then mouthed my name. "Silas." Then something stole her attention away from me. She turned to look toward the ledge above her. Her expression turned to one of terror. My eyes followed her gaze.

"Oh, God!" I flipped my rifle to take aim. The gray wolf snarled its sharp incisors at Nan. I steadied my arm and held my breath. Then I squeezed the trigger.

Click.

Click, click. It failed to shoot. I threw my rifle aside and ran for my sister. Her arms came up defensively, protecting her face from a wolf that leapt toward her. I witnessed this as a moment taken out of time—frozen among the snowflakes that fell about her and the wolf. I ran faster toward her. I refused to let her die. Faster! As if I suddenly had the power to fly, I leapt into the air as the wolf leaped down upon her. The three of us fell to the ground in a loud, crashing commotion. Time whirled ahead, as we rolled into the river. The stinging icy waters covered my head. I reached to the floor of the riverbed to push off and stand. I slipped. I regained my footing and stood in the water. Knee-deep, the wolf came at me, undeterred. I lost my balance, slipped and regained my footing. I saw for just a second, the wolf in all its glory stretched on hind legs; it stood nearly as tall as a man. His underbelly looked lean and raw with hunger. His teeth gleamed. In another second the wolf's body soared. He lunged and took hold of my arm. Sharp teeth ripped easily through my shirt and his brute strength hurled me around.

I struggled to unsheathe my knife at my side. The wolf slammed me into the waters below. Releasing his grip on my arm, so that he could feed on my stomach or grind his teeth into my neck, he backed away only a step, in order to make his assault. Then suddenly he was pushed into the water. Nan was on his back. He turned with a snap. She screamed.

I plunged my knife into his back. He yelped and turned on me with insane desperation. He would not be kept from this meal. He stood again and threw his body forward taking both of us toward the middle of the river. I lost hold of my knife. A current caught us grappling; I jammed my arm under his chin staving off his ferocious teeth. The waters swept us along. Banging against rocks and gulping swirling water, we gripped each other. Afraid to let go, I held tight to his fur and kept my arm forced up against his throat, until we hit the embankment on the other side of the river.

There he released me, but only in order to make a stronger stance. He came at me while I was scrambling up the embankment. This time, I used my left arm against his throat and reached with my right to rip his eye from its socket. I caught only the corner of his eye. He howled in pain; released me, only to leap again before I could scamper away. I threw my bloody arm up and lodged my knuckles into his throat. Coming down hard on me, he refused to die. My arm buckled.

The weight of him nearly knocked the wind from my lungs. My back crushed, my arm bleeding badly. My strength abated, I feared I wouldn't outlast him. And then the moment came. I no longer feared that I wouldn't outlast him; I now knew that I couldn't outlast him. An acceptance of death came over me, perhaps not with as much bravery as the confederate officer, but acceptance nonetheless. The feeling of inevitability filled with peace. I nearly relaxed my arm that still locked his ferocious teeth away from me.

"Silas!" I heard my name. Then just as it had come upon me, the feeling passed over me, like an eagle soaring on currents of wind. I tightened my fist to fight again. Simultaneously, the wolf arched his body and howled a screeching scream, falling sideways with a tremendous thud.

I looked up to see Nan pull my knife from the back of the wolf's neck and then plunge it in again, this time, piercing the under belly of the beast. The animal screeched. The blood sprayed forward. She dislodged the knife again, and plunged it in once more. Then I heard a slow gurgling noise. She raised the blade above her head and brought it down again. The blood that had coursed through his veins flowed down the front of him as he lay on the embankment.

Nan fell to her side, exhausted. She had swum the river's current to me, managed the embankment, and hurled herself at the wolf. I will never know how she managed to extract my knife from the beast under such circumstances, but she had, and she had delivered the deathblow before collapsing in the snow. We each lay there, our hearts racing, our breath coming in great giant heaves, listening to the animal between us take its last breaths, while we took contrasting breaths of life and relief.

Eventually, she sighed. As did I.

"Next time, perhaps, ...," she panted the words between breaths, "you could warn me that there are wolves in the area or that it's not the best time to go to water."

I laughed, gulped another breath of air, and laughed again. We continued to catch our breath.

"Remember?" she asked and took another deep breath.

"Remember when we were kids and we used to swim together, brothers and sister, friends and cousins? Back when we were 'Indians,'" she added playfully.

"We're still Indians, Nan, especially you."

"You think so?"

"Without a doubt. As brave as any Warrior Woman, as smart and clever as any Beloved Woman."

"*Wado*," she thanked me. We lay there letting the snowflakes fall on us for a while.

"I don't think I can stand," she finally admitted.

"I'm not surprised," I told her as I raised myself up. "Here," I reached out my hand to her. Then turning around, I squatted low. She climbed onto my back and I carried her along the riverbank.

"So, you wanted to go for a swim?" I teased her.

"Actually, I wanted to *go to water*. I wanted to pray. I thought it might cure me."

"Or kill you."

She laughed at my statement, adding, "Yes, there's that."

When we reached the shallow area, I forded the river and returned to the spot where my rifle lay discarded. I picked it up without putting her down.

"What happened?" she asked.

"I forgot to reload."

"That's not like you."

"No, it's not," I saw the brave Confederate, bloody and dying, in my mind's eye. A man whose body, now, would surely not receive a grave. After we made our way back and into the cabin, I set Nan in front of the fire.

"Here," she handed my knife to me. I put it on the table. I helped her remove her wet clothes and hung them from a hook on the mantel. I dressed her in one of my father's old shirts from the bag that I had found in the buckboard and put her to rest on the floor again. Then I stripped off my wet powder bag, my soaked leather sheath and shirt and pants and found clothing for myself. Redressed, I scavenged through William's things to find dry powder and minié balls.

"Is she all right?" William asked gripping my sleeve as my hand rummaged through his haversack.

"She'll be fine."

"I'm sorry, Silas," he said taking responsibility for Nan's departure and his own oversight.

"I know," I acknowledged. He released me. I made my way to the other side of the cabin.

"Silas," my mother beckoned. I went to her side and leaned down. "You're a good son," she whispered, noticing the blood that fell from my torn sleeve. I nodded.

"Help me up," she added. I did. She made her way to the door. "I want to sit outside." She unlatched the door. As it opened I could see that the snow had stopped.

"Come along," she said to me.

"Mama, I'm tired."

"I know," she told me. "Come along anyway." Her words beckoned; I countered.

"Mama, there are wolves out tonight."

"Then you best bring your rifle," she concluded, as she stepped out the door.

I followed her.

PART 3

THE FINAL BATTLE

CHAPTER 37

SEVEN BOYS

The Night of December 22, 1865

I followed my mother. My rifle, reloaded and ready, at my side. She walked in her usual scuffling style from the porch, down the steps and toward the buckboard, carrying two blankets in her arms. Her long calico skirt swished unevenly with her awkward gait. Her hair fell loose from its knot at the nape of her neck and looked both thick and coarse, but I had stroked it once as a child and could still recall its silky feeling. Now, the tangled raven and snowy tresses matched the bare tree branches that interlaced each other in the winter woods that surrounded us. I thought, she is the forest. My mother.

Standing at the wagon's side, she let the blankets drop to the ground by the buckboard and then she reached into the back. As a petite woman, her first attempt to retrieve whatever it was that she was after failed. She stretched again feeling bundles, but not what she wanted. Then she stepped up higher on the wagon wheel and peered into the back. Bending over the side, her waist pressed against the buckboard railing. Balancing at the waist, she moved bags and bundles, rearranging containers and baskets, until she came upon her medicine bag.

"There," she said as she climbed down off the wagon wheel. "Now, let me see your arm." I held out my arm. She turned it palm up and then over again.

"Puncture wounds can be dangerous. Bobcat or wolf?" she asked.

"Wolf," I told her. She nodded.

"Different medicines for each," she added letting my arm go. "Get me two more blankets and a lit ember from the fire or hot stick. I didn't like the sound of that, but I went back into the cabin, gathered two more blankets and selected a slender branch from the dried wood and put its tip into the fire. In time, it blazed on the end and I carried it with the collection of blankets outside.

My mother no longer stood by the wagon. I looked around and found her near Willie's grave. She had placed one blanket on the hillside and wrapped the other one around her shoulders. I hesitated.

"Join me," she said, patting the ground next to her. I placed both blankets on the one that she had already spread out, but I didn't sit down. I glanced quickly at Willie's grave and then down at the ground. I poked the branch into the ground and twisted it to secure it, with the lit end up, like a miniature torch.

"You need to finish saying good-bye to Willie." I wavered, feeling that I never want to let go of Willie. An aching in my stomach followed. I swallowed hard. She waited without further word. Eventually, I crossed one foot in front of the other and lowered myself, Cherokee-style.

My mother spread several pouches in front of her, saying, "Puncture wounds. Did it bleed much in the beginning?

I shrugged my shoulders. It wasn't important, I thought. It didn't compare to losing one's life, like Willie, or like the Confederate officer who was mangled by the wolf. My mother must have agreed. She let the question go.

Although she selected a pouch on her right and sprinkled a dry powder on my arm with great care, she dismissed serious concern, "This is nothing but a frog that has passed by and put into you." I nodded. Then she sang:

Dunu'wa, dunu'wa, dunu'wa, dunu'wa, dunu'wa, dunu'wa, dunu'wa
Sge! Ha-Wala'si-gwu tsu lu taniga
Dunu'wa, dunu'wa, dunu'wa, dunu'wa, dunu'wa, dunu'wa, dunu'wa
Sge! Ha-Wala'si-gwu tsu lu taniga
A'hawi Akata!

She took snow from the ground and rubbed it over my wound. After cleansing it, she dried it with the hem of her skirt. Taking a second pouch she sprinkled its substance, which smelled like tobacco, and then spit on my arm. She rubbed the tobacco juice in circles, four times on each of the puncture wounds before reaching for another pouch.

"*Utistugi*," she informed me as she poured this substance into her free hand. Then she mixed the snow and powder forming a paste, which she plastered onto my arm. The crushed herb made a healing poultice. "There," she noted completing her ritual.[1]

"And the fire?" I asked nodding toward the branch, steadying myself for the burn.

"Oh, yes," she spoke as if she'd almost forgotten something. My mother stood up, took the branch, and looked at me. I held out my arm and turned my face away. Nothing happened. I waited. Still nothing. I opened my eyes and turned to see my mother bending over a pile of brush that sat between Willie's grave and us. Placing the hot tip into the leaves, she started a fire. I laughed at myself. She smiled. "Now we sit and wait for Willie's spirit to cross to the seventh height and then onto the land in the West. Like Selu, when her sons murdered her. She traveled through the night sky and made her home on Brother Moon, some nights you can see Selu's face on the Moon. She is looking down on us. Willie will look down on us tonight if we keep a good vigil. We mustn't betray his love." I nodded. At that moment, I thought I should have had my mother cure Willie. Why had I asked for a doctor? My mother knew all the medicines; she'd been trained by Tsiskwa'gwa and as if she could hear my thoughts, she informed me that, "We have no cure for small pox or for measles."

The word measles, triggered a thought of my father. I heard again in my mind the stories that he told me before he died. All the stories that had unfolded over such a short time; each one answering specific questions and yet each one giving rise to new questions. I realized then how much I had learned and how much more I needed in order to fully understand.

Now, I knew how my mother's cousin had betrayed her and how she had come to walk with a limp. I lay that blame on myself; my mother lay that blame on Kilakeena; and I suspect that if my father had had the time to tell me, he would have laid that blame at the feet of Andrew Jackson. I also understood why we moved from one abandoned village to another. At least I knew my mother's truth. She searched for her family and friends, her homeland. My father's reasons may have been different. Perhaps, he was an opportunist. Perhaps, not.

Tonight, it didn't matter. Tonight, we focused on sending Willie's soul to heaven. Darkness enveloped us. I stared up at the stars.

"I buried Papa as well," I said at last.

"I know," my mother acknowledged softly, nodding. We sat quietly for a while before she raised her hand and pointed to a constellation.

"Do you see that one? The Seven Boys?" she asked, turning to look and see if I was looking in the right direction. This time I responded by nodding.

"Your father loved the story of the Seven Boys," she smiled wistfully. "Did he ever tell you this story?"

"I don't think so," I lied, acting as if I couldn't recall. He had told me the story, *Seven Boys*, I liked it as much as he did. I sat thinking about all the times he used to sit on a front porch and parcel out stories, the same way he'd hand out apple slices from the edge of his knife. I wasn't ready to return to the cabin. For obvious reasons, I couldn't bear the thought of looking upon Julia with only two babes sleeping by her side. I let my mother tell me about seven boys. And so she began:

"Long ago there were seven boys who loved to play the *gatayu'sti* game, which involved rolling a stone wheel along the ground and sliding a curved stick after it to strike it. They spent all their time playing this game by the townhouse. These boys were so absorbed in their playing that they neglected to help their mothers in the cornfield. Their mothers scolded them, but they wouldn't listen. So one day the mothers thought of a plan to teach their boys a lesson. They collected some *gatayu'sti* stones and put them in a pot of boiling water. They sprinkled in a bit of corn and let the soup cook. When the boys returned home because they were hungry, the mothers ladled out the stone soup, saying here is your dinner since you prefer *gatayu'sti* instead of work.

"The boys grew angry and gathered at the townhouse to discuss their displeasure over this stone-soup dinner. They agreed that if this is the way their mothers would treat them, then they'd go where they'd never be trouble to their mothers again. And so they began to dance, a magical dance. Round and round the townhouse, they went, praying to the spirits as they danced.

They were gone so long that their mothers began to worry and went in search of their sons; but, by the time they arrived at the townhouse it was too late. The mothers saw their boys dancing, but their feet were off the ground and they were quickly rising into the evening sky. The mothers ran to get their children, desperately reaching into the air, but the boys were up too high. The mothers couldn't reach their sons, except for one mother. This one mother quickly grabbed a *gatayu 'sti* stick and strained in an attempt to catch hold of her son and bring him back to earth. She pulled him downward with such force that the boy struck the earth and was sucked underground. The other six boys circled higher and higher into the night sky where they became the constellation you see now. We call this group of stars, *Ani 'tsutsa*, The Boys.

"It is easiest to spot in the wintertime, on a cold, clear night like tonight." She stretched and turned her head upward, before speaking again.

"The people of the village grieved for a very long time. The mothers felt their stone-soup punishment had been too harsh. And the mother, whose son went down under the earth, returned to the spot by the townhouse every day, where she cried tears that fell on the earth that had swallowed her son. Eventually, a green shoot sprang from the ground. It grew taller and taller each day until at last it developed into an elegant pine tree, made of the same nature as the stars and it holds within itself the same bright light,"[2] she finished and turned to look at me.

"I wish that I could pull them back to us—both your father and Willie. Like the mother in the story, I would strain with all my might, but I would be careful." I nodded. We slipped into silence again. My thoughts drifted toward Willie and my father.

I never would've been cross with Willie, just like my mother has never been harsh with me. This reminded of something my father had told me, that the first time he visited a Cherokee festival a very strange scene had surprised him. He had been walking about taking in the uniqueness of the festival: Cherokee traders, both men and women, dressed in colorful clothing exchanged peacock feathers for turtle shells, iron pots for fox fur or deer pelts. Cherokee men, sitting cross-legged on woolen blankets, gambled in games of chance. Cherokee women in calico dresses stirred pots filled with rabbit and corn stew.

231

His head was turned; he wasn't watching where he was going when a voice yelled out.

Tsundige wi! My father looked up bewildered, but quickly discovered he had almost walked into a woman with wild eyes and matted, black hair. He stopped abruptly.

Tsundige wi! she yelled again. He didn't understand, but suddenly realized that the woman was tied to a stake, her hands bound behind her back. She yelled her taunt once more. Helpless to understand her words, my father looked to Two-Turtles, he had told me. His friend pointed behind them. My father turned to see that she wasn't yelling at him, but at the man behind him, who was also tied to a post.

Tskili! The man yelled back at the woman. Then my father saw that between the two posts sat a kindly grandmother who shook her head at the arguing couple as she watched a small child play with stones in the dirt.[3]

Perplexed, my father had turned to Two-Turtles, who explained:

If a child takes even one step onto scared ground during a festival because the parents are not watching closely, then it is the parents who are punished by being tied to posts for one night.

But it's the child who must learn a lesson, my father had disagreed.

Cherokee believe that children are innocent and should never be punished.

I miss Willie, I thought as I remembered the story. I would gladly be tied to a post to have Willie back. And I should have told him that the doctor was wrong about monkeys. *Monkeys are wherever you want them to be, Willie, even in Tennessee.* I held back tears.

"Pine trees," my mother announced pulling me back again to the present moment, to the current place, with her words.

NOTES

[1] This remedy was more widely used for snake bites (Mooney, 1891, 1900/1992).
[2] The story of The Seven Boys is adapted from Mooney (1891, 1900/1992). The Seven Boys is the same constellation that the Greeks named Pleiades.
[3] *Tskili* means witch; *Tsundegi wi'* means closed-anus, closed ears, closed mouth in short, someone who was not paying attention (Mooney, 1891, 1900/1992).

CHAPTER 38

PINE TREES

Midnight Hour of December 22, 1865

"My friend Tsiskwa'gwa was a medicine woman who taught me that plants hold all the medicines. But pine trees are the most promising for unexplained diseases. She told me that long ago the animals became angry with the people who had been acting greedily. Greediness is the worst of all sins," my mother asserted. "Anyway, in the olden days, quadrupeds, birds, fishes and insects could all talk, and they and the human race lived together in peace and friendship. But as time went on, the number of people increased so rapidly that their settlements spread over the whole earth and the poor animals found themselves cramped for space. Adding to their misfortunes, man discovered the usefulness of bows and arrows, knives, blowguns, spears and hooks. Men began to slaughter the larger animals, birds, and fishes for the sake of their flesh and their skins, while the smaller creatures, such as the frogs and worms, were crushed and trodden upon without mercy, out of pure carelessness or contempt. Men became insensitive and selfish, taking more than they could use. Because of this state of affairs, the animals resolved to consult about measures for their common safety and perhaps for a bit of revenge.

"The bears met in council at their town-house in *Kuwa'hi*. The old white bear presided as Chief. After presenting an introduction, he asked each bear to state his or her case against the human beings. After each, in turn, had made formal complaints, the Bears unanimously decided to declare war against the human race.

"One bear asked what weapons men relied on most to accomplish their destruction. *Bows and arrows, of course,* cried all the bears in chorus. *And what are they made of?* The first bear asked. *The bow is made of wood and the string of our own entrails,* replied one of the bears. It was then proposed that the bears should make a bow and some arrows and see if they could turn man's weapons against him. So, one bear got a nice piece of locust wood and another sacrificed himself for the good of the rest in order to furnish a piece of his intestines for the string. But when everything was ready and the first bear stepped up to make the trial, to their disappointment, they discovered that in letting the arrow fly, after drawing back the bow, the bear's long claws caught in the string and spoiled the shot. Annoyed, but not altogether stymied, another bear suggested that he could overcome this difficulty by cutting his claws. And so it was done; his claws were cut off. A second and successful trial demonstrated that the bear could shoot the arrow straight to the mark. The bears cheered their success. But the Chief, the old White Bear, looked worried. He insisted that bears must have long claws in order to be able to climb trees and catch fish. *One of us has already died to furnish the bowstring, and if we now cut off our claws we shall all starve. It's better to trust to the teeth and claws which nature has given us, for it is evident that man's weapons weren't intended for us.*

"No one could suggest a better plan, so the old Chief dismissed the council and the bears dispersed to their forest haunts. Had the result of the council been otherwise, we should now be at war with the bears, but as it is, the hunter does not even ask the bear's pardon when he kills one.

"Next, the deer held a council with their Chief, who is called Little Deer. Little Deer and his followers, after lengthy deliberation, resolved to inflict rheumatism upon every hunter who dared kill one of their number; unless, he took care to ask pardon for the offense. They sent notice of their decision to the nearest settlement of the real people and told them at the same time how to make propitiation when necessity forced them to kill one of the Deer Tribe. Now, whenever the hunter brings down a deer, Little Deer, who is swift as the wind and cannot be wounded, runs quickly to the spot and, bending over the blood stains, asks the spirit of the deer if it has heard the prayer of the hunter for pardon. If the reply be 'yes,' then all is well and Little Deer goes on his way, but if the reply be in the negative, he follows on the trail of the hunter until he arrives invisibly at the cabin in the settlement and strikes the neglectful hunter with rheumatism, so that he is rendered on the instant a cripple. No hunter who has regard for his health ever fails to ask pardon of the deer for killing it.

"Next came the fishes and the reptiles, who had their own grievances against humanity," she continued. "They held a joint council and determined to make their victims dream of snakes twining about them or of eating raw decaying fish, so that they would lose their appetite, sicken, and die. Thus, it is that snake and fish dreams are accounted for.

"Finally, the birds, insects, and smaller animals came together for a like purpose, and Grubworm presided over the deliberations. Each, in turn, expressed an opinion as to whether or not man is guilty of reckless murder. Then they voted on man's innocence or guilt. The verdict—Guilty!" my mother announced.

"*Wala'si*, Frog spoke first: *Man has kicked me about because I'm ugly, until my back is covered with sores.*Next came *Tsi'skwa*, Bird, who also condemned man. The birds decided that they would bring illness on the people by casting shadows over them, for they were tired of being scorched over their open fires. Others followed in the same vein. They each told their particular stories of abuse until the ground squirrel came forward. The tiniest of squirrels alone ventured to say a word on behalf of man, who seldom hurt him because he was so small; but this so enraged the others that they fell upon the ground squirrel and tore him with their teeth and claws, and the stripes remain on his back to this day.

"The assembly then began to devise and name various diseases, one after another, to set upon people. And had not their invention finally failed them, not one of the human race would have been able to survive.

"The Grubworm, in his place of honor, hailed each new malady with delight, until at last they had reached the end of the list, when someone suggested that it be arranged so that menstruation should sometimes prove fatal to women. On this note, he rose in his place and cried: *Wata'! Thanks! I'm glad some of them will die, for they are getting so thick that they tread on me.* He fairly shook with joy at the thought, so that he fell over backward and could not get on his feet again, but had to wriggle off on his back, as the Grubworm has done ever since.

"When the plants, who are friendly to people, heard what had been done by the animals, the birds, and the insects, they determined to defeat the evil designs. Each tree, shrub, and herb down to the grasses and mosses, agreed to furnish a remedy for the diseases named. Thus, medicine originated. And the plants, every one of which has its use, if we only knew it, furnished the antidotes to counteract the evil wrought by the revengeful animals."[1] My mother finished the story, but continued to talk about medicines.

"But of all the plants, the plants that stay green all winter hold the strongest medicines. The holly, the sage, the hemlock, the pine— the permanently green plants were the only ones that kept vigil all night during the Creation. And of those, only the pine tree sprouted from the tears of a mother and a boy who had touched the magic of the stars." My mother systematically returned her pouches of herbs to her medicine bag. She raised herself up, slung the haversack filled with herbs over her shoulder and across her chest, and under the light of the celestial bodies made her way to a pine tree near the edge of the cabin.

"Come along," she instructed me. I followed. "We need to help the others now. Pine bark, sage, and willow bark, if we can find it," she instructed, as she searched. "The problem is that our plants weren't expecting the Europeans to bring new diseases. We'll do our best."

I followed her lead, breaking branches of pine, collecting needles and cones under the light of a full winter's moon. Clouds drifted in after a time. My mother stuffed sage in the folds of her skirt as she lifted it up like a basket in front of her. She still limped, but her gait seemed stronger. In time, she headed for the cabin as if she would go in.

"What about Willie?" I worried.

"You'll keep vigil. You'll see." She led me back to the cabin and I entered without hesitation.

NOTE

[1] "The Origin of Disease and Medicine" relies on Mooney's (1981, 1900/1992) collection (see Sacred Formula of Cherokees, pp. 319–322).

CHAPTER 39

A SCREAMING DECISION

Night Turns to the Morning of December 23, 1865

"Whittle the bark, like so," my mother directed. We were in the cabin and sitting comfortably by the fire. I had laid Nan's and my wet clothes aside.

"So Nan went to water?" my mother asked. "You both came back soaked to the skin."

"Yes," I affirmed, stripping the outer bark in long strings from the pine branch, revealing the green inner layer.

"Did she pray?"

"No, I don't think so. I don't think she had time, before—"

"Before that frog came by and put his tiny teeth into you?" my mother interrupted me.

"Yes," I answered, handing her a stripped pine branch. She broke it so that the pulp released a fragrance into the cabin. The scent refreshed the air that had grown stale with sickly odors. My mother set the broken twigs onto the table and reached for the sage leaves. She pulverized them by rubbing them in her palms, back and forth. The crushed herbs fell into her skirt, which she then cupped carefully and lifted to a height just above the table ledge where she had placed a flat rock. She let the crushed leaves fall onto the rock.

"Hand me a stick," she pointed to the fire. I pulled a lit branch from the fire, she held the ember end to the sage, occasionally blowing breaths near or over it slightly, while protecting it with her other hand, cupped around the rock. Eventually, it began to burn. A trail of incense snaked into the air.

"Can you find a pot?"

"Sure." I set my pine-whittling aside to get a pot from the kitchen. I reached tentatively, wary of the mice, which had been living in this open cupboard. I found a large iron pot and brought it back to her.

"Fill it with snow." I took it to the front door, which I unlatched quietly and closed just as carefully. From the front porch, I looked in the direction of Willie's grave, but it was too dark and cloudy to see. Then I did as I was told and I returned to the fire with a pot filled with snow.

My mother hung it over the fire and the two of us took our seats. I resumed my job of stripping bark and she returned to breaking pine bark into small pieces and tossing them into the kettle.

The fragrance—pine and sage warmed my heart, bringing back memories of past yuletides. We'd not had a Christmas celebration this past year. We were too busy making our way through enemy lines and lingering battles. But previously, Julia had insisted on a tree being brought into the house. We'd strung popcorn and cranberries on it and eaten those decorations like gluttons on Christmas day. Willie had turned three that year and Julia had taught him about baby Jesus. For the most part, the war was raging elsewhere and I was able to sneak back to my parents' home and spend a few days with my wife and children.

I say for the most part, because I did encounter one loud blast of a canon as I made my way across a snow-covered trail. I admit that I was plum startled by it for I had heard Julia's all-clear signal beaten out on the hollowed log and I myself had heard no other enemy action in the area for some time. Nevertheless, a blast had resounded through those woods and clearly stopped me in my tracks, which was one of the luckiest moments I had in those woods. For not more than forty yards away three deer also stood frozen in their tracks. It took me only a second to register the possibility that lay in front of me. I swung my rifle to the crook of my arm, took aim, and fired. Almost instantly, the buck dropped with a thud. While wholly expecting the other two deer to dash off, I was amazed by the fact that they were completely stricken still, paralyzed by the excitement. I reloaded and brought down the second one with one shot. It would've been downright greedy to take all three. I let the third one be.[1]

After hog-tying the first and placing it on a rough, hand-built litter, I tied the second and hoisted it over my shoulders. So it was, that I carried one deer and dragged the other all the way to my family's house. A thin trail of blood through the pure white snow followed me. My mother was a woman a few words or excitement, but when she saw me arrive with those deer, tears filled her eyes.

Silas, she asked, *did you thank Little Deer?* I hadn't.

Silas?

I shook my head.

My mother began immediately gathering wood from the woodpile by the house. Neatly stacked, it had been cut by my own axe. I watched as she carried one log at a time, until she had three logs together, situated a good one hundred paces from the house and directly on the trail that I had made. Then she began gathering kindling.

Get your father's tinderbox, she instructed. I went into the house and retrieved it. We built a fire and let the two deer lay near-by while my mother began her prayers.

Little Deer, do you see what has happened? A hunter has taken one of your people from you. Little Deer, do you see what has happened? A hunter has taken another of your people. The hunter let his excitement and his hunger invade his thoughts. The hunter is not greedy, nor vengeful. The hunter is grateful that your deer people are willing to sustain his people in their time of need.

I listened to my mother's words, which oddly turned to a different prayer.

Our father who art in heaven hallowed be thy name, give us this day our daily bread and forgive us our trespasses as we forgive those who trespass against us. I had looked up then to see Julia standing in the doorway of our old home in Georgia, Willie at her side. She smiled at my mother's praying. And I smiled at the sight of my wife and son.

Silas, my mother had called me away from the beatific vision. *Son, you need to pray.* I will never forget the sweet, sweet smile on Julia's face as I turned away to pray with my mother. Not then, but much later, I realized that the two prayers are the same.

In Cherokee style, she made us wait three days before cutting into the hides of those deer. She kept her fires going day and night, day and night, day and night, until the morning of the fourth day at which time she stripped one deer while I skinned the other. My mother took

239

the skins to the river where she washed them in preparation for tanning; while I gutted the carcasses, broke the bones and prepared the meat. But before any of that was done, my mother and I ate the livers, raw, and I cracked the skulls and extracted the brains for tanning purposes.[2] Later, that day, we roasted the meat over an open fire; such a succulent meal we hadn't had since before the war began.

I remember we ate the roasted venison with sweet potatoes on the side and later that evening we topped it off with the popcorn and cranberries, the ones from the Christmas tree. Willie's chin ran red with cranberry juice.

Come here, son, I had said, and Willie had climbed up into my lap. I wiped his chin with my fingers and licked my fingers clean. Julia led us in a series of Christmas carols and I bounced Willie on my knee. Later, my father had told the nativity tale with at least a half a dozen interruptions from Willie.

How did the star know where the baby Jesus was going to be born?

Way'll, I reckon the star was made by the hand of God and God gave the star the ability to see right down into that stable.

So, stars have eyes? Willie asked.

Way'll, now, I don't know about that, my father had answered.

Did baby Jesus have teeth? Willie asked and we laughed in response. My mother had leaned over toward me and pronounced, *He reminds me of Malachi when he was a boy. Every story was greeted with a basketful of questions.* And I thought of Malachi, off to war. I remembered how Willie's questions slowed and he rubbed his eyes. I knew that I should leave before daybreak in case the soldiers were heading back into our region, but my mother lit a pipe of tobacco and she and my father and I shared a smoke. Then mother and father sipped a bit of corn whiskey, while Willie snoozed in my lap.

When everyone returns, all my brothers, from William to Malachi, I swear to you that I'll bring down two more deer for such an occasion, I told my parents as I roused Willie and rose to take my leave. Julia and Willie followed me to the door. I stroked Julia's auburn hair and smelled the top of Willie's head. *It smells like pine,* I said of Willie's hair. Julia turned to me, adding, *He smells like Christmas.*

"Silas,"

"Silas," my mother interrupted these memories. "Take the lantern," she said, "and bring more pine branches." I did as I was told and she sent me twice more, with lantern in hand, for other herbs and more pine bark. Each time, I returned and opened the cabin door the air smelled sweeter and I felt better. By morning, the air had warmed outside. And on my last trip outdoors, I sprinkled pine needles on Willie's grave. The sun was trying to shine through the thick morning haze so common to these mountain parts.

It'd be a while before the sun would be able to burn the fog away. And that was fine with me. My memories of the good days with Willie and my father seemed to sit well in a soft cloud floating around my mind with images of the Blue Ridge Mountains. Exhausted I knew now that I could sleep.

When I returned from my last trip, I had no sooner latched the door behind me than William spoke up.

"Do you hear that?"

"What?" I said, dumping a load of pine branches to the floor.

"A wailing, in the distance," he said.

"No, it's the wind whistling through the chinking," I told my brother. "Go back to sleep."

"No, Silas, I hear it, too," Nan interjected, reinforcing William's concern. She sat up. Julia rustled beneath her blanket. My mother looked up from her skirt full of herbs.

"Please, Silas," Lydia added without finishing her thought.

At their request I went to the door; cracked it a bit; and looked down the long road that wound its way eventually to Mister Dodd's estate. At first, I saw nothing except the fog of blues, greens, and grays surrounding the mist-covered evergreens and winter bare trees; but then, like them, I did hear something. Quickly, kicking the pine branches out of my way, I got my rifle.

"They've come back," William warned.

"No! Don't let them get us," my sister Lydia begged.

"Silas," Nan called out from her place, too weak to stand. "Your rifle is it loaded?" Her voice higher pitched than usual, edged closed to frantic. The whooping and hollering became louder. Everyone in the cabin awoke. Most were stirring one way or the other.

"What is it?" some were saying. "Tell us," others commanded. They were all astir. My youngest sisters clinging to each other, William trying to raise himself upward, Reuben rolling for I don't know what, all caused a commotion within the cabin. I looked again through the opening of the door that I'd left ajar; I searched and strained my eyes to see through the dense blue haze. I heard a wail.

I flung the door wide open. A mountain mist blurred my vision so that I both squinted and strained my eye-sight while taking aim.

"I see one. I see one," I said. "Whooping and hollering like a madman."

"He's getting closer," Lydia cried. Some of my sisters were standing behind me now.

"He's wearing gray," I told the others.

"Somethin' sparkling above his head," I announced, lowering my rifle just a tad.

"They've come to burn us down," William yelled at me. "They've come to finish the job!"

The rider came into view. He was swinging something above his head. His screams were tortuous and contorted—neither Indian, nor white; neither Southern, nor Northern. They were the cries of a madman. I raised my rifle.

"Shoot him!" William yelled. Suddenly Julia began to wail. Then Reuben cried out in mournful tones. "Shoot him! Shoot him!" William screamed at me. The baby cried. The noises intensified to one gigantic screaming sound. Wailing and crying and screaming filled the cabin and the madman shouted outside. I feared my head would burst. I couldn't think. "Shoot! Damn it," William cried again. I took aim.

"Damn it! Shoot!"

I pulled the trigger. The blast jolted me back a step. The shot blazed through the air. The rider fell from his horse with a resounding thud. Suddenly, the madness stopped. Screams turned into soft cries and William gasped a bit of relief.

After reloading my musket, I walked outside and carefully approached the downed rider. His horse circled aimlessly about. I used my rifle to see if there was any life left by poking his side. No sound ushered forth. I leaned down and turned his head to see his face.

"Oh, Sweet Jesus!" I proclaimed in horror and regret.

I ran to the cabin doorway. I stood there. My jaw seemed frozen; I was unable to speak. Tears filled my eyes. My mother took a step toward me, dropping sprigs of sage to her feet.

"Silas?"

"Oh, Sweet Jesus! I've shot Malachi."

NOTES

[1] Silas' hunting story can be found in Shackelford Sims (1978).

[2] The process of brain-tanning was explained to me by a historical re-enactor at the Feast of the Hunter's Moon held in Lafayette, IN. After skinning the deer, scrape the hide with stones, remove the hair and epidermis, (save the brain and tendons), cook the brain until it turns white, let it cool until it is just warm to the touch, rub it on both sides of the hide, wash the hide to remove blood and dirt, stretch the hide over a frame and poke it with a stick; smoke the hide. Then make needles from deer bone and thread from the tendons (i.e., sinew).

A REALITY MORE DREADFUL THAN DREAMS

December 23, 1865

"Why was he screaming so?" Nan begged to know as if it was his fault for being shot, but the tone of her voice lamented her complicity.

"He's burning with fever," my mother told us as she touched his forehead. I had dragged his limp body into the cabin and laid him next to William.

"It's just a shoulder wound," she added. William rose up on one elbow to look.

"If anything kills him, it'll be the fever," he reassured me, making light of the wound in Malachi's shoulder. We took off his jacket. I supported his head and neck.

"Malachi, I'm sorry; I'm sorry," I cried.

"Silas?" he answered me with a question.

"Yes," I said, but no response followed. For a second, only the whites of his eyes showed and then his eyelids fluttered shut.

"Nan," my mother instructed, "get me some cloth." She nodded her head in the direction of the clothing bag.

Nan brought a cotton skirt to my mother, who took it in her hands, but also held it with her teeth and ripped. Tearing the skirt into strips, she made a long bandage.

"Now, get my medicine bag." Nan brought it to my mother who dumped the contents with far less care than she had handled them before. She shoved small pouches aside, until she found what she wanted—aloe leaves. She split one down the center with a long motion of her thumbnail and peeled apart the halves. She laid the open leaf, still moist with aloe, on Malachi's wound.

"Hold it there, gently," she told me. I pressed it lightly against his skin.

My mother began sorting through her pouches checking this one and that, sometimes by its aroma rather than its look, sniffing at each. As soon as she had the three that she wanted, she took them to the table and sprinkled a bit of each onto one of the sage-covered rocks. She used her finger to mix the ingredients and spat on it to moisten the powders and get them to stick. She brought the mixture to Malachi's side and carefully applied the poultice to his wound. After dabbing it on the front, she said, "Lean him forward," which I did. My mother reached around and applied the paste to his back, to the exit wound. I propped Malachi up as my mother wrapped the bandage over his shoulder, down his back, circling it around his waist, and back up to his shoulder. It stretched around, but thrice.

"Are you leaving the bullet in?" William asked.

"I think it's gone clean through him," my mother reported.

"Oh, Jesus," I muttered under my breath.

"Look here," my mother pointed to a rash on his chest and abdomen. William and I both leaned forward.

"It's different from either the measles or the small pox," I said.

"I heard they had an outbreak of typhoid fever in Oklahoma and Arkansas," William reported. That concluded the diagnosis and the discussion. We completed bandaging his wound and listening to him mumble deranged thoughts, barely audible, something about *Stand Watie*. He winced again as we put his shirt back on him.

"Malachi," I held him in my arms as I spoke. "Malachi, can you hear me?" He neither answered nor seemed to recognize me anymore. Although his eyes opened again, it was but for a moment.

"Amazing that he found the strength to get to us," William figured. And I thought, *and then to be shot by me, his older brother, the one he'd stood up for when William had called me a …* I couldn't finish that thought. Yet, at the same time, I could think of nothing else.

This is William's fault, I thought. *If he hadn't been yelling at me to shoot and putting such fearful thoughts in everyone's heads about the Rebs burning our cabin down, it would've been quieter. I could've thought things through. I could've shot above his head or waited to see what was gleaming in his hand.* At this point, I surmised the gleaming must've been something on his hat, but I didn't go out in search of his

Confederate cap; or who knows, maybe he was carrying a torch to find his way through the fog.

William, I thought, *not only instigated the panic, but also sounded like a coward himself. What man makes women and children cry during such duress? He should've left it to me. I could've handled it; I would've protected him. But I suppose that was his deepest fear, entrusting his life to me—a man who refused to go to war. A coward! But the war was a pretense—people pretending to take a moral stance, when it really came down to politics and economics. Power and greed! It's not like the North has been the bastion of equality for Negroes. In the meantime, it wasn't like the whole of the South was courting slavery. After all, there were people like Nate Butler, freed slaves, working men and women.[1] Not that I'm saying slavery is right, I'm just saying that the war wasn't fought only over slavery. My brother wasn't fighting to save the Negroes. He didn't even know a Negro. He was fighting to be a part of something else. Whatever it was, it was no reason for him to make me out to be a coward, a coward because I wouldn't fight in this dang blasted war. Damn the war! Damn the North and the South! Damn them all to hell, including William, especially William!*

William should've known better than to call me a coward. I'd told him that I'd protect my family if it came to that point. He knew that or he should've known that, damn it. When did I ever let him down? He knew that I wasn't a coward.

Oh God, I thought as I held Malachi and rocked him in my arms, *perhaps, William didn't know it. After all, I didn't shoot those Confederate bastards who entered the cabin when I had the chance.*

Maybe, I am a coward. Maybe I shot today because I was afraid of what William would think of me. Now look at me. Brave enough to shoot my younger brother, but not brave enough to shoot two conniving strangers. I questioned every action I had taken. Even mercifully killing that confederate who had been attacked by wolves. That officer had challenged me, too. And I can only wonder as to whether it was easier to shoot him because I was angry at those damn blasted Confederates who had assaulted my sister and my wife, or whether it was because his bravery commanded me to do so. Either way, somehow it didn't feel as though I had made the decision. It'd just happened.

Malachi, Oh, Malachi. I was even angry at Nan. She hadn't been any help at all. *Are you sure your rifle's loaded? What testament was that to faith in me? She should've trusted me. Some Beloved Woman she turned out to be. Oh, Lord, what am I saying? She's only seventeen. She saved my life, not once but twice. What kind of man am I?* I continued to rock Malachi.

I never should've shot. I had promised to never shoot a man. *Julia. This is Julia's doing,* I decided, *for swearing me to such a vow that no man could keep and then at the same time I find my wife wailing insanely when the crucial test arrives.*

"Julia," I said.

"Silas," she answered me. And the sound of her sweet voice, weak but quick and supportive, sent aches of regret through my bones for what I had thought, for what I'd been about to say. I hung my head backward.

My mother remained next to me, staring at Malachi. *She said nothing. Not a single word. She could've told them all to be quiet; they would've listened to her. They always listen to her. But instead she sat dumbstruck in her chair, crumpling dried leaves between her palms. To what end? Why hadn't she spoken? Why hadn't she told them to hush? Her silence had sealed our fate! How hard would it have been for her to say, Hush! Can't you see the man needs quiet? Hush, now. Let the man think. But no! Not a word! And now she stares, silently, at Malachi's weak and innocent form. I loathe her. I hate her.*

Oh sweet Jesus, take pity, I thought and pursed my lips. *How could I have shot my own brother?*

"Oh Malachi, what were you thinking?" I said aloud. What *was* he thinking, I wondered, wearing a Rebel uniform and shouting to the winds, of course someone would shoot him. Malachi mumbled something. "Oh, Malachi, I'm sorry," I said releasing him quickly from the seat of the scapegoat; after all, he was deranged with fever and, now a bullet wound as well, blood oozed through the bandage. "I know, you didn't understand," I whispered to him. "How could you've known what we'd been through?" I expected no answer and received none.

This is no one's fault but mine. I resolved long ago never to raise my rifle against another man, unless absolutely necessary. Was this necessary?

Malachi is the only one of my brothers who hadn't looked at me with judgmental eyes, the only one who didn't think I was a coward. *Oh, Malachi, why did you have to ride in here screaming like a madman,* I thought again as I stroked his hair and watched over him. I tried to blame someone else, anyone, but me. I wrestled with my thoughts to the point of exhaustion.

"Malachi. Oh, Malachi, I'm sorry," I breathed over him.

He mumbled more, and at times, I think he was reliving battles he'd seen and at other moments he became almost tranquil. Bursts of excitement sometimes came with yells of *Look out!* And I became lost in memories of Malachi as a boy. *What a scrappy lad he was, always challenging me to a dare. I always took him on, too. That's how Malachi knew that I wasn't a coward, at least, not by his standards. Malachi thought bravery was proving that you weren't afraid to climb the highest sycamore or balance on the weakest elm branch hanging over the gorge. I recalled the two of us swinging on a rope over Stone Man Falls one day. Malachi knew first hand that I wasn't afraid to catch a snake with my bare hands and that I'd shoot just about any wild edible thing with my blow gun or my bow and arrow. I could scamper up any mountain-side faster than Malachi or any of my other brothers. I had to admit though that Reuben and William were faster runners than I could ever be. And John and Joseph could probably best me at wrestling, although I do have strong legs and solid wrestling moves. As for shooting, Thomas was a ten out of ten, too; we often tied. Malachi could best me at marbles and holler louder than I could, but that didn't keep me from trying to outdo him nor him trying to outdo me. I'd never back down from a dare—No, sir. To Malachi, I suppose that meant I was brave and most definitely not a coward, but what does a young'un know about bravery or cowardice. More likely they're just fool-hardy, not brave. And is that how I came to shoot Malachi? By a dare? Had William's words and Nan's concern and Julia's scream along with my mother's silence all dared me to fire my weapon? Or was it something else?*

"Oh, Malachi," I whispered again, lamenting my actions. I shot because I was afraid. I searched his young face—seamless and fresh, thinking there was nothing brave at all about my shooting Malachi.

Sweet Jesus, I can't blame anyone but myself; I'm the one who pulled the trigger. I'm the one who shot Malachi. I scooted around and laid Malachi's head on a folded blanket. Then I rested my head on Malachi's chest. I tried to use William's assessment to help me sleep—that if he dies, it'll be the fever that kills him, not the bullet. Nevertheless, my thoughts tossed and turned. I slept fretfully. Later, at the sound of my mother's voice, I sat up again.

"Silas." I answered with silence.

"It's not your fault," she said.

"Whose fault is it?" I asked her.

She didn't answer me. The silence continued to hang like a heavy wave of humidity on a summer's day, but it was cold. So cold."Was I wrong not to pick a side, not to go to war?" I asked her.

"The night you boys left home, before the war started, your father said to me—*Our sons are headed in three different directions, North, South, and to the hills.* I said right back at him—*Our sons are headed in seven directions. We Cherokee have always believed that there are seven directions—The cardinal four—East, South, West, and North; plus, there is above you and of course there is what's below you, and ...,*" she paused before adding, "Look at me, now, Silas." I looked up at my mother who sat in the glow of the fire and the shafts of the morning sunlight creeping through cracks in the cabin walls. She placed her hand over her heart, saying "and then there's here;" she tapped her heart gently, "the seventh direction—the path that your heart tells you to follow. You and your brothers each took the seventh direction.[2]I nodded, forcing back my tears, and stared up at the cabin ceiling.

"Lay down," she said. I, once again, placed my head on Malachi's chest. The heat of his body kept me warm. Eventually, the emotional turmoil slipped into pure exhaustion; I lowered my eye-lids and fell asleep.

My early dreams found me standing on a path with several branching ways to go. I kept asking which path is the one that will take me back home, to Willie. Strangers kept coming and going and making all different kinds of decisions, but none of them knew the way to Willie. My legs ached in the dream from not being able to take a step. I was sure of only one thing in my dream—that I had to walk down one of those paths because I couldn't stand still and I couldn't go back.

My later dreams were filled with the faces of gaunt-faced Negroes who were walking down the path, singing softly, spirituals, I think. I saw the soldiers, blue and gray alike, missing legs or arms, carrying their appendages, and yet, walking down a path. I saw Julia and Nan walking different paths but holding hands, somehow. One image after another either tortured me or confused me. I sensed myself lying in the hole under the floorboards of the house in Georgia and it became a grave. I sat up with a start only to see myself staring at Malachi, he slept peacefully and I, too, then fell back to sleep.

And in my next dream I saw Malachi's face, my youngest brother, the one who said that I wasn't a coward—half of his face was missing and part of his arm. He was trying to put his face back on, but it wouldn't stick. I saw his bullet-shredded shoulder, hanging skin with muscle and tendon flopping about. I screamed or tried to scream but no sound came forth. Then in my dream Malachi screamed. And as he screamed I raised my rifle and shot Willie. Then Willie was screaming and Malachi was screaming and my mother was screaming and the whole world became one awful screeching scream. I jerked awake.

"Ahhh! No, Lord! No!" Julia cried out. It was Julia who was screaming, not the Malachi of my dreams. She seemed to be flinging herself about, an arm, a leg. I rushed to her aid. Her screams awakened my mother.

"What is it?" my mother asked, concerned.

"Julia, Julia," I tried to calm her, but she writhed and wailed. I caught her arms and tried to hold them down, but to no avail. I couldn't see what the problem was until at last she gathered up our baby daughter Sara in her arms and tried to take up Nannie, as well. Not a single motion or a simple cry emanated from my children. I could only hear Julia's cries.

"My babies. Oh, God, not my babies."

"What is it?" I shouted at her. "Talk to me, woman!" I demanded.

"What's wrong with the children?" My mother sat up.

"My babies, my babies!" Julia wailed. Like rag-dolls, their limbs were lifeless, their heads bobbed about without strength as Julia held one in each arm, sobbing, and pulling them to her chest. At last, it became clear to me; my daughters were dead.

NOTES

[1] See *Incidents in the Life of a Slave Girl* written under the pseudonym of Linda Brent, so as not to jeopardize her hard fought freedom and life in the North (Jacobs, 1861/1988).

[2] I first learned about the seven directions from a presenter at the Fall Festival that I attended on the Qualla Boundary, 1997. I apologize for not recalling the presenter's name.

CHAPTER 41

GRIEVING IN TIME

December 24, 1865

Julia's lip quivered as she tried to stop crying. She looked up at me as if begging me to do something, anything. I stood there, my arms at my sides, watching her.

"Silas, Silas," she pleaded. She rose to a sitting position and draped one child across her lap, the other in her arms. She sobbed and wailed. Tears rolled down her cheeks and snot from her nose. She sniffled and wiped her face smearing her grief across her cheek. In time, what seemed an unbearable eternity, her body slowed to a soft mourning sound, like that of a dove, as she rocked back and forth. From time to time, she would realize again that her babies were gone. Her whole body would renew its trembling and crying, until she could take control again. And then, she would take short breaths trying to stave off tears, but they came anyway.

She cried for hours until she fell into a fitful slumber. I took my place in my chair by the table and watched her sleep with dead children now beneath her protective arm. I stared for a long time. The fire died out. No one spoke.

There's no explaining what made me eventually stand, determining that I could wait no longer, but I did. At first I tried not to wake her, while reaching for the baby. But as I tried to pull our infant from her grasp, she screamed; startling me as did the feel of my baby girl, whose rigid body, gave a hint of warmth. Life and death seemed to exist simultaneously.

A sweat broke out across my forehead; I wiped it away and went about the gruesome task, extracting a baby, now like a wooden doll, from the desperate hands of her mother.

"No! No!" Julia held tight to our baby girl. The sound of Julia's voice tore my heart further, but just the same, I continued trying to free

Sara from my wife's grip. I nearly had the baby when Julia suddenly screamed wildly, stirring the others, who had been sleeping."Shh, shh, Julia," I let go of the infant and reached for our toddler, but Julia screamed again. And then upon seeing that rigor mortis had set in, she wailed all the more. I went to the table where I'd left the Bible.

"Julia, Julia," I begged. Placing the Bible in her hand as I slid the baby from her grip, I added "Pray, Julia." Instead of holy ejaculations, a dreadful mourning sound oozed out of her like a demon from the depths of hell. She raised her arm, attempting to hurl the Bible across the cabin, but in her weakened state it fell fruitlessly to the floor and she sobbed again. Then reaching up, she tore at me with her fingernails. I set my lifeless daughter down and caught Julia about the wrists, holding her tight. She flailed her arms and her fiery hair swung wildly as she fought against me, but she wore out quickly. Her head dropped backward exposing her cream-colored neck with pale blue veins pulsing with life, but also covered with spots. She dropped her head against my chest.

"Oh, Silas," is all that she said. I stroked her hair and wrapped my other arm around her.

As I rocked Julia in my arms, I realized that it had indeed surprised me that she would turn on me and throw the Bible with such vehemence. She had all but dedicated her life to Jesus and she had never been anything but kind to me. Now I sat by her side, thinking that this time I faced too many intervening obstacles to stay the path of the Holy Spirit. And so did Julia. What nightmare had been unleashed? No parable could explain or take away my pain. Don't even speak of Job to me, I thought with anger.

I looked at the Bible, on the floor, where Julia had thrown it and considered that Bible was as stiff and cold as those babies and offered not a thread of warmth for a woman in such a crisis. Nevertheless, knowing how fervently religious Julia is I hoped she could be coaxed by the name of Jesus. I decided to try again.

With my arm still around her shoulders, I turned her face toward mine. "Julia," I whispered. She whimpered softly.

"Julia, it's time to give the children to Jesus," I told her, knowing that eventually she would find solace in her religion, even if I now could find none. Tears ran down her cheeks, but the sobbing subsided. She sniffled as if she were putting the tears back inside her.

"Silas, where will you bury them?" she wanted to know, still sniffling. "I can take them to Mister Dodd's cemetery," I told her.

"But Willie," she said. "Please, don't leave Willie here, all alone." I nodded. She must have heard me speaking with my mother or realized that we hadn't gone far to bury Willie.

"No, I won't leave Willie," I promised her.

"They need to be buried together," my wife determined, squaring her shoulders. I stood, ready to prepare their bodies.

"I'll help," Julia meekly added when she realized what I was doing. She got to her feet with some trouble. Then each of us lifted a stiff infant into our arms.

"Oh, oh my," she whimpered. Julia set Sara down on the table and straightened her nightgown.

"Do you have a comb?" she asked. "One of the small ones," she added, speaking with difficulty, and meaning the kind that I had whittled during the war days. I handed one to her. She gently combed through the child's hair. Soft hair with ringlets at the nape of the baby's neck, the comb tugged a bit at the end.

"It always did tangle here," Julia reminisced. She lifted the child and looked at me. We exchanged bodies. Julia combed Nannie's hair. I took the children, one after the other, and wrapped each in a blanket."I'll go with you," she told me. I nodded. "But I need to bathe and change."

"Of course." I understood that she wanted to be properly dressed for a funeral. "Julia, there were wolves out the other day. But in all likelihood they are well fed by now," I said thinking regretfully of the Confederate officer whom I hadn't had the time or opportunity to bury. "Or dead," I added, thinking of the one lone wolf that Nan had killed.

"Just the same, I think you should take the rifle," I told her. "I'll be right behind you." After she gathered clothes from the surplus bag, we quietly made our way outside. I sent her to the river before I returned to the cabin to gather my blanketed babies. I could have carried them together in one trip; one under each arm or stacked on top of each other rigid as they were, but each image seemed sacrilegious. I made two trips.

When I was done I went to dig up Willie. It was the hardest task that I've ever undertaken, not physically, but of the heart, a matter of love and loss and loss again. I pierced the shovel blade into the earth with vigor at first, but adjusted my intensity, as I grew closer to Willie's body. It wasn't like digging a well, trying to go deeper, trying to go faster. I took small scoops, often holding the shovel at a sideways slant rather than a sharp driving angle. I didn't want to discover Willie's body with the edge of the shovel blade. But after several more shovelfuls, that is exactly what I did.

When I felt the resistance, I stopped immediately, fell to my knees, and brushed the dirt from him with my hands. Eventually, I saw the blanket clad figure and lifted the small corpse from the grave.

As I carried Willie's body to the buckboard, the blanket came loose. I shifted my grip and felt squirming and crawling between the blanket and his skin. The blanket slipped away exposing centipedes on Willie's face.

"Oh Jesus!" I exclaimed. One climbed across his eye. My stomach curdled and my skin pimpled up with goose bumps. My cheeks puckered involuntarily and then I heaved a dry heave. I snatched the blanket as quickly as I could and covered him again. Closing my eyes against the image, I waited a second, then taking a deep breath to clear my head, I discovered the putrid smell of human decay. *Oh God,* I wanted to cover my mouth and nose, but my hands were full with Willie. I quickly made my way to the buckboard, holding him stretched out in front of me. I began to load the figure into the back. The odor of decomposing organs permeated the blanket and wafted into the air; I turned my face away from the rank smell as I set him in the back of the wagon next to his sisters.

Following that ungodly task, I set off to join Julia at the river wash and bathe myself. I made my way through the thickets and down the slope. Sister Sun had regained her full force by mid-day and now in the early afternoon, a nearly springtime warmth spread across the woods. Horizontal shadows of tree trunks and branches decorated the barren, brown soil. As I came in view of the river, I caught sight of Julia as she pulled water toward her face in cupped hands.

I joined her at the river's edge, pulled my hunting shirt over my head. Checked for the rifle; she had leaned it against the tree. I rolled up my pant legs and stepped into the chilly water.

"Good Lord, it's cold!" I came toward her with outstretched arms. She looked at my hands. Dirt still caked under my fingernails and in the creases of my palms. I swished them clean. I took her hand and led her into deeper waters, where I submerged myself and shook my head as I resurfaced from cold waters. I scrubbed more thoroughly and picked the dirt from my nails. Now clean, I reached out for her and pulled her toward me. The water, waist deep, curled around us. I noticed that her rash was clearing. This alone brought a joy to my heart. I pulled her closer and submerged us both to the neck.

She surfaced with a scream. It had life in it.

"Silas Mercer Beasley, Jr.," she scolded and started to leave me. "Stay," I begged. She stopped, lingered sympathetically for a moment, before turning away again, making her way through the water to the bank where she had laid out fresh clothes on a blanket for herself and she'd brought clothes for me. She'd washed her dress and stockings and undergarments and left them on a rock. I watched her as I slowly made my way from the chilly waters. She slipped a white cotton blouse over her head and stepped gently into a calico skirt.

God forgive me, I thought later, for even though my three children lay dead and stiff in the back of the buckboard at the top of this hill, I could think of nothing else than the fact that my wife stood before me without wearing a single undergarment. Her hair hung wet and clumped down her back. She pulled it up in an attempt to keep her blouse dry. I left the water, discarded my wet trousers, dried myself with a blanket, and dressed in the clothes that Julia had brought for me.

I was *Kana'ti* at that moment, the only man on earth and one who had suffered immeasurable unhappiness; she was *Selu*, the woman who returned *Kana'ti* to a gentle and kind man. "You are the reason the sun shines," I said to her, a saying I had learned, or stolen, from a friend or acquaintance.

She cried. I took her chin in my hand, turning her face toward me. She wept for her children. I searched her eyes. At last, she threw her arms around me and held tight. I wrapped the two of us into that blanket. We held each other. We stayed until the sun slid into late afternoon and I remember thinking that I never wanted her to leave me, ever.

After we returned to the cabin, I double checked the rifle, making sure that it was loaded. I told William and Reuben that it was by the door should they need it. Julia strung her wet clothes over the backs of the chairs by the fire and then slumped onto one of the chairs. She didn't have the strength that she thought she had. I laid her back on the floor and covered her with a fresh blanket.

"I should go," she noted with remorse.

"You're not strong enough," I told her. I kissed her on the forehead and pulled the blanket over her shoulders. I started to leave, but she quickly caught my sleeve.

"Stay, please," she pleaded. I nodded.

"Close your eyes," I told her as I took her in my arms. I stayed until Julia fell asleep. This was a gift I gave my wife, sparing her the smell of death and the sorrow of burial. I would take her to the gravesite when she was well.

As I left the cabin, however, my heart sank with a feeling of loneliness, realizing that once again I would stand, solo, at the foot of a grave, actually three fresh graves. Although Julia's love had given me some strength, an ineffable form of despair washed over me as I walked to the buckboard, hitched the horse and climbed onto the seat.

I couldn't even muster a "Heeyah;" instead, I gave the mare a rap with a light snap of the reins; she started with a jolt despite my weak efforts. I turned to check on my children as the wagon lurched forward. A part of me wanted to ask them if they were all right, but another part of me accepted that they were dead, that they would never answer me again. The only sounds I heard from the back were the squeaks of the rickety buckboard and the wagon-wheels. All I saw besides the blankets was a wisp of Willie's blonde hair. I made my way to Mister Dodd's home again.

"Silas?" Mister Dodd called to me as I climbed down from the buckboard seat.

"Sir," I said barely able to hold my head up. I swallowed hard. I sniffled back tears.

"Silas, what's happened?" he asked approaching me. I held my hand up to stop him from coming any closer to the wagon. No need to expose him to this disease. He stopped and looked at the back of the wagon and then at me.

"My children, sir."

"Oh, Beasley," he said with as much sorrow as if they were his own grandchildren. I pursed my lips and turned away. I regained my composure, turned to face him, and then in a tone absent of any emotion, I spoke to him.

"Would you mind if I buried them in your cemetery, next to my father?"

"I'll send someone to help you."

"Thank you, sir." Turning around, I boarded the wagon seat and headed the horse and wagon with its contents toward the cemetery. The road was bumpy; my three lifeless children bounced in the back of the wagon. I felt like I was hurting them even more and was anxious to bring this buggy to a halt. To a dead stop. I hopped down, looped the reins around a tree branch and went to the back of the wagon. I had the shovel with me and began to dig the graves next to my father's grave.

In a short time, a Negro arrived. It was the same man who I had come upon by the river earlier.

"I'm sorry fo' ya' loss, sir," he said respectfully.

"And I for yours," I said to him.

"What do you mean, sir?"

I couldn't explain; I don't know what I was thinking exactly at the time, except that our family had determined that slavery was not a godly institution. Well, most of the family. I assumed he had experienced more pain than I had ever known, more loss than I could imagine. I began to dig. I continued to dig. He looked at me from time to time, probably wondering if I'd gone crazy from my grief. I shoveled without speaking, until the holes were deep.

Eventually, I lowered my children, each, individually into their graves. He helped me. Such small graves. Shallow, tiny graves. I said nothing as I began to shovel dirt over their lifeless forms. He politely stood back. This was not his responsibility. To shovel dirt onto another man's children's graves. Earth. Soil. Blanket of death. It is the sound that rips one's heart from the body—the spray of pebbles and dirt hitting what was once one's joy. When the task was done, I stood, a shell, so filled with emptiness that I couldn't speak, couldn't move. I couldn't even say Willie's name; no man should have to bury his child twice. And my daughters.

"Sir, would you like to say somethin'," the nameless man asked me, concerned.

I only shook my head. Then he took it upon himself to say something kindly. I must have spent all my energy on saving Julia from her grief. There was nothing left in me, except sorrow.

"Jesus, take unto you the little children," the Negro prayed. His kindness overwhelmed me; my lips trembled.

We both stood for a time at the graves. Eventually, I turned to leave, taking the shovel with me. It wasn't my shovel, but I guess I figured I wasn't done with it, yet.

CHAPTER 42

THE LAST BATTLE

December 24, 1865

My journey back with the empty buckboard behind me sent my mind into a deep depression that I couldn't control or express in words. I had thought that listening to my children's lifeless bodies bounce in the back of that wagon was a dreadfully lonely sound, it didn't compare to the silence that echoed behind me now. I wanted to return and dig up those graves; I imagined peeling back the dirt with my fingernails, scoop after scoop to get my Willie back, to get my daughters. I couldn't let go of them and I couldn't go on without them. An image flashed in my mind of the anger that *Kana'ti* must have felt when he found out that his sons had killed *Selu*. I pictured him conspiring to kill them at every turn, throwing one after the other onto the ground, flailing at them. The desire to squeeze the life out of them with a strangling grip pulsed in my veins. I don't know why such violent images came over me, but I couldn't stop them. So I pulled my wagon off the road and walked. I needed to walk before I went back to that cabin.

Down a deer trail I found a sturdy stick and used it to steady my gait until I felt that I was out of view of the Dodd estate and then I took that heavy branch and beat it against a boulder that jutted from the hillside. Whacking it! Smashing it! Pounding it! All I knew is that I needed to break something. I needed to crack the branch so that it cried out loud, so that I wouldn't hear the silence that came from the back of that wagon. I thrashed that old tree limb against the rock until it all but pulverized into sawdust. Then I walked some more.

I followed a curve in the path, which brought me to a steep incline with an old overhanging sycamore tree. This reminded me of one of the most challenging places in which I had made my home during the war years—in a small cave perched on a high bluff. The only way to reach it required that I climb some distance and at a particular point leap to one branch and then take hold by swinging onto the next and finally swinging again onto the bluff. Each day, I marveled at the joy that climbing and swinging would bring me. It was such a simple feat, requiring so little skill and which included as a small reward—a rush of wind through my hair and a blast of sunshine on my face. I remembered how the sun would always shine its brightest into my eyes as I swung upward, blinding me momentarily, until my feet landed me solidly on the ground.

The sun, my father once told me, is a beautiful woman who burns with intensity as the day wears on because she is growing frustrated and angry. *Why*, I asked my father? *Oh, because the sun is so beautiful that no one can look upon her without squinting or having to turn away. This means that no one can look long enough to give her a compliment. She would never hear anyone say—You're beautiful.* I don't know why I remembered that story at that time, but for some reason it brought a calm back to me. *It's a Cherokee story,* he had told me when he was done.[1] I thought of Julia's face and the expression, *You are the reason the sun shines.*

I eventually retraced my steps to the boulder that I had beaten earlier with the tree limb and sat down there. I leaned my head back. Sister Sun was settling down into the folds of the rolling mountains. I pretended that I could feel her warmth on my face, although it was growing chillier. The blood red sunset filled the sky with magenta clouds. I thought of Julia, her hair. I returned to the wagon and climbed onto the buckboard. I gave the reins a snap.

Although I might well have succumbed to the sorrow I was feeling and just kept walking until darkness shrouded the day, I believe that it is some kind of providence that I arrived back home when I did. Just as I turned the reins of the horse toward the clearing in front of the cabin, I viewed a man, stepping toward the cabin door.

"Whoa, whoa!" I yelled to him as I jumped from the buckboard. I saw his face; the scar under his right eye stood out against his fleshy cheek. He turned and grinned as if I was a joke, a fool, like someone he'd cheated at poker who never saw the malevolence of his evil game. He was one of those troublesome Rebs who had violated my family when we first came to this cabin. What gave him such gall as to grin, such audacity, was beyond me. At least until I felt the lightning sting of a rifle butt against my back. The pain seared across my shoulder blades. Dizziness enveloped me. As the initial assault became clear, I forced my eyes to open and tried to steady my legs. He's not alone, that grinning bastard is not alone, I realized. A second wallop knocked the wind from my lungs. I fell. Staggered to all fours. Regained my breath. Scrambled to my feet. And moved as quickly as I could toward the back of the buckboard.

I flew with rage toward the second drifter after grabbing the shovel from the back of the wagon. He came at me again swinging his rifle. He must've been out of dry gunpowder or surely he would've shot me.

The clash of the rifle against the shovel reverberated down my arm. The clanging noise echoed through the valley. It gave warning to my family. I swung again as fast as I could, catching his arm and relieving him of his rifle. It flew toward my horse; she whinnied and reared.

Without a second thought I smashed the shovel into the man's head and leveled him with one swoop. He dropped sideways curling into a ball. Groaning.

I ran for the cabin where I found the other bastard holding my grief-stricken Julia. I dropped the shovel and threw him toward the door. He banged against it. Then I threw him into the yard in front of the cabin. He could see that I had bested his friend and now by God I would best him, as well.

He came at me. Madness swelled inside my brain and I swung at him with a fist made from anger and hate.

"Vengeance is mine, not the Lord's," I screamed. He didn't have a chance. As he backed away, I witnessed him assessing his own bloodied nose. But something changed in him, he now flew toward me like a madman. He too carried a hatred that had been boiling for far too long. But my rage could not be matched by any man!

I forced his body, pushing and shoving, until I had him up against the side of the cabin. I throttled his head and punched his nose again. Then I dug my fingernails into his face, just missing his eyes. I gorged his scarred tissue. He screamed with pain and suddenly broke my grip.He didn't get far before I grabbed him and punched him full force against his jaw. I couldn't tell if the cracking noise was my fist or his jaw. I didn't care. He came back at me. His fist clobbered me. I felt the sting against my eye. And then another blow took me by surprise. It knocked me to the ground.

He dove on top of me. We wrestled there, turning and rolling, twisting. His arms were thicker than mine and maybe longer and he suddenly got a grip at my throat. I found I couldn't reach his neck. Like hands from a drowning man reaching into air my fingers stretched, but they touched nothing. He was fast and strong, but he hadn't learned to wrestle as I had. I realized he was fighting only with his upper body. His legs were a wasted resource. I threw my legs up hard and fast catching my right leg around his neck. I yanked him backward and flipped him over. At last, I had the upper position. I pinned his legs with my legs and then one of his arms with one of mine. He flailed with his free hand. I knocked his arm away and cracked him one in the face. Then I grabbed my knife from my side and held it quick above him, ready to stab his throat. Ready. I was so very, very ready to kill him, but my hand remained on high.

He was knocked silly. I could see it in his eyes. He blinked twice, recovering his senses. He looked at the knife gleaming in my hand.

"Please," he winced. Begging.

"You coward," I spit through gritted teeth. He closed his eyes. I brought my raised hand, with knife in solid grip, down as fast and as hard as I could.

I stabbed the ground beside his head, and then pulled my knife back up. I made sure it was close enough that he heard the air split beside his ear.

"Get out of here! Get out before I kill you. And take him with you," I commanded as I got off of the miserable bastard and pointed to his scoundrel of a friend.

He gathered his senses. Pulled himself to his feet.

"My hat," he said and turned the other way. I looked to see if his companion could stand. That's when I heard it—the crack of the rifle, smelled it—the scent of the gun powder. The sound echoed. The smell spread. For a moment, I wasn't sure if I'd been shot or not.

I turned.

The second Confederate drifter fell to his knees, his hand still held the knife that he had been about to wield at me.

Behind him, standing in the doorway of the cabin, Julia held the rifle.

NOTE

[1]   Mooney (1891, 1900/1992).

REMEMBERING NATE BUTLER

December 24, 1865

It took me a minute to register the whole scene. The drifter had been ready to wield his knife into my back. Julia stood in the cabin doorway holding the rifle up, and my sister Nan stood behind her, holding Julia up. My mother appeared beside the two of them, with gunpowder bag and minié balls in hand. As the knife-wielding Rebel teetered in his kneeling position, holding his shoulder and crying in pain, I realized that no smoke emanated from the rifle that Julia held.

I turned the other way.

Behind me, some fifty paces, with a smoking rifle in his hands, sat the Negro man on a horse.

"Mister Dodd says he want you two Rebels off his property." He pointed his rifle from one Rebel to the other while controlling his horse with the strength of his knees and the skill of trained soldier. *Had he served in the 'Colored troops,'* I wondered later, for at the time my head was still swimming.

Stunned, and of course grateful, I looked to that man with immense gratitude. He nodded at me while he kept an eye on those two no good characters. I walked over and picked up the Reb's hat. His wound was surface, not serious. Not even as bad as Malachi's bullet wound. He whimpered just the same. I shoved his hat into his hands. Then I went over to the other fellow and picked him up by the nape of his shirt. I gave him a good shove to be on his way, as well. I looked back to the man on the horse, the man who had saved my life. He spoke first.

"You just take care of your family, sir. I'll keep an eye out from here."

As I looked at him, with the smoking rifle, I was instantly reminded of Nate Butler, the only other Negro I'd ever had the pleasure of meeting. I met him years ago, on my way to Charleston. I had left our secluded mountain home when I turned twenty-one years of age. That was expected by custom—my father's family's custom. A man went in search of a wife. I think I went more in search of an adventure, but I was lucky enough to find a wife. I had wanted to see things that I had only heard talked about like cities, ships, and the ocean. I never even thought about the fact that I'd never seen a White man other than my father, and one other relative once, much less a Negro. Cherokee were all we knew.

I recalled that the time that I had left home and headed toward Charleston, I realized that my hardtack wouldn't last long. I figured if I wanted to obtain luxuries like coffee, I'd have to find odd jobs along the way. So I kept an eye out for such possibilities. I traveled along the Hiwassee River southeast toward the Georgia/South Carolina border. I slept near Tallulah Falls the second night. By the third day, I'd reached Red Creek. On the fourth day, my traveling eased with the mountains behind me. I slept in Elberton. I met a man there who advised me to follow the road south to Augusta and then to take a ferry across the Savannah River. He told me that after crossing the river, a man could get to Charleston by following the road in a southeasterly direction. He also said that a man could probably find some work in that area.

Somewhere between Augusta and Charleston a farmer accosted me on the road and offered me a day's work. My father had prepared me that I wouldn't be able to get more than 50 cents for a day's work and to plan accordingly. After all, a pound of coffee cost nearly 40 cents and a pound of bacon roughly 12 ½ cents.[1] So when that farmer offered me a whole dollar for a day's work, I quickly agreed and felt most beholden' to him. Then he explained:

My horse took lame and I need to plow a field. I'll pay you the whole dollar at the end of the day, but you'll have to work side by side with Negroes, don't you see? Now, I won't make you stand in the middle and they're free Negroes from Mister Butler's place, he said as though that should mean something to me.

In the middle? I asked.

It takes three men to equal the strength of one good plow horse. The three of you get harnessed to the plow and then I'll direct you, but you won't have to stand in the middle. That's how it came to pass that I worked like a horse, literally, for an entire day directly next to a freed Negro slave by the name of Nate Butler.

We didn't speak a word during the plowing hours, but at the end of the day, I mentioned, *I didn't know there were any freed slaves in South Carolina that weren't in Cherokee Territory.* To which Nate Butler said, *I'm no man's slave.*

Yes, I apologized for my ignorance and explained that I'd come from the mountains and never met a Negro before. *Matter of fact,* I told him, *I hardly have ever met a white man, 'cept for one uncle on my father's side who came to visit.* I told him, *we mostly lived with the Cherokee. And there was one occasion where we left the mountains and I interacted with a few white Christians.* Nate and I had a decent chat after that while we sat in the shade and waited for the farmer to return with our money.

Well, sir, if ya don't mind my askin,' what you doin' workin' next to a Negro, anyway? Nate asked me.

I explained, that I needed money to see me on my way to Charleston. Then it was my turn to ask a question. "*What kind of work do you do when plantin' season is over?*

I takes whatever I can git. I work for the smithy once. Hot work, sir! Sometime I shovel dung for Misser Courtright, who sells it to farmers for fertilizer. Yes, sir, I save every penny I earn. So's I can buy my Elizabet's freedom. My grandmother bought my freedom, an' I'm gonna buy Elizabet's freedom.

Who's Elizabet? I had asked Nate.

Why, sir, she is the reason that the sun shines, he said with a smile. Nate Butler leaned back against the jagged bark of the elm tree, closed his eyes and presumably, pictured Elizabet. After his reverie, he sat forward and asked me, *Why you goin' to Charleston, sir? I reckon' I just want to see it—the city, the ocean, Fort Sumter—things I've never seen before.*

That's right, you from the mountains. That's how they got you to work besides a Negro. He said this and laughed at my expense or was it his expense, I wasn't quite sure. *Maybe ya'll find a pretty woman in Charleston, like my Elizabet.* He smiled.

I don't know much about courting, I confessed.

Oh, ain't much to it, he said and laughed again.

I don't even know where to start, I added.

Oh, that's easy, sir. You got to go to Sunday Meetin'. That's all there is to it. I remember that he laughed again, a deep, rich, rolling laugh. Then the farmer returned. He paid Nate and his silent, companion 15 cents. He put a dollar into my hand. Not a single one of us mentioned the injustice of that act. I reckon, I didn't even think of it as an injustice at the time, just a strange and curious practice. I was new to this world. Just the way things are here, I had supposed. Now, I stood looking at a different Negro, one who'd suffered similar or worse injustices in his lifetime. This kindly man, who helped me to bury my children and later saved my life, stood sentry over our cabin for the next ten days. His woman brought him food and extra for us. And later, he helped me with Malachi.

NOTE

[1] The amounts may be somewhat inflated as they come from a story in S. M. Beasley Story with a later date (Shackelford Sims, 1978).

CHAPTER 44

MALACHI

December 25, 1865

There was something so comforting in having that nameless Negro sit sentry for me that after I escorted Julia and Nan and my mother back into the cabin, I left my rifle at the door and I lay down and fell into a deep sleep. I didn't awake until the next morning when I heard a rapping on the door.

"Mister Dodd says this is for you and yours," the Negro stood in the doorway, holding a chicken within his grip and dressed more properly for the weather than he had been before. His thinly clad attire had been replaced, beginning with a solid cotton shirt which was covered by a woolen jacket. His new trousers, second-hand as they might be, were still an improvement as they reached to his ankles. Further, he wore leather boots upon his feet. He may well have been dressed like this the day before when he had shot that cowardly Rebel, but if so, it had gone unnoticed by me.

"Sir," he looked at me, holding out a feisty chicken that fluttered and squawked within the man's hand.

"Yes, oh yes, thank you. Please pass along my gratitude to Mister Dodd," I thanked him, taking hold of the chicken, with one hand, gripping its neck, and the other hand under its base.

"Mister Dodd says, it's not a layer. So you all should use it to make soup. See if that'll help ya family." I nodded, and once my grip was firm, the Negro released his hold on it, turned and walked away.

As I turned, I found my mother already standing at my side, ready to take the bird from me. The exchange was quick and the next thing I knew she stood on the front porch with the squawking bird. She gripped the bird's neck with both her hands and twisted it like a wet towel. The squawking ceased. The chicken went limp. My mother

271

carried the dead fowl to the edge of the porch where she stood and looked toward a near-by tree stump.

"Mister Dodd says to make a soup," I told her.

"I wish I had a vulture. I don't know how a chicken wash can help Malachi? He needs something much stronger," she spoke without looking at me. [1]

"Not a wash, a soup," I repeated. "Mister Dodd wants you to make soup."

She didn't answer me.

"It was kind of him, don't you think?"

"If you see any vultures, or an eagle, don't hesitate, Silas. I know how to appease the Great Buzzard and the Father Eagle." [2] I nodded.

"Did you bring your father's hatchet?"

"It's in the wagon." I started down the porch steps.

"Stoke the fire first, son."

I turned around, entered the cabin and put the few remaining branches into the fire. The pine-scented water still hung above the fire in an iron pot. I peered into it; the water level was high and the pot big enough to hold a whole chicken.

As soon as the flames were strong enough to catch the thicker branches, I left, leaving the door ajar, just a crack. I went to the wagon and moved bundles around to uncover the farming tools we'd brought with us, a hoe and a hatchet, an axe and a sickle. I selected the hatchet. I returned to my mother's side and simply stretched out my hand. She extended the bird. I took it by its feet, carried it to the tree stump and laid its head sideways. I gave it a good whack with the hatchet then fetched it up quickly again by the feet, held it away from me and let the blood pour out the neck whole. My mother joined me at the stump.

"You'll have to wash it; I can't make it to the river. I'm as tired as the Great Buzzard searching for a homeland. Remember, this may only be a chicken but it deserves the respect of the deer." I nodded, noticing that she did look weary. At that moment, I remembered a time that she told us children to always respect the Cherokee after our Cherokee neighbors had watched our house and cared for our things when we went to a meeting, a tent revival. She said it, as if she herself was not Cherokee. It struck me odd. I would have asked her but I had work to do.

"Hold this for a minute," I said, handing the chicken by its feet to her. I walked to the edge of the woods and took up a thick tree limb I had espied earlier, brought it back and used my hatchet to chop it into smaller pieces.

"Can you put these on the fire?" I asked her. We made the exchange again, I took the chicken back and she nodded taking the firewood. I left her heading into the cabin as I went off to the river.I thought of what she'd said to me as I walked down the now familiar path to the river. I remembered the story of *Selu* washing the blood from the deer that *Kana'ti* had killed; and from it came a magical boy, who grew up wild in the forest. I pictured Malachi as I thought of the two boys—Little Boy and One-Who-Grew-Up Wild. But the image of Malachi gave way to another image related to the blood being washed into the river. I thought of the blood of the Confederate officer, whom I'd shot, becoming a part of the woods. I pictured his blood, the color of berries, rivulets, seeping into the ground, feeding the earth.

When I reached the river I washed the bird, letting water flow in through the neck hole and then drain away with my hand cupped over the opening so that the fluid ran between my fingers. I repeated this task several times, leaving its innards in-tact, until the thick, red blood turned thin and pink, eventually running like clear water through my fingers. Making my way back to the cabin I continued to hold the fowl by its talons, before taking it to the stump to cut off its feet. When I looked up from this task, I saw my mother waiting on the porch for me.

"Is the water boiling, yet?" I asked as I approached her. She nodded. Taking the bird, which now looked like a ball of feathers, she disappeared into the cabin.

"Did you find tongs, of some kind?" I called after her. She didn't answer me. I figured if she needed them, then she'd let me know. I waited on the front porch, as I knew my mother would return soon after boiling the bird for a few minutes.

She had indeed found the pincers in the wagon while I was gone, as I could see when she stepped out of the cabin a few moments later holding the boiled bird by the tongs, into the air to cool. A water-soaked ball of feathers, dripped down her sleeve.

"Want me to take that?" I asked. She held it out to me. I took the bird by the tongs and held it to cool a bit more in the December air. My mother went inside briefly and returned with a blanket around her and one in her hand. She sat on the front porch step, placed the folded blanket on her lap and then looked up to me with one outstretched hand. I gave her the wet, headless, footless bird, which she took into her lap and began plucking.

"I'll check on the others." I left her to her work. She still looked weak.

I returned to the cabin to undertake my duties. I tended the fire, keeping an eye on the water, a rolling boil continued to spit and hiss from time to time. I checked and found the water bucket empty, which meant another trip to the river. I covered Julia and stroked her hair before leaving and I sat down by Malachi's side.

"We'll get you well, Malachi. I promise," I whispered, but he felt dangerously feverish to me.

"Don't promise, what you can't deliver," he whispered weakly and I was surprised to hear him speak so coherently.

"Oh, Malachi," I exclaimed.

"Silas, could I have some water. It's burning hot in here."

"I was just going for fresh water; I'll be right back." I told him. "William," I said with some enthusiasm. "Are you awake?"

William mumbled groggily.

"William, the rifle is by the door and mother is on the porch. I'll be back soon."

My trip to the river went quickly. *Malachi is awake*, I thought, *that's a good sign.* I rinsed the bucket in the icy water and filled it again. The sun sparkled on the droplets; the river seemed dappled with diamond glints. I thought of the magical boy and his brother. Malachi and I had played a pretend game when we were youngsters. I was Little Boy and he was the wild brother, we would play in the woods, swim in the river and wrestle in the leaves. Malachi, with his black hair streaming down his bare back was the epitome of what Julia had come to call *a real Indian*. We climbed trees and went on adventures in search of *Kana'ti*'s cave and we shot our blowguns at birds, pretending they were big game. These happy thoughts gave me strength at the river and carried me back again.

I returned to the cabin with a lighter spirit. I passed my mother on the stoop, still plucking feathers, a pile of chicken plumes at her feet. I entered the cabin and immediately snatched up the ladle and took the water bucket to Malachi's side.

"Malachi?" He didn't answer me.

"Malachi?"

I put my ear to his chest; I heard his heart still beating. But his consciousness had slipped away. I let him rest. I passed out water to the others.

"Silas," my mother called to me.

I went to the open doorway. She had finished plucking the bird. I knew what she needed. I took a slender branch from the pile and whittled the end to a sharp point. Then I gathered some dried cornhusks, I'd found in the kitchen and poked them onto the spear. I set them afire and brought this makeshift torch out to the porch, where I carefully singed the fine hairs from the plucked chicken while my mother rotated the bird around in her hands. When we were done, I took the singed creature back to the tree stump, where I used my hunting knife to split it down the breastbone. I reached in with my knife and sliced out the liver, the heart, and the gizzard, setting them in one pile, and the entrails, stomach, esophagus and lungs and tossed them aside. I carried the chicken in one hand and the giblets in the other to my mother, who waited by the fire. She took the giblets and dropped them into the boiling water. I broke the neck with my hands and dropped it into the pot. Finally, I let the whole bird slide into the boiling water with a bit of a splash. We both jumped back.

"Silas," Malachi's voice came to us.

"Silas, why won't you give me water?" I went to him. I dipped the ladle and reached behind him to help him sit up. He groaned with misery and touched his shoulder. He looked to his wound and then back at me.

"Silas, who shot me?"

The room remained intolerably quiet. I breathed deeply.

"I did," I said at last. Again he looked to his wound and back at me.

"Why, Silas?" His eyes searched my soul. No words ushered forth. I put the ladle to his lips. He took a sip and then lay back down. My mother tended the soup. William watched without saying a word. The others slept.

NOTES

[1] During the smallpox epidemic of 1866 the Eastern Cherokee called on the spirit of the buzzard who is believed to be immune to all illness as he is able to eat any carrion and survive. Some Eastern Cherokee used a buzzard soup wash to help fight the smallpox (Mooney, 1891, 1900/1992, p. 284). Reimer (2004) of The National Museum of Civil War Medicine provides a history of inoculation, vaccination, and isolation among "White and Colored" troops in the Union and Confederate armies and civilians but does not mention the Cherokee concerning the 1866 small pox epidemic even though they had known of and should be credited with quarantine as a method for centuries.

[2] Eagles were very special to the Cherokee. Few ceremonies required eagle feathers. Eagle killers were trained by the shamans and were the only ones allowed to take the life of an eagle. By the 1800s, there were no trained eagle killers left among the Cherokee (Mails, 1996).

WHY?

January 3, 1866

Why, indeed, I wondered to myself, as the days went by and Malachi's question went unanswered. I sat in my chair by the table watching them all as I had on that first evening when my mother had sat by my side. I had asked my mother on that first evening about her limp and been told the story of how Sister Sun betrayed Brother Moon by placing ashes on his face to discover his identity. Was it the Sun who betrayed the Moon or the Moon who betrayed the Sun by pretending to be something he wasn't?

Now I sat wondering whether I had betrayed Malachi? He had trusted me, believed in me. Had I shown my true face, a coward, after all? I thought of the Confederate officer and I thought of those Confederate bastards. I realized then that I had helped a brave man die and let two fools live. And neither act redeemed me from my sin—shooting my brother Malachi.

"Silas," my mother called to me in the dark, later that evening.

"Silas," she repeated. "Julia looked better today. Maybe we should take Malachi and Thomas to the river, too."

"Why?" I asked not understanding.

"If we take them to water and let them cleanse themselves and pray to the spirits maybe they'll get stronger. Julia went to water. It seems to be working for her. Nan looked stronger today also. She went to water."

"If you think it will help," I said.

"In the morning?"

"Yes, first thing, if you like." I didn't put much faith into going to water, but what could it hurt, I decided.

"Silas?" my mother called out again. I didn't answer her.

"Are you all right?" A silence followed.

"Yes," I finally told her.

"Do you want me to sit with you?" she offered.

"No, I'm fine."

Nevertheless, her shadowy form raised itself up from its place on the floor. She carefully made her way around sleeping bundles and joined me at the table. She said nothing; she simply sat beside me. Eventually, she rose again and gathered two mugs and the dipper. She ladled us each a bit of chicken broth and brought it to the table. I sipped it slowly. After a time, I spoke.

"I love you," I told her at last.

"I love you too, son."

"Tell me the rest of the story. What happened to Kilakeena?"

She nodded, saying, "Yes, indeed, what became of Kilakeena? For that matter what became of the infamous three?" I knew she meant the Treaty Party and I knew she also knew the answer to my question. I waited. She inhaled deeply before beginning.

"Shortly after daybreak, on June 22, 1839, twenty-five men surrounded the home of Scaleeloskee, Kilakeena's cousin and the son of Major Ridge. Inside, Scaleloskee and his wife slept somewhat fitfully, but the children were deep in their dreams, when three of these men crashed in the door, disrupting the calm of pre-dawn. They rushed up the stairs, pushing the bedroom door open, in time to see Scaleeloskee attempting to raise himself from his bed. Weak with an illness, he was unable to reach his rifle before the men forced him back to his sheets. Scaleeloskee's wife let out a scream.

"One of the Cherokee men held a pistol to Scaleeloskee's head and without a word, pulled the trigger. They all heard the click. The faulty pistol failed to fire. The man pulled the trigger again and again, click, click, click, but to no avail.

"He grabbed Scaleeloskee by his night shirt and the others grabbed his arms. Scaleeeloskee struggled, but the three men dragged him downstairs and out the front door, where his assailants forced him to face the other twenty-two men. Scaleeloskee wrenched and jerked his body, but could not get free from his attackers. His wife wailed. Scaleeloskee pleaded to be heard. The children awakened and came running. Alarmed by the noise and what they discovered; they tried to come to their father's aid, but Cherokee warriors caught them and held them back.

"Scaleeloskee tried again to be heard, shouting, *Let me explain;* but the Cherokee warriors shouted him down as they cried out *Justice!* and *Blood law!* The Cherokee warriors unsheathed their knives and stabbed Scaleeloskee twenty-five times as the children watched.

"When his body slumped, they stood and took their leave. Scaleeloskee raised himself up on his elbow, looking to his wife and tried to speak, but only blood gurgled forth.

"At the same time, in a different place, twenty-five Cherokee warriors sat stoically on their horses, hiding in the thick foliage of the Arkansas woods. They waited and watched, knowing that Major Ridge would soon pass by on his way to the general store. He traveled each day, via this route, with his friend, his Negro servant named Peter.

"Just as predicted, Major Ridge and Peter rode along the path that wound by the river. And just as predicted, they stopped to water their horses. As Major Ridge's horse dipped his head to drink, five of the Cherokee warriors leveled their rifles, took aim and shot Ridge. His horse, frightened by the commotion, went scurrying in circles, as did Peter's horse. But Peter reined in his horse first, then turning to see Major Ridge slumped in the saddle, he reached out for Ridge's horse's bridle, only to watch Ridge fall from the steed. Peter listened as the twenty-five warriors rode away.

"On that same morning, an otherwise peaceful day, Kilakeena, who was overseeing the building of his new home west of the Mississippi, was accosted by three men. The strangers told Kilakeena that they had recently come from the east and needed medicine. He cordially agreed to take them to Worcester's home where medical supplies were stored. As Kilakeena walked down the path, escorting the three men, he realized that one had dropped back. Just about to turn around, Kilakeena felt the hatchet's blade slice the center of his back. He cried out for his wife and fell to his knees. The executioners then drove a tomahawk into the back of Kilakeena's skull. When he dropped to the ground, they turned him face up, his eyes still seeing, they slashed his perfectly beautiful face seven times, for the death of the seven clans. When the deed was done, they ran off to the woods where twenty-two men waited with three extra ponies. The executioners mounted the horses and rode away, leaving Kilakeena in the arms of his new wife who had come running from their cabin." My mother took a breath as deep as eternity, then sipped her chicken broth, and stared into the night.

I found myself speechless. My mother the Beloved Woman had made a decision perhaps far more difficult than any decision that I had ever made. We sat for a long time in the darkness, much like the first night in this cabin.

After a spell of silence, my mother stood. I looked toward her.

"Get some sleep, son," she advised as she made her way back to her spot on the floor.

I nodded in the dark, but remained in my seat.

"The Treaty Party betrayed us; they did us in, the traitorous three were our kin," Thomas sang.

Thomas still talked in rhyming riddles and Malachi remained feverish. Everyone else slept except for my mother and me.

"Why don't we blame Jackson?" I asked my mother.

"And accept defeat?"

I didn't understand. She continued, "If a Nation of People is beaten by a mightier Nation, then those People accept their defeat. But if a Nation of People is betrayed by a few of their own People then they do not accept their defeat; they live with hope and the possibility that they will rise again."

"From the ashes?" I said.

"Yes, from the ashes."

"But wasn't it Kilakeena who believed in the *Cherokee Phoenix*?"

"Yes," she paused. "Silas, get some sleep."

But I couldn't sleep. I sat for a long time, thinking about how Kilakeena had betrayed the people and how I had betrayed Malachi. Eventually, I went to Malachi's side.

"Malachi?" He didn't answer me.

"Malachi, I'm sorry," I whispered. I laid my head on Malachi's chest. This time, I heard no heartbeat.

"Oh, Malachi."

CHAPTER 46

WE DO MOVE ON

January 4, 1866

Esquire Dodd gave me a burial plot for Malachi. I had stripped his uniform, washed his body and carefully wrapped him in a union army blanket that was left from my brother William's belongings. So in the end, my father, my brother, my son and my daughters came to rest at that place. Mister Dodd came to the cemetery for the final funeral— for my youngest brother Malachi's burial. The Negro and his woman attended, also. They helped me piece together a fine service. And I fulfilled my father's last request by singing all of the song, '*I am free. Washed in the Blood of the Lamb.'* My voice broke only once with sorrow.

When it was over, I handed Mr. Dodd his shovel.

"Sir, please, will you furnish me with work so that I might repay the debt I owe you for your kindness." But with tears in his eyes, he refused to let me pay him.

"You owe me nothing, Beasley. I'm the one who has given too little to a man who has lost so much," he determined. I right then and there broke down and wept as I had never wept before. Esquire Dodd held me to him as if he were my father or my longtime friend. I thanked him for everything he had done.

Then I turned to the Negro, the man who had been nameless to me for too long now. Putting out my hand, I said, "I don't even know your name, sir."

"Don't matter," he told me. "It wasn't really my name anyway."

I didn't understand at the time, not really. "I'll choose a new name," he added.

Next to my brother's grave was another, a fairly fresh grave. One I hadn't noticed when I buried my children, but perhaps it had been there. I looked to the Negro with questioning eyes.

"A Confederate, or rather what was left of 'im. I come across him in the woods."

"You didn't mind burying a Confederate?" I asked.

"The war's over, sir," he told me. I could hear forgiveness in his tone. I agreed, nodded to him and his woman, realizing that it was probably she who had laid out the pillow for my father's grave. I turned to leave, when the Negro's voice stopped me.

"Sir?"

I turned toward him again.

"Sir, you don't mind, do you, … that I buried them together? A Confederate and a Union man, next to each other?"

I shook my head no in response. I didn't bother to tell him that Malachi had fought for the South; it simply didn't seem to matter.

When all was done, I made my solitary journey back to the cabin. This time, on my way, I resolved not to stay in this cabin another day.

I began packing. While I was escorting everyone out I told Julia and Nan, "About the Negro saying he would take a new name," I added, "Maybe he'll think Malachi is a fine name." It seemed fitting, I thought for the man who had protected me to take the name of the brother who had stood up for me.

"Not Malachi," William put forth, "A freed man wouldn't want to have a Confederate's name."

But Julia took it a different way, saying "It's an omen." Julia proceeded to explain; "the name Malachi means *My Messenger.* "And the Messenger calls out for the God of justice and the judgment day and tells the people to prepare themselves for they have been wicked and vile by succumbing to temptations of pagan gods. Slavery was vile." She continued as I loaded Thomas and my sisters into the back of the wagon,

> *"Lo, I am sending my messenger*
> *to prepare the way before me;*
> *And suddenly there will come to the temple*
> *the LORD whom you seek,*
> *And the messenger of the covenant whom*
> *You desire.*
> *Yes, he is coming, says the LORD of hosts.* [1]

I helped Julia up onto the buckboard; she continued to preach.

"For a freed slave to become the messenger of the Lord must prove the wickedness of slavery, the justice of the war, and the need to prepare for the final Judgment Day. And likewise we should prepare the Indians, as well. All need to come to Jesus," Julia reminded us. Now, I knew she was feeling better.

As usual my sister Nan had something to say about that as she boarded the seat and took up the reins:

Now! We must call on the Ancient White to bring us health and help us move forward in a new way, without any slavery.[2]

"Heathen talk," Julia announced as Nan finished.

"Nan, move over," I said ignoring her and Julia's debate. I wanted them to make room for William.

"William," I called to my older brother. "Here," I said helping him up on the buckboard. I then gave Lydia, Elizabeth, and Mary aid into the back of the wagon. Finally, Martha took my hand, "Thank you for taking care of us," she said as she climbed aboard and I studied her face. The beauty of Kilakeena etched in the delicacy of her features struck me as promising in some hopeful way. I nodded to her. Maybe our family will get another chance through her.

William then clarified the naming of the unnamed Negro, "Wanting to name him Malachi is your way, our way, of wanting to keep our younger brother alive."

"I suppose you're right." I appreciated that he added, *our way.*

"Silas, do you know why I have been angry at you?" I shook my head, but figured he was angry because he thought I was a coward and a poor source of protection.

"You'll raise your gun to protect yourself and your family, but you've drawn the lines too close. I'd say that unnamed Negro is a part of your family. You feel it too, don't you?"

My quarrel with my conscience may not have been fully reconciled at that moment; indeed, I would add that Negro to the people I would protect and Mister Dodd, too, but I still wasn't sure about war, in general. What I did feel, was my brother's forgiveness at that moment. Instead of cursing my cowardice, he was trying to teach me a way of seeing humanity, the way Lincoln saw it, as one family.

Joseph and John settled Thomas into the buckboard so that he could lay down. Then they sat at the edge, dangling their feet from the back of the wagon.

"What name do you think he'll choose?"[3]

"Hard to say."

I walked alongside the wagon as we left that cabin. The darkest days of my life were now behind me. A nightmare I wished not to revisit.

My mother walked by my side, limping in her usual way. I now understood why my mother had been reluctant to discuss her limp. I recalled her saying that she wouldn't part with it, or the pain, because it reminds her of who she is and what she's lost along the way. I left that cabin without a visible limp, but I knew that I'd never forget what I'd learned and what I'd lost along the way.

After a time, I asked my mother a question. "Do you remember telling me the story of Kana'ti and Selu?"

"Yes."

"And after Kana'ti found out that the boys had killed Selu, he left them with the Wolf Clan?"

"Yes."

"What did the Beloved Women decide?"

"The Beloved Women of the Wolf Clan spared Kana'ti's sons. And from that day forward, the Nation flourished, from the children of Kana'ti and Selu to the seven clans: The Potato Clan, The Wolf Clan, The Paint Clan, the Blue Clan, The Deer Clan, The Long Hair Clan and the Bird Clan."

I walked feeling more at peace with each step.

"And each clan has its purpose," my mother told me. "It's the role of the Bird Clan to carry the stories and the messages from the Chief to the people, from one clan to another, from one person to the next, and in some cases, from one generation to another." I nodded as we walked, knowing that she must have been a member of the Bird Clan.

"What happened to us after the Cherokee were forced west and after Kilakeena was executed?"

"I told you before, we came out of the caves," she touched her heart or maybe she was touching that black talisman beneath her calico blouse—a reminder of her own dark days.

"And after that?"

"We moved on."

And so did we, move on.

NOTES

[1] Book of Malachi, Chapter 3: verse 1

[2] Nan is making the same claim as Julia only for her Cherokee ways of being, but it should be noted that the Cherokee also held slaves (see Perdue, 1983).

[3] Several stories of keeping the old name or taking a new name can be found in a variety of sources, one of the most famous being Booker T. Washington's story—*Up from Slavery* (Washington, 1902). For a contemporary story see the documentary, "Family Name" by Mackey Alston and Leonard Cox (1997) (winner of the Freedom of Speech award at the Sundance film festival).

CHAPTER 47

A FEW FINAL THOUGHTS

From an Old Man, 1908

By now I am sure that any sensible reader of this narrative is asking why a man would take the whole of his family through disease-infested lands where the festering sores of a hard fought war could erupt at any time. Why hadn't I gone alone to gather my brothers, you might be asking. Originally that is exactly what I had planned. In fairness, the reader deserves to know the details of my circumstances.

As I mentioned earlier, the lot of us lived in a two-story clapboard northeast of the old Cherokee capital of New Echota, Georgia, near the mountains of North Carolina, when the war came upon us. There I hid from conscription and made a living with my comb factory in the caves and could visit my family when no regiments from the North or from the South were close at hand. But in December of 1865, Georgian confederate veterans descended on our fair house, threatening my parents and telling my wife Julia that they intended to kill my brothers for having fought for the Union army, if they returned. In addition, they labeled me a traitor by cowardice and planned the same untimely end for me. I was surprised that they gave my wife warning. Perhaps, these men thought that we were already home from war and had planned to hang us that very day.

Julia brought me this news. I promptly gathered my family and we traveled west to Decatur, Alabama. This is where I had gone to a Church Meeting once, under my father's supervision. There I met White men for the first time. Although I found most of them brutes, there was one preacher who seemed kind-hearted. As it happened, at the meeting, we learned Christian songs, prayers and customs. The meeting lasted a good three days. On the last day, I was introduced to a custom that set my heart against both White men and red beets.

While sitting around a fire, one of the White men handed me a new food that I had never been exposed to as yet. He told me it was called a beet and that it had a fine sweet taste to it. He seemed a generous man as he handed me a beet and told me to take a liberal bite, which I did. Suddenly, my lips and tongue and even my fingers where I had held the 'beet' and caught the feel of fire. I felt sure that the blaze would rupture my throat and it brought tears to my eyes. My suffering was doubled by the humiliation I felt as these men laughed heartily at my misfortune. It was the preacher who'd come from Decatur that put an end to their spiteful joke. *Come along, son,* he entreated me. *I'll give you a bite of bread.*

White men have given me grief on more than one occasion. When I turned twenty-one and left home I decided that when the time came that year I would cast my ballot, but I found that even then I had to stand my ground against the White men of this Southern region, who told me I looked "mother silly and boyish."[1] I announced that I was twenty-one and that was all that was necessary for me to cast a vote. They asked me if I would swear to it and I said, *no*. All in attendance looked aghast. *Why not*, they demanded. I told them that I would swear to the fact that, that is what my parents told me, but I have not been one to keep track of my birth or the years that followed. They bloodied my nose before I was able to make my mark, but I did. I felt "like yelling the Indian War Whoop, but refrained."[2] I was opposed to secession and determined to raise my voice against it.

On another occasion, I had a long walk to my family's home one afternoon before the war had broken out and a fella offered me a ride in his buggy. I accepted, climbed aboard only to have the gentleman insist that I drink whiskey with him. I declined in a polite way. He insisted again, and again I declined, telling him that I didn't want my family to smell whiskey on my breath. This went on for a bit until the gentleman became angry and threw whiskey on my clothes. I was ashamed to walk into my home. And have ever since preached against the evils of liquor. Although I must admit that sauerkraut with a sip of whiskey has a mighty fine taste to it if you only partake of it on special occasions.

But not all White men had such vile personalities. As I was saying, the preacher from Decatur, Alabama had seemed a kind and virtuous man. So when I heard that these Southern veterans aimed to kill me and my brothers, I took my family and headed west to find the preacher in hopes that he would shelter my family; while, I went off to find my brothers and warn them.

When we reached Decatur, I hid my family before I proceeded to locate the Preacher. Having found him, I went hesitantly toward him. He was hoeing his garden. I have always been an agile and silent man of the woods and so I drew upon those skills and stealthily made my way until I stood near enough to speak to the preacher. A fence separated us. He was taken slightly aback by my suddenly being on him.

"Hey, what in the name of … Well there, aren't you Beasley's son?" He remembered me.

"I am, sir. I've come to ask your help."

"Beasley, the South asked for your help. Don't you think I heard what you and your brothers did! Traitors and cowards! Except the two." With that said, he took his hoe above his head and if that fence had not separated us I think he would have bashed my skull right then and there. Although I had my rifle in my arms, I wouldn't raise it against him. I had taken an oath. I ran as fast as my scrawny legs would carry me. I organized my family. What a pitiful bunch of refugees we were; thin clothing on our backs, little in the way of coffee, clothes, and food, only one rifle to our name.

I saw no other way to go but north.

I collected my brothers along the way. The last, with the exception of Malachi, was in Gallatin.[3] This is where all took ill and I hid us in an abandoned boxcar, before being taken in by the generous Esquire Dodd.

You dear reader, know what happened after that, except for what I learned later about Malachi's life. I heard that Malachi had survived the last battle of the Civil War.[4] It would seem that Stand Watie's Cherokee regiment was the last to be notified of the Southern surrender. At first, I shook my head at this assuming that the Cherokee hadn't been told because the White generals didn't think they were important enough to tell, or that they had simply been forgotten. But it'd seem that I was wrong about that; instead, it was Cornelius Elias Boudinot, Kilakeena's son, who kept word of the surrender from his uncle, General Stand Watie and even managed to keep a few Southern White generals from receiving the news that he intercepted. It turns out it was a calculated maneuver on Cornelius's part to ensure as many provisions as possible be delivered to the impoverished Western Cherokee from the Confederacy before the Northern troops took everything for themselves.[5] But before the reader think that Cornelius spent his life making up for the debt owed to the Cherokee by his father, Kilakeena, I would warn you that the acorn doesn't fall from the tree and Cornelius's life was no less conflicted, and just as intriguing and complex as his father's life had been. But that's another story, for another day.

As for the Eastern Cherokee, they suffered terribly from the small pox epidemic of 1865–66 as did those who fought on the western front in Arkansas and Oklahoma. According to the Cherokee historical records, over one fourth of all Cherokee men fighting with Thomas's Legion died from small pox following the Civil War.[6]

As for me, I'm not sure why I was the only one not to take sick during those troubling times, but what I do know is that I learned a good deal about life and death, about my family and about myself during those days. I still admire the bravery with which that Confederate officer not only faced death, but commanded it to come his way. And to this day, I'm not sure why I gave those miserable Rebel soldiers a second chance, but times have led me to believe that it wasn't so much them as it was me who was given the second chance. Perhaps, it wasn't Malachi who fought on the final battlefield, the Cherokee being the last to hear of the war's end; it was me, when my convictions came under siege. In the face of my greatest test, when I held a knife above that Rebel's head, I chose not to take a life.

My brothers had chosen otherwise, with some offering their services to the North and some to the South. Each paid dearly. So whether my brothers and I are heroes and saints or traitors and cowards, I cannot be the judge, but I know that we were each men of conviction. And except for my blind eye to the Negro situation, I finally decided that I had little to be ashamed of that I did during those days. And since then, between Nate Butler and the nameless Negro and the woman by his side who saved my life, I have, with open mind and a good heart, formed a conviction—to fully respect my fellow human beings, of all races.

One final note is worth mentioning. As we left that cabin and traveled through the cold, winter's night, I looked up and saw a full moon with Selu's forgiving face. I do believe that Malachi sent me a message.

NOTES

[1] Shackelford Sims (1978, p. 13).
[2] Shackelford Sims (1978, p. 13).
[3] According to Shackelford Sims (1978), William enlisted in the Union Army and became an officer in Thomas' Union Army. Thomas' Legion was a Southern unit; Thomas' Army was a Northern unit.
[4] With regard to Malachi Beasley I have taken great liberty as Shackelford Sims (1978) reports, other than his birthdate nothing is known of Malachi. I did find one Malachi Beasley of the same age mentioned as a Confederate soldier, but I cannot be sure it is the same Malachi Beasley; These websites were helpful but not definitive: https://www.fold3.com/document/29197262/
https://co.currituck.nc.us/wp-content/uploads/currituck-military-civil-war.pdf   Compiled Service Records of Confederate Soldiers Who Served in Organizations from the State of North Carolina Fourth Cavalry (59th State Troops) B. Beasley, Malachi W (19).
[5] See Colbert (1982) for the life story of Kilakeena's son.
[6] See Mooney (1891, 1900/1992, pp.169–172) on the smallpox epidemic.

EPILOGUE

March 2020–March 2021

Following the small pox epidemic of 1865–66, my great, great, grand-uncle Silas Mercer Beasley Jr. and his mother, my great, great, great grandmother Sarah Elizabeth Reese led the family from a cabin on Mister Dodd's estate near Gallatin, Tennessee, where they had been quarantined, to Lawrenceburg, Tennessee, where they built a cabin in an area that Silas described as the most beautiful land he'd ever seen. Silas declared that he and his family would remain there for the rest of their lives. And that they did.

Historical fiction allows for the creation of characters, situations and invented dialogue to bring an underdeveloped, but true story to life. Although I have taken such liberties I have also footnoted facts as they are contained in my uncle's diary or as contained in historical and archival sources. During and following the quarantine of 1865–66, my ancestors met the following fates. Silas Mercer Beasley Sr. died of measles, three days following the move from the boxcar in Gallatin to the cabin on Mr. Dodd's estate. He was actually buried with the help of the Commander of the Union forces in the Gallatin cemetery. Silas Jr.'s children were buried in the Dodd estate cemetery. Julia's sister was also with them and passed away. She was also buried on the Dodd estate.

One of the liberties that I took in this novel includes that of Malachi Beasley's return. There are contested stories. Silas Beasley Jr. wrote that ten days after the burial of his children, "my youngest brother came home from war only to take small pox and die."[1] Silas also wrote that his youngest brother is buried in the Dodd family cemetery. Malachi is listed as his youngest brother, but other family stories suggest that Malachi may have died of typhoid fever before making it home to his family and may be buried in Arkansas. Why such a contested claim exists is unclear. In addition, Thomas who was in poor condition when they left the cabin, passed away before they reached Nashville. Silas also reported that of the family members who survived, some fared well following their illnesses, some became worse with typhoid fever, and others were left with chronic conditions that plagued them long afterward. But of note, is that Silas never shot his brother.

Again, this is an historical novel, and as such other liberties were taken. I developed several fictional characters to demonstrate how Silas Jr. might have struggled with the decision to be a conscientious objector. Those fictional characters include the unnamed couple that Silas encounters at the river and who later help him survive, the two troublesome Confederates who attack the cabin, and the Confederate officer who was attacked by wolves. Each of these characters and the storyline surrounding them, was used to address the thesis, but beyond that they were employed to represent the issue of slavery as real in a more tangible way than Silas' family actually encountered. For Silas and his brothers, for the most part, slavery was an abstract notion as they lived in the mountains, rarely encountered a White man, and lived only among the Cherokee. In addition, the novel makes it appear as though the unnamed man may have taken a job working for Mr. Dodd. In actuality, Silas worked for Mr. Dodd before leaving in order to repay him for his generosity.

With regard to Sarah Reese's limp, it was in reality Silas who acquired a limp following an accident. But applying the limp to Sarah provided a motive to reach into her past. A past that is still contested. And one that I have imagined, as Sarah Reese's ethnicity is still very much in question.

CONTESTED ETHNICITY

In the introduction of this book I wrote of *narrative ethnicity and contested histories*. Narrative ethnicity refers to beliefs based on the stories one has inherited from relatives about one's ancestors. And these narratives of ethnicity can be contested. Henry Louis Gates Jr. dedicated his research and television program, "Finding Your Roots" to exploring the racial/ancestral histories of people via archival data and DNA, which exposed the fragility of family narratives. His own family story had relied on a Cherokee history which he debunked, much to the dismay of his relatives, through DNA testing and analysis. He also reported that in 2009, it cost $50,000.00 to have his and his father's full genome typing assessed and that this was a deal given to him. In recent years, Gates Jr. suggested that one might be able to get the tests for around $5,000. In other words, confirming or disconfirming family narratives of ethnicity via DNA, especially those that date back six generations, is difficult, if not impossible, and not very affordable. A simple ancestry test would not provide such specifics, according to Gates Jr. (Gross, 2019).

For my family, a contested narrative about Sarah Elizabeth Reese surfaced. The debate was that she was not of Cherokee heritage, but rather African-American and Welsh. Had I written this novel as though Sarah Reese's ethnicity were African American, a completely different background would have emerged. And it is quite possible that she was African American. Her father, it is thought, was George Reese from South Carolina who fought in the Revolutionary War.[2] Her mother remains unnamed. George Reese, if it is the same George Reese, followed his brother from Pennsylvania to Cherokee territory where the brother preached, among other topics, on the evils of the institution of slavery. But he simultaneously held slaves. It is possible that the unnamed mother of Sarah Reese was a slave in which case most would presume the relationship was nonconsensual, violent even. But again, it is Professor Henry Louis Gates Jr. who discovered in his own family history the biracial relationship was not a violent one; rather, it developed into common law marriage which he discovered at his ancestors' grave site, where the couple was buried together.

Unlike Gates' ancestors' relationship, George Reese does not acknowledge a relationship of any kind with Sarah's mother or with Sarah. Later in life, he signed a testament that he served during the Revolutionary War in order for his family to receive the government pension. His family is then listed. There is no mention of Sarah Elizabeth as a descendant. There is mention of having served in Cherokee Territory as the Americans fought against the Cherokee who had supported the British and an admission that he left the service for six months during that time, "absent in this expedition" but may have remained in the Territory.[3] It is less these sorts of documents that persuaded me that Sarah Elizabeth Reese was Cherokee and more the family resemblance between her daughter, Martha and that of Kilakeena Elias Boudinot. Kilakeena's mother was Welsh and Cherokee, her name was Susannah Reese and his father was Oowatie. Photographs of Martha, the daughter Sarah Reese and Silas Beasley Sr. are compared to Kilakeena in the introduction of this book.

Of course there is another possibility, that Sarah (Sallie) Elizabeth Reese was entirely of Welsh heritage. As a White girl it would have been odd for her to have married at the age of fifteen; indeed, none of Silas Sr.'s daughters married before the age of 20 and most married between 20 and 24 years of age. So Sarah's marriage at 15 years does not follow the White norm (but rather the Cherokee norm), but certainly it is not impossible. Second, as Silas Jr. notes, his mother was a Christian. He does not know when she became a Christian, but she once spoke to the older children with tears in her eyes of Jesus' love and knew the words to a hymn that she sang to them. She was also aware of clothing that White boys wore (a frock) until they were older to save on having to sew clothes frequently. Thus, she was familiar with White settlements. Furthermore, Silas reports that the family owned a table which made them more "advanced" materially than most Cherokee. In short, Sarah Reese's ethnicity remains contested to this day.

Susannah Reese and her son Kilakeena were mixed ethnicity (Cherokee and Welsh). It is highly likely that Sarah Reese and her children were also of mixed race/ethnicity. Yet, there is no record of Sarah Reese being related to Susannah Reese, although both lived in Cherokee territory.

As Henry Louis Gates Jr. suggests, we are all an "admixture" of races with intriguing pasts.[4] We are one family; the Family of Man[5] as the poet Carl Sandburg wrote in reference to Lincoln's "Address to Congress." One humanity.

Finally, I believe this book would benefit readers through follow up discussions, whether in the classroom or in book clubs. I am happy to supply readers, teachers, and professors with discussion questions beyond those listed below, especially linking the past to the present on subjects of quarantine, civil unrest, social justice, such as Black Lives Matter and Native American rights, victimhood, cancel culture, voter suppression, conscientious objectors, and more. Indeed, this book that speaks of a quarantine of the past can certainly be related to the Covid-19 quarantine of 2020–21. And more so, this novel can be related and discussed in light of the incidents at the U.S. Capitol in 2021. What language should we use, noting the power of words, to describe January 6, 2021 (e.g., protest, demonstration, riot, domestic terrorism) and how do we explain the preceding events, when iconic figures were taken off their pedestal, literally and figuratively (e.g., vandalism, rhetorical acts of resistance, de-constructing and dismantling racism)? These are questions that hopefully lead to communication agency, guiding us to a better future, a regeneration. May the next generation be the re-generation.

FAMILY RECORDS
(BIRTHS AND DEATHS)

Sarah (Sallie) Elizabeth Reese, b. 1809–d. 1888, buried in Lawrence County, Tennessee (Silas' mother).

Died during the quarantine in the cabin on Mr. Dodd's estate in Tennessee:

Silas Mercer Beasley, Sr.	b. 1795–d. 1865
William (Willie) J. Beasley	b. 1859–d. 1865
Nancy (Nannie) G. Beasley	b. 1861–d. 1865
Sara A. Beasley	b. 1863–d. 1865

Julia Hood's sister is believed to be the fifth person buried in Dodd Cemetery from the Beasley group.

Other family members:

Reuben Beasley	b. NC 1825–d.?
William Fletcher Beasley	b. NC 1827–d.?
John Wesley Beasley	b. NC 1829–d. 1873 buried in Tennessee
Joseph Beasley	b. NC 1831–d.1929 buried in Arkansas

Silas Mercer Beasley Jr.	b. NC 1834–d. 1914, buried in Lawrence County, Tennessee
Mary Pastell Beasley	b. NC 1835–d. 1906 buried in Tennessee
Martha Ann Beasley	b. AL 1837–d. 1892?
Thomas Fletcher Beasley	b. 1841–d. 1865 died and was buried in Nashville after leaving the cabin on Mr. Dodd's estate.
Malachi Beasley	b. SC 1843–d. date unknown and was possibly buried in Arkansas, but also may have rejoined the family, died, and was buried at the Dodd estate in 1865 or 1866.
Elizabeth Beasley	b. SC 1847–d.?
Nancy (Nan) C. Beasley	b. GA 1848–d. 1929 buried in Tennessee
Lydia Beasley	b. GA 1850–d. 1878 buried in Tennessee

NOTES

[1] Shackelford Sims (1978, p. 25).
[2] Shackelford Sims (1978).
[3] Documents of George Reese (1833/2009), Pension application.
[4] Henry Louis Gates Jr. referencing his television show and his roots in an interview with Terry Gross (January 1, 2019).
[5] Carl Sandburg (1970) drew from Lincoln's address to Congress on December 1, 1862 to create his poem, *The Long Shadow of Lincoln: A Litany* in which he "dreams of the Family of Man" [sic].

DISCUSSION QUESTIONS

1. The main thesis of this novel addresses the question of the morality of taking a human life. Silas' brother William calls him a coward for choosing to be a conscientious objector, but in the end reveals that it is not so much cowardice as Silas' failure to see African Americans as his extended family and worthy of his protection that irks William. Is William's point valid and if so, in what ways? How does this position complicate the killing of Confederate soldiers? What does this say about the current day Black Lives Matter movement?
2. Malachi argues that William is taking up the side of the North, but points out that the North will surely turn on Native Americans later so that they can grab more land in the West. Malachi chooses to do whatever the Cherokee decide. How does this decision reflect on various positions concerning slavery, reservations and treaties, and the choice of political positions based on immediate and exigent needs versus likely future outcomes?
3. Two factions developed within the Cherokee Nation (i.e., the progressive and the traditionalist). Sarah Reese espoused the philosophy that to follow Kilakeena's way (becoming Christian, dressing and acting as Whites) will only make the 'Cherokee' disappear in a different way. Chief Ross told the people to stay on their land, but the "treaty party" (a.k.a. progressive party) argued that all would be killed if they stayed. In short, the Cherokee appear to be doomed by the paradox. Chief Ross also suggested moving the Cherokee to Mexico. Would this have saved the Nation? What if any recourse could have been proposed? Is Kilakeena a traitor or a voice of realism?
4. Spirituality and religion are part of most cultures. In this case, both Cherokee spirituality and Christianity are taught through stories. Are the stories moral education lived by the characters who espouse them? How do Julia and Nan represent two sides of the same coin? How do they differ in their world views? How is Julia's faith tested during the quarantine?

5. Silas was stopped by men who did not want him to vote (whether his voting was for the 1860 presidential election or the January 1861 secession of the State of Georgia is not completely clear). What is clear is that he was punched in the face and left with a bloody nose, but marked his ballot anyway. Does voter suppression exist today? If so, how have voter suppression tactics changed? How do various democracies attempt to safeguard the right to vote?

A FINAL NOTE

According to Hattie Shackelford Sims (1978), these are the exact words inscribed in Silas's Bible:

I am determined that I will not shed human blood except
in defense of myself or my family.
– Silas Mercer Beasley, Jr.

REFERENCES

Alston, M., & Cox, L. (1997). *Family name.* Documentary. New York, NY: River Films. PBS.

American Battlefield Trust. (2021). *Fort Sumter.* Retrieved from https://www.battlefields.org/learn/civil-war/battles/fort-sumter

"An experiment in Evangelization: Cornwall's Foreign Mission School". (2020, November 10). *A pamphlet.* Retrieved from https://connecticuthistory.org/an-experiment-in-evangelization-cornwalls-foreign-mission-school/

Anderson-Douoning, J. (June 21, 2020). *Why Black Life Matters.* Lecture. Central Presbyterian Church, Lafayette, IN. Retrieved from https://www.youtube.com/watch?v=pudsDBJes4g&t=33s

Awiakta, M. (1993). *Selu: Seeking the Corn Mother's wisdom.* Golden, CO: Fulcrum Press.

Bell Sr., G. M. (1972). *Genealogy of old and new Cherokee Indian families.* Bartlesville, OK: G. M. Bell Sr.

Beasley Jr., S. M. (1906–1908). The Silas Mercer Beasley Jr. memoirs (article series). *Lawrence Democrat,* Lawrenceburg, TN.

Cherokee and Sioux Courtship. (2020). Retrieved from www.aaanativearts.com.

Clair, R. P. (1997). Organizing silence: Silence as voice and voice as silence in the narrative exploration of the Treaty of New Echota. *Western Journal of Communication, 61,* 315–337.

Clair, R. P. (2003). Starvin' Marvin's got an injun. In R. P. Clair (Ed.), *Expressions of ethnography: Novel approaches to qualitative methods.* Albany, NY: State University of New York Press.

Clair, R. P., & Hearit, L. B. (2017). The meaning of work and the absence of workers in *Les Mandarins:* Irony at work through the 'essential accessory.' *TAMARA: Journal of Critical PostmodernOrganizationScience, 15,* 203–215. http://tamarajournal.com/index.php/tamara/article/viewFile/415/pdf_1

Clair, R. P., Wilhoit, E., Green, R. J., Palmer, C., Russell, T., & Swope, S. (2016). Occlusion, confusion and collusion in the conversion narrative, "Religion exemplified in the life of 'Poor Sarah.'" *Journal of Communication and Religion, 38,* 54–72.

Clifford, J. (1984). Introduction: Partial truths. In J. Clifford & G. E. Marcus (Eds.), *Writing culture: The poetics and politics of ethnography* (pp. 1–26). Berkeley, CA: University of California Press.

Colbert, T. B. (1982). *Prophet of progress: The life and times of Elias Cornelius Boudinot.* Unpublished dissertation. Stillwater, OK: Oklahoma State University. Retrieved from https://shareok.org/handle/11244/20248

Counting in Cherokee. (2020). Retrieved from https://www.languagesandnumbers.com/how-to-count-in-cherokee/en/chr/

Ehle, J. (1988). *Trail of tears: The rise and fall of the Cherokee Nation.* New York, NY: Anchor Books. Finger, J. R. (1984). *The Eastern Band of Cherokees 1819–1900.* Knoxville, TN: University of Tennessee Press.

Gridley, M. E. (1974). *American Indian women.* New York, NY: Hawthorne Books.

Gross, T. (January 1, 2019). *Historian Henry Louis Gates Jr. on DNA testing and finding his own roots.* NPR. Retrieved from https://www.npr.org/2019/01/21/686531998/historian-henry-louis-gates-jr-on-dna-testing-and-finding-his-own-roots

REFERENCES

Hall, S. (1985). Signification, representation, ideology: Althusser and the post-structuralist debate. *Critical Studies in Mass Communication, 2,* 91–114.

Hamel, P., & Chiltosky, M. (1975). *Cherokee plants and their uses—A 400 year history.* Walker, MI: Herald Publishing Company, Silva.

Jacobs, H. (a.k.a. Linda Brent). (1988). *Incidents in the life of a slave girl.* Oxford, UK: Library Oxford University Press. (Original published in 1861)

John Ross. (2021). Retrieved from https://en.wikipedia.org/wiki/John_Ross_(Cherokee_ chief)#American_Civil_War

Josephy Jr., A. M. (1994). *500 Nations: An illustrated history of North American Indians,* New York, NY; Knopf.

Klausner, J. (1993). *Sequoyah's gift: A portrait of a Cherokee leader.* New York, NY: HarperCollins.

Las Casas, B. (1552). *A brief account of the destruction of the Indies.* Project Gutenberg. Retrieved from https://www.gutenberg.org/ebooks/20321

Lincoln, A. (December 1, 1862). Annual message to congress – Concluding remarks. Retrieved from http://www.abrahamlincolnonline.org/lincoln/speeches/congress.htm

Mails, T. E. (1996). *The Cherokee people: The story of the Cherokee from earliest origins to contemporary times.* Tulsa, OK: Council Oaks Books.

McLoughlin, W. G. (1984). *Cherokees and missionaries, 1789–1839.* New Haven, CT: Yale University Press.

Mooney, J. (1975). *Historical sketch of the Cherokee.* Chicago: Aldine. Reprint of portions of 1900 ethnology reports to the U.S. Bureau of American Ethnology, transferred to Washington D.C.: Smithsonian.

Mooney, J. (1992). *History, Myths, and Sacred Formulas of the Cherokee (1891–1900/1992).* Fairview, N.C.: Bright Mountain Books. (Original works published 1891, 1900)

Moore, J. D. (1997). *Visions of culture: An introduction to anthropological theories and theorists.* Walnut Creek, CA: Alta Mira Press.

Perdue, T. (1983). *Cherokee editor: The writings of Elias Boudinot.* Knoxville, TN: University of Tennessee Press.

Reese, G. (2009, December 28). *Southern Campaign American Revolution and Pensions Statements and Rosters. Pension application of George Reese-W8548* (W. Graves, Trans.). Original document written and recorded in 1833. Retrieved from http://revwarapps.org/w8548.pdf

Reimer, T. (2004, November 9). *Smallpox and vaccination in the Civil War.* The National Museum of Civil War Medicine. Retrieved from http://www.civilwarmed.org/surgeons-call/small_pox/

Romans, B. (1775). A concise natural history of East and West Florida. New York, NY: James Rivington.

Sandburg, C. (1970). The long shadow of man; A litany. In *The complete poems of Carl Sandburg.* New York, NY: Houghton, Mifflin, Harcourt. Retrieved from https://www.poetryfoundation.org/poems/53250/the-long-shadow-of-lincoln-a-litany

Shackelford Sims, H. (1978). *The Silas Mercer Beasley Jr. story: A brief family history, 1725–1978.* Lawrence County, TN Archives. Retrieved from http://www.tngenweb.org/lawrence/lawrbknv.htm

Stein, B. (2002). *Lecture on herbs.* Lafayatte , IN.

Thomas' Legion. (2020). Retrieved from https://en.wikipedia.org/wiki/Thomas%27_Legion
Washington, B. T. (1902). *Up from slavery: An autobiography.* New York, NY: Doubleday, Page & Co.
Wilkins, T. (1986). *The Cherokee tragedy: The Ridge family and the decimation of a people* (2nd ed.). Norman, OK: University of Oklahoma Press.
Wood, L. M. (n.d.). Marriage in North Carolina. *Anchor.* Retrieved from https://www.ncpedia.org/anchor/marriage-colonial-north

ABOUT THE AUTHOR

Robin Patric Clair (Ph.D.) is a Full Professor in the Brian Lamb School of Communication, College of Liberal Arts, at Purdue University and a descendent of Sarah Elizabeth Reece. She is an award-winning researcher, a two-time recipient of the Fellow to the Center for Artistic Endeavors, a Diversity Fellow, has received two Outstanding Book of the Year Awards and a Golden Anniversary Award from the National Communication Association for research on narrative and sexual harassment as well as for her work on novel approaches to ethnography. Also, she has been named to the Book of Great Teachers at Purdue University. She teaches rhetoric, narrative theory and practice, ethnography, and "Transformative Texts," a course offered in the Cornerstone Program at Purdue University. This is her third novel in the Social Fictions series (*Zombie Seed and the Butterfly Blues: A Case of Social Justice*, 2013; *Blood into Water: A Case of Social Justice*, 2021).

Printed in the United States
by Baker & Taylor Publisher Services